MERCHANT
FLEETS

MERCHANT FLEETS 6

BLUE
FUNNEL
LINE

Duncan Haws

Illustrations by author

© 1984 Duncan Haws

First Published 1984
Reprinted, Updated Edition, 1986
Reprinted, Updated Edition, 1988

British Library Cataloguing Publication Data

Haws, Duncan
  Merchant Fleets 6
  Blue Funnel Line.
  1. Merchant Marine — History
  1. Title

  ISBN 0 946378 01 0

Text photoset in 9 on 10 English Times by En to En, Tunbridge Wells, Kent.
Printed by White Burton & Co. Ltd., Edenbridge, Kent.
TCL Publications, Travel Creatours Ltd, 1 Meadowbank Road, Hereford HR1 2ST

Dedicated to
John Dodd Soulsby, a lifelong Holt Chief Engineer who knew the precise state of his ship's machinery by the merest whisper of a change in engine noise.

Introduction

No fleet of ships can ever have evoked greater affection and regard than those of Alfred Holt. Graced with the characteristic distinction of that tall, almost always vertical, ethereally blue funnel and deep black top, the Blue Funnel ships were the aristocrats of the ports which they served.

Only with the coming of the 'Box Boats' has the Holt silhouette disappeared from the oceans.

Even the name of the illustrious founder has gone from the scene. But the company that Alfred Holt created continues in the finest traditions of maritime history and endeavour; this work seeks to set down the story of Blue Funnel and to place on record the ships that bore that distinguished funnel. They served their country well under the men who manned them through all the vicissitudes of both peace and war.

I am indebted to the World Ship Society's Central Records for their aid in filling in some of the missing detail. Also to three charming ladies, Sally Furlong of Ocean Transport and Trading with Julie Doran and Deborah J. Lindsay of Merseyside County Council's Modern Records Centre. To each is accorded my thanks and appreciation.

Contents

Funnel and flag colour details .. .. *Front Cover*

Introduction.. 5

Explanatory notes 9

BLUE FUNNEL LINE

Chronological History 11

Livery 34

Routes.. 34

Fleet Index 36

Illustrated Fleet List 39

CHINA MUTUAL STEAM NAVIGATION CO.

List of vessels owned prior to acquisition 147

Explanatory Notes

1 Company histories are arranged chronologically.

2 The ships owned are listed virtually chronologically except that sister ships are grouped together even when the period of their building covers more than one year.

3 Tonnage: the method of calculating tonnage has changed several times since 1830 and very few ships kept their initial tonnage. The gross and net tonnages shown are generally those recorded when the ship first entered service.

4 Dimensions: unless recorded as 'overall' the figures given are the registered dimensions between perpendiculars.

5 The speed given is service speed. This could vary according to route and ports of call.

6 Abbreviations: to assist all readers as few as possible have been used —

Apr	*April*	ft	*Feet*
Aug	*August*	fwd	*Forward*
BHP	*Brake horse power*	g	*Gross*
Blr	*boiler*	GP	*Goal post masts*
B	*Built*	GRT	*Gross registered tonnage*
B	*Bridgedeck*	**H**	*Hull*
cabin	*Cabin class*	HP	*Horse power/High pressure*
cm	*Centimetres*	IHP	*Indicated horse power*
cu m	*Cubic metres*	in	*Inch(es)*
cu ft	*Cubic feet*	Jan	*January*
Cyl(s)	*Cylinder(s)*	K.K.	*Kabusiki Kaisya*
D	*Dimensions*	kts	*Knots*
dbl	*Double*	lb	*Pound(s)*
Dec	*December*	LP	*Low Pressure*
Dft	*Draught/draft*	m	*Metre*
diam	*Diameter*	Mar	*March*
disp	*Displacement*	mm	*Millimetres*
dwt	*Dead weight*	MP	*Medium pressure*
E	*East*	mph	*Miles per hour*
E	*Engine*	n	*Net*
exp	*expansion*	N	*North*
F	*Forecastle*	NHP	*Nominal horse power*
Feb	*February*	Nov	*November*

oa	Overall	S.SA	Stroke. Sgl acting
obb	over bulbous bow	S.DA	Stroke. Dbl acting
Oct	October	scr	Screw
Pad	Paddle	Sept	September
P	Passengers	sgl	Single
P	Poop	SHP	Shaft horse power
Prom	Promenade	Stm	Steam
Q	Quarterdeck	Stm P	Steam pressure
quad	Quadruple/four	SV	Sailing vessel
refrig	Refrigerated	**T**	Tons
reg	Registered	tpl	Triple/three
RHP	Registered horse power	tst	Tourist
rpm	Revolutions per minute	tw	Twin/two
S	South	W	West

7 The technical data follows the same pattern throughout —

B (built); **T** (tons), g (gross), n (net), dwt (dead weight). **Dim** (dimensions) oa (overall) length × breadth × depth; *Dft:* (draught). **Eng** (engine) Pad (Paddle), sgl (single) dbl (double), scr (screw); Cyls: (cylinders); IHP, NHP, SHP, BHP, RHP, HP; Boilers; *Stm P:* (steam pressure) lb (pounds); kts (knots); By (engine builder). **H** (hull details); *Coal; Cargo; Pass:* (passengers), 1st (first class), 2nd (second class), 3rd (third class), tst (tourist class); Crew.

ALFRED HOLT

Chronological History

The story of the Blue Funnel Line properly commences with Alfred Holt's father George Holt (1790—1861). The Holt family at that time resided in Rochdale, a Lancashire textile town, where George was born on June 27, 1790. Liverpool came into the picture in October 1807 when, during a visit by George's father Oliver Holt, he heard that the Liverpool cotton broker Samuel Hope was in need of a young apprentice. Within days the seventeen-year-old George was commencing a month's probationary period which was, in turn, followed by a five year apprenticeship at Hope's office in Water Street, Liverpool.

1812 November 28: George Holt, now aged 21, accepted a junior partnership in the business which was re-styled Samuel Hope & Company; thus George Holt became a cotton broker and the city of Liverpool thereafter became his permanent place of residence and it was here that his five sons were born and brought up. Now that he was established in the city a cottage was rented from Robert Durning and George Holt moved into Rake Lane, Edge Hill. From here, then a country home, the journey into the city was made by horse and carriage.

1820 George Holt married Emma Durning (1802—1871) from whose family the Rake Lane cottage was rented. Emma was a fervant Unitarian and George changed his allegiance from his Nonconformist church to hers.

1823 June 30: By amicable and mutual agreement George Holt and Samuel Hope separated in their business ways with Hope moving into banking to form the Borough Bank of Liverpool. George Holt remained in cotton; he did however maintain a keen interest in banking which he regarded as being essential to the growth of trade into the seaport of Liverpool.

1829 On June 13 Alfred Holt was born. He was the third son of George Holt, his elder brothers being William and George, junior. His younger brothers were Philip and Robert. Alfred's education commenced at the age of five when he was sent to Mr Browne's school in High Street, Edge Hill. Two years later, in 1836, he went as a boarder to Miss Hunt's (there were three of them) school at Gateacre before being sent to complete his education at the Unitarian School located in Heathfield, Knutsford.

1834 George Holt, senior, built the India Buildings which was to become, and still is, the headquarters of the Blue Funnel Line. His accounts for 1837 show that £28,000 was invested in the property.
In the same year the East India Company's monopoly to the Far East was abolished thereby opening the way for private trading to China.

1836 London had, until now, been the central source of insurance premiums for cotton both at sea and in storage. Like so many distantly controlled activities the premiums were higher and the settlement slow. In this year George Holt, snr, helped to found the Liverpool Fire and Life Assurance company (later 'and London' was inserted into the title). The new company was innovative in that lower premiums were payable for the least hazardous categories of goods with pro rata increases to match the level of risk being covered. Liverpool, by this action, became the paramount cotton insurance centre and actively engaged in the re-insurance of the high risk elements of the business. This enabled premiums to be kept at a rate that was a shade lower than could be obtained elsewhere.

1845 After final private tutoring in his home city Alfred Holt was apprenticed not in shipping but in railways with Edward Woods, the Liverpool engineer for the Liverpool & Manchester Railway Company at Edge Hill.
He therefore actually became in 1846 one of the original employees of the London & North Western Railway Company when it was formed by the amalgamation of his parent concern and the London & Birmingham and Manchester & Birmingham Railway Companies.

1850 December 31: With the competion of his five year apprenticeship Alfred Holt was noted by Edward Woods as being a technically brilliant locomotive engineer with an instinctive appreciation of the potential − and the limitations − of the steam driven locomotive. His particular skill lay in boiler design which, in the railroad business, was well ahead of all other contemporary uses of steam including more especially the sea. The year 1850, nevertheless, saw the introduction of William Inman's transatlantic steamer *City of Glasgow* which brought iron hulled screwdriven propulsion to the scene.
Alfred Holt's coming of age as an engineer coincided with a slump in railway development and no worthwhile position was available for him on the engineering staff at Edge Hill.

1851 In January Alfred Holt joined the engineering department of the Lamport and Holt organisation. He was in fact already connected with the firm because elder brother George was a founding partner with William James Lamport. George had entered the firm of T & J Brocklebank and there had met Lamport, then a clerk in Gibbs, Bright & Co. The two men joined forces to found the organisation which Alfred now joined.
His first work for them is recorded as being in connection with the planning specifications and contractual work for the screw steamer *Scamander*.
By the end of that year Alfred Holt was to be seen attending to the completion, at Denny's Dumbarton yard, of Lamport and Holt's second steamer *Orontes* and when she entered Mediterranean service during the following month Holt sailed in her on her maiden voyage as a supernumery engineer. This voyage to Sicily, Egypt and Syria gave him his first real insight into practical marine engineering under sea-going conditions. Until now Alfred Holt had regarded his work in shipping merely in the light of a temporary occupation until the time came when he could resume his railway career. Now, aware of his son's ability and sea experience, George Holt, senior, suggested that Alfred set up in Liverpool as a consultant engineer to advise the ever growing number of sailing ship owners who were now turning to steam driven propulsion for their vessels.

1852 Jan 18: Alfred Holt took over an office in number one India Building and put up his brass nameplate. It became the office that he was to occupy for the remainder of his working life. The rental was £45 per annum but his father fixed the sum payable by Alfred at £40. The staff of the office other than himself comprised only one person − Francis Young − the office keeper.

Oddly enough much of Holt's initial work came from his former master Edward Woods and consisted of carrying out the proving trials and bollard pull calculations for a series of L&N W R locomotives. He did, however, supervise the engine design and its installation into the steamer *William S Lindsay* at Newcastle-upon-Tyne. Within the year Alfred Holt's steamship business had expanded to the point where his work on the railways had to be given up and to which he was never to return.

He himself, recognised that the main problems besetting steamship owners arose from the techniques involved in building iron hulled ships coupled with the casting of the propeller shafts and stern tubes. At that time iron was brittle and in service there were many metal fatigue failures; all of this despite the slow rotating speed of a ship's engine compared with his experience of the fast engine used in a railway locomotive. The compounding system, whereby steam was passed sequentially through two consecutive cylinders, one high pressure the other low, thereby effectively using the steam pressure twice, had been patented by Jonathan Hornblower back in 1781. Railway engines were already being successfully compounded but at sea the lower mandatory boiler pressures (15—20 pounds per square inch) effectively prevented the re-use of the residual steam power.

To Alfred Holt the concept of redesigning the whole idea of ship size, engine capacity and, above all, boiler pressure and efficiency became the answer to the problem of economical steamship practice at sea. Only by the application of this concept could long sea passages become economically viable. He was aware, too, that, as things stood in 1853, fuel consumption to drive the ships of the time was such that 4 lb of coal was needed per hour for each indicated horse power; a ratio which was far too great.

Armed with this knowledge Alfred Holt began to plan his new era propulsion, but a decade was to pass before he was able to put his ideas to the test. In the interim, iron hull and engine design preoccupied his talents.

1853 March 12: The coal merchant Thomas Ainsworth, a resident of the Cumbrian village of Cleator, engaged Holt as consultant to his screw driven collier which plied between Whitehaven and Cardiff at a loss.

Rebuilt to Alfred Holt's specification *Alpha* became a modest money maker and between the young Holt and *Alpha's* captain Isaac Middleton there developed a life long friendship which resulted, later, in Middleton joining Alfred Holt's first Ocean S. S. Company's ship as her captain.

Thomas Ainsworth was so impressed with Holt's work that he suggested to Alfred a joint venture. *Alpha* could not be made really profitable because of her elementary design. New building to the hull and engine design of Alfred Holt was suggested. Father George Holt went further and extended the idea: Ainsworth and George Holt would purchase a newly built steamer if Alfred would act as consultant engineer and agent to the ship. Subject then to the venture becoming feasible he proposed that new ships to Alfred's design be built.

As a result the William Denny built home-waters screw steamer *Dumbarton Youth* was acquired. The story has it that when Alfred Holt saw the gaunt black funnel he used a few tins of powder blue paint out of the ship's store with which to repaint it. No one explains the intended use of paint of this colour and as for Alfred Holt his only recording of the event is "She was the first to have a blue funnel". What ever the truth may be *Dumbarton Youth* set a colour scheme which has persisted to this day and served well to make the vessels of the Blue Funnel Line the most instantly recognizable of all the world's great shipping companies.

1854 Encouraged by the profits from their venture Thomas Ainsworth and George Holt put up the capital for the envisaged new ship which was duly named *Cleator* in honour of the home of the Ainsworth family.

Cleator was constructed by Cato & Miller at Liverpool's Brunswick Dock under the eagle

eye of Alfred Holt. Compounding had still not arrived at sea but the new ship had the capability built into her to enable later modification should the opportunity arise — which it eventually did.

During the year the Crimean War broke out and led to the ship being chartered profitably to the French Government at the good rate of 62s 6d per registered ton per month for the duration.

1855 To capitalise on the needs of the war, the group of men, which now included Philip Holt who came across from Lamport and Holt, ordered a second ship, similar to *Cleator* but with a slightly greater carrying capacity. Named *Saladin*, because Turkey was one of the allies against Russia, the new ship was incomplete when the war ended. An attribute of the ship was her larger bunkerage to enable the extra cargo loading for the longish voyage to the Black Sea. To use her on European coastal voyages appeared unnecessarily wasteful and, instead *Saladin* was placed on the similarly distanced West Indies route to Jamaica.

On the face of it this was an unwise move because competing steamers carried the subsidised Royal Mails.

Holt's entry into the business was in fact inauspicious and within months he almost gave up his shipping interests to join his father's cotton business. Alfred Holt, apart from being the consultant engineer, was also the commercial agent for the ships and he had become keenly aware of the over competition on the route; *Cleator* and *Saladin* were not the only ex-Crimea ships dumped on the service.

However at the vital juncture, her third voyage, *Saladin* propitiously came up with an encouragingly good voyage profit and the flagging enthusiasm of Alfred (and Philip) was re-kindled.

1857 A new ship was added: *Plantagenet* to be followed in quite quick succession by *Askalon, Talisman* and *Crusader*. It almost seemed as if Holt ships were assuming names linked with the crusading days of the Holy Land.

With these five steamers trade grew and the ships, each trading as individual enterprises with shared voyage profits, continued to turn in voyage profits. It is perhaps of interest to observe that in shipping throughout the ages the individual ship system of ownership had predominated and few merchants combined to pool investment and to share out an averaged profit such as now practised by joint stock limited liability companies. Seamen like Sir Francis Drake operated in just such a manner and like so many others was his own 'Board of Directors' and issued voyage share certificates to investors like Queen Elizabeth I. In ordering four new ships in 1857 Alfred Holt, by now the leading figure in the consortium, began a practice which he was to follow for the remainder of his career; building ships in times of dockyard depression. As a result of the recent war there was a glut of tonnage available and new building plummeted. Holt was, therefore, able to negotiate excellent construction rates allied to low levels of repayment interest on the loans. He frequently pointed out that a low purchase price stayed with a ship all its life and did not merely apply to the year of its building.

Interestingly, too, Alfred Holt saw no purpose in buying low priced secondhand tonnage, a widespread phenomenon; he preferred to lay down his own hull specifications which gave a better coefficient to engine power with a resultant saving in the cost per ton of propulsion.

1859 The very circumstances that led to the Holt building spree also saw a marked and growing increase in competition to the West Indies. Surplus available tonnage unbalanced supply and demand so that forward freight rates fell and spot rates for loading per any available sailing, steam or sail, reached rock bottom. In such conditions as these it is the financially strong who are able to hold out the longest. Three such companies existed on the route; they were the Royal Mail Steam Packet Company, the West India & Pacific Steamship Company and the Spanish American Steamship Company. Against such as these the Holt finances were scant notwithstanding the wealth of George Holt, senior.

1861 Aged 71 George Holt died and with his passing also went the ready flow of capital that had been at his command. In parallel Alfred's elder brother George was fully involved financially in the building up of the Lamport and Holt fortunes — aided at times by Philip Holt.

1864 Faced with the problems of under-financing, over-competition and inevitably dwindling returns on the capital employed Alfred Holt, on behalf of the partners, sold out to the West India & Pacific concern retaining for his own sole account the *Cleator*. Her retention was deliberate. Holt needed her for trying out the new style of compound engine which he had envisaged 11 years earlier. This was his two cylinder compound tandem engine built with integral auxilliaries coupled to a boiler which drew upon his railway experience of working with higher steam pressures. At 60 lbs per square inch this was three times that of a normal steamer of the day.

The Holt engine contained two major improvements; the first was the double injection of steam into a high and then into a low pressure cylinder. This replaced the so-called simple engine with one cylinder per steam inlet. The second feature was that the cylinders were placed in tandem and operated a single balanced crankshaft with a fly wheel counterweight; thus both cylinders applied propulsion together instead of sequentially thereby doubling their shaft drive thrust per revolution.

By December of 1864 *Cleator* was at sea where her new engine cut coal consumption and therefore fuel costs, by 40 per cent. In addition she was a reliable 2 knots faster. Her proud commander was Holt's friend Captain Isaac Middleton of the *Alpha* back in 1853.

The experimental *Cleator* was not merely a whim. Alfred and Philip had discussed exhaustively the Liverpool mercantile scene. The West Indies and North America were out as far as they were concerned. Brother George had advised against taking on either Lamport and Holt or the Pacific Steam Navigation Company on the South American routes. Africa as far as the Cape of Good Hope was saturated. All that remained was the last true stronghold of the sailing ship — India and the Far East.

Indeed at this time the numerical and capacity zenith of the sailing ship era was still over a decade ahead and opinion, Europe wide, held that with fuel consumption cutting into cargo capacity sail was the only currently viable means of transport to and from the Pacific.

Samuel Rathbone, the Liverpool merchant, once addressed an audience thus:

"Steamships may occupy the Mediterranean, may tentatively go to Brazil and the River Plate — But China at least is safe for sailing ships".

Steam existed west of Good Hope but almost entirely on a port to port shuttle basis where steam overcame the vagaries of wind reliant vessels. The long voyage home concept would only prevail if Holt's economical compound engine could be relied upon.

Such was Alfred Holt's faith in his engine that even before *Cleator* commenced her proving voyage the decision to enter the China trade had been taken by he and his brother Philip. And to back their determination three revolutionary ships had been ordered, at a total cost of £156,000, from Scotts of Greenock for delivery commencing six months hence in April 1865.

1865 *Cleator* during the first six months of the year made reliable and profitable voyages to the Gulf of Biscay area of France, then to Archangel and finally two round trips to Brazil.

Jan 11: The Ocean Steam Ship Company was registered using as working capital the £156,000 involved in building *Agamemnon* (I), *Ajax* (I) and *Achilles* (I).

Jan 16: The first announcing circular to the shippers was issued in which the date for commencement of sailings was given as July 1st. The advertised route being via the Cape of Good Hope calling at Mauritius, Penang, Singapore, Hong Kong and Shanghai. Time 77 days, Inbound Foochow was added.

April: *Agamemnon* ran her trials and recorded the best fuel results of any vessel then afloat.

On each 24 hour run her coal consumption was 20 tons 6 cwt 3 quarters (45,610 lbs). This was better than engine specification because Holt had also re-designed the hull on a beam ratio of 1:8 against length and with a slimmer bow water flow coefficient.

April 19: Ahead of start up date *Agamemnon* took the maiden sailing to China. In command was Alfred Holt's long time friend and associate Captain Issac Middleton who transferred across from *Cleator*.

The outbound freight rate was £6 plus 10% per ton of 40 cubic feet volume. Inbound the freightage was to be variable according to demand. This was a calculated attempt to offset the competitiveness of the sailing ship, especially the fast tea clippers which averaged only one week longer than a Holt ship but whose freight charges for tea were only about 2/3rds of the Blue Funneller.

1866 Alfred and Philip Holt were appointed Managers of the Ocean Steam Ship Company. Alfred served 38 years until 1904 and Philip 31 years.

1867 *Achilles* arriving at Shanghai on Christmas Eve 1866 was then, like other Holt vessels, handled by Preston, Bruell & Co. They unfortunately had no cargo offering and it seemed as if a voyage home in ballast was inevitable.

Fortuitously on January 1st the new firm of Butterfield and Swire opened its office in Shanghai. Unlike Preston, Bruell & Co. their main trade was in cotton and not tea (the tea contracts were then still tied to clipper sailing ships). As a result a cargo of 600 bales of grey shirtings, consigned to Thomas Barlow & Bros., Manchester, was carried. This marked the beginning of a close and extremely important liaison between the Holts and John Samuel Swire.

Butterfield and Swire was descended from the Liverpool firm of John Swire & Sons whose principal areas of trade were from the cotton States of America and the wool exporting ports of Australia via Liverpool into the adjacent Lancashire mills. When John Swire, the founder, died in 1847 his two sons John Samuel Swire and William Hudson Swire took over control of the company.

The advent of the American Civil War cut off their main source of supply and thereby the more profitable portion of their trade. As a result John S. Swire voyaged out to China where he met, liked and entered into partnership with Richard Butterfield. John Swire was a man of undoubted vision who saw that within China the goods that he required were readily available provided someone went to fetch them. For this he proposed to establish steamer services up the main rivers of that vast continent sized country.

The Holt brothers recognised the validity of his views but asserted that their Liverpool venture had to be the priority. However as a result of the dialogue John Swire firmly established himself as one of the prime movers in the history of the development of the Blue Funnel Line.

It remains only to record that in 1872 Butterfield and Swire formed the China Navigation Company, capital £360,000, to open up the hinterland of China.

1867 The Ocean Steam Ship Co. put in a tender against P&O for the carriage of the mails to the Far East.

November 29: P&O had their three year contract renewed, by the Government (the Admiralty) for £400,000 but with an additional sliding scale of payment, not to exceed £500,000, being the sum necessary to ensure the payment by P&O of a dividend of 6% to its shareholders. This contract was higher than that put in by Holts and, backed by the Liverpool Steamship Owners' Association, a parliamentary row followed. The outcome was that clearly P&O's passenger liners carried more weight with the India Office and Colonial Office than did the Blue Funnel Freighters.

Holts, and their backers, continued to harry the Government over the contract for the ensuing decade or more.

1868 Initial experience with the *Agamemnon* class indicated that the initial trio were over engine powered for the China service. Holt's next ship *Diomed* was shorter by almost 20 feet but with a beam ratio that was increased to 8:5 and with a smaller engine. At this time the Bibby Line were building (or converting) ships which were long and narrow at a beam ratio of 1:10.

Other companies commenced a spate of ship lengthening. The main trading advantage being additional cargo capacity on the same basic engine horse power.

To test the concept further *Nestor* was constructed, also by Andrew Leslie & Co., Hebburn-on-Tyne, with a 1:9.6 beam to length ratio with an even smaller engine.

During 1868 Bibby's lost two long-ships *Calpe* and *Catalonian* (both 1:10) and Alfred Holt abandoned the attempt to emulate this thinking. However experience with *Nestor* indicated that a ratio of 1:9.6 was an improvement on the *Agamemnon* class particularly if stability was gained by the hull being made bluffer rather than yacht-like. This had as a bonus greater cargo capacity in relationship to the now smaller engine style. Alfred Holt now had the formula right and stuck to it from 1868 until 1880. The other important feature was a progressive increase in cargo carrying as hull designs improved class by class.

Sept 16: *Ajax* sank at Shanghai. The incident was to change the design concept of future Blue Funnel ships. The shaft coupling the propeller shaft to the engine had worked loose and the engineer removed it for the necessary repairs. This left the propeller and its driving shaft unattached. During that night the outgoing tide 'unscrewed' the propeller with the result that the vessel filled and settled with her uppers above water at high tide. She was quickly back in service but Alfred Holt was furious. Not with the engineer but with his own lack of design foresight. Thereafter his ships had a water tight gland installed in the propeller shaft tunnel; in addition as a precaution the coupling flange was made larger than the stern tube.

1869 The opening of the Suez Canal shortened the route to China by 3300 miles; it also cut the voyage time by between ten and twelve days — reducing it to 55 days outbound and 60 inbound (being the effect of the spin of the earth plus the consequent winds).

Metaphorically it took the wind out of the sails of the traditionalists and made it economic to introduce more steamer services to China, Japan and the Pacific and especially to the Persian Gulf or India.

Thus overnight the whole of the trade beyond Suez and the Cape of Good Hope was transformed.

As far as Alfred Holt was concerned there were two main factors: His long voyage compound ships had too much bunker space and, more importantly with the establishment of bunkering facilities at Aden, ships previously unable to compete with him were now able to steam through the Canal. The effect of this Holt knew would be a rate war. Granted there would be more cargo offering now that the sailing ship was virtually out of the race (here he was far from being correct; sailing ship owners took a quarter of a century to fade out and many of them merely moved into steam). But voyage profits would fall by virtue of the price cutting that would follow.

To counteract this competitive threat the Managers of the Company decided to inaugurate regular sailings at shorter fixed intervals. To achieve this five new ships were ordered for delivery during the ensuing two years.

1869 Holt's Far East trade was beset by two main competitors. The Peninsular & Oriental SN Co. from Britain and, following the opening of the Suez Canal the French mail steamers of Messageries Imperiales (Messageries Maritimes).

Agamemnon loaded at Hankow 2,516,000 lbs of tea, then the largest cargo ever loaded into a single ship; the freightage was also a record at £28,087. Her voyage to London was achieved in 77 days (not a record) so that the first of the new season tea sold in London at a premium of 2d per pound.

1870 *Priam* (I) and *Sarpedon* (I) were delivered.
At Singapore Walter Mansfield & Co. replaced Symes & Co as agents.
Seven ships owned.

1871 *Hector,* (I) *Ulysses* (I), *Menelaus* (I) and *Glaucus* (I) came into service. The new vessel *Ulysses* went ashore in the Red Sea. The damage necessitated a return to Liverpool for repairs and a voyage loss of substantial proportions was suffered.

1872 *Patroclus* (I), *Deucalion* (I) and *Antenor* (I) were completed. *Ulysses* continued with her unlucky spell. Near to Singapore her propeller shaft snapped and, without power, she drifted ashore. This incident was the forerunner of four broken shafts which caused considerable anxiety to the Managers.
Cleator and *Saladin* were sold out of the fleet.

1873 Competition to the Far East increased with the advent of services to Shanghai operated by Glen Line. Castle Line (Thomas Skinner & Co.) and Watts Milburn & Co. This year saw the commencement of a six year period of recession and trading slump.

1874 Transpacific trading between San Francisco and Chinese ports commenced with the Pacific Mail Steamship Company's twice monthly service.

1875 Oct 4: *Hector* was lost in the approaches to Amoy harbour when she struck a reef and sank. Worth £36,000 *Hector* was the company's first total loss.
Voyage gross earnings before shore expenses reached £145,217 and reserves stood at £283,000. Other business — such as deposit interest and rentals added a further £70,000. The annual dividend stood at 15%. Because of the general level of financial stability Holt's now decided to carry their own vessel insurance risk. Until 1875 each subscriber had been responsible for insuring his own share in the venture; the company assuming liability for the hull only, this was limited to £500 per hull until 1870 when the figure had been increased to £2,000. By 1875 the insurance account stood at £36.225, and so that annual risk per vessel was increased to £20,000. In all the insurance account contained a sum equivalent to one total loss replacement every 14 months. For this reason the company decided to underwrite its own ships.
Three new ships were ordered — all with two funnels — they were *Orestes* (I), *Stentor* (I) and *Anchises* (I). The Ocean SS Co now owned 16 ships. Japan entered the trading arena with the opening of a service by Mitsubishi KK across the Pacific to U.S. Pacific ports — mainly San Francisco.

1876 Mar 7: *Orestes* (I) was sunk off Galle Face harbour Ceylon. Sept 4: Off Ushant *Sarpedon* sank after being in collision with the Belgian steamer *Julia David*. A tribunal, chaired by Justice Sir Robert Phillimore found *Sarpedon* solely to blame and awarded £20,000 compensation to the Belgians.
Suspecting collusion Alfred Holt went to Antwerp, following a tip off by *Julia David's* steward named Meyer.
On March 12, 1877 the Appeal Courts gave permission for the re-opening of the case. In the process most of the opposing witnesses were proved guilty of perjury. An attempt to silence Meyer, Holt's principal witness, on a trumped up charge, was thwarted and on August 7, 1877 the court found in favour of *Sarpedon*. Only £2,000 was recovered from *Julia David's*

owners but Alfred Holt was wholly satisfied in that right had prevailed.

During this year the first signs of a change in the Britons tea drinking habits manifested itself. The lower priced Indian and Ceylonese teas dominated the market and the demand for the weaker scented China teas commenced to decline.

Voyage profits for the year were the lowest yet recorded. *Antenor* (I) was actually chartered to Lamport & Holt and traded to the River Plate.

For the very first time, too, a Holt ship had no outward cargo and sailed as far as Jeddah in ballast. Rates fell to as low as 30/- per ton.

1877 Philip Holt together with John Swire and accompanied by Captain Isaac Middleton, now the firm's Shipping Superintendent, made a fact finding tour of their Far East bases and set about overhauling their methods and procedures.

A number of accounting changes were made — the foremost being that of apportioning overheads against each voyage so as to give a truer cumulative picture of any particular sailing. Commodity accounts — coal, tin, cotton seed etc. — kept separate from voyage accounts because of their dependence upon the fluctuating Liverpool commodity markets were revitalised and made to trade for the company in their own right. Holt's entered the future's market, selling forward and using their foreign based local management expertise to buy effectively as well as in time to meet delivery deadlines.

1878 On the voyage home from China Captain Isaac Middleton died at sea.

1879 The tiny coasting vessel *Fantee* of only 120 ft (36.57 m) and 167 gross registered tons was taken out from the Clyde to Singapore under her own steam by Captain Highton. She spent her career of 20 years in these waters.

August saw the establishment of the Far Eastern Conference. It had been the brain child of the indomitable John Swire (although he in fact copied the Calcutta Conference of 1875). Over competition to the East was rife and freight rates fluctuated not only by the voyage but by the actual competition available at the overcrowded ports on loading day.

Swire warned Holts, in 1878, that Thomas Skinner's 'Castles' and McGregor Gow's 'Glens' were faster, served London, or Southampton, and seemed more efficient. The only way Holts could master this competition was, Swire said, by regular sailings. Not just by Holt ships, who had insufficient of them, but by a common pooling agreement operated at fixed rates per commodity per ton. Sailings would be regulated (even rationed in times of necessity) and supporting shippers would receive a deferred loyalty rebate payable 6 months in arrears. Initially Alfred and Philip turned the suggestion down. In April 1879 Swire was back with his calculations which proved that a loss of £500 per steamer was his share of the present situation but Holts, themselves, were down by £1,000 — "and" he added "without any necessity or thanks". Philip became convinced and joined the John Swire camp.

Finally the managers agreed but with a caution and reluctance that left John Swire to do the negotiating with the competition. The result in August 1879 was the first Far Eastern Conference. Its members consisted of P&O, Glen, Castle, Messageries Maritimes — and Blue Funnel. It's title perhaps should have included the word 'freight' for passenger fares were excluded — an omission that was to cause later trouble.

1880 Tobacco production in North Sumatra had in 1865 seen the first exports to Europe all carried in sailing ships operated by the Dutchman Pieter van den Arend.

When Philip Holt was in Singapore three years earlier George Mansfield had pointed out the opportunity that existed. On his return home Philip proceeded to persuade the Managers to enter the trade.

By early 1880 the venture was underway. The *Ganymede*, ordered in 1879, was on station ready to carry the season's tobacco from Belawan-Deli, Sumatra, to Singapore. At Deli the hulk *Sarah Nicholson* was installed to act as a storage depot. A second steamer the tug *Ascanius* (I) was delivered and, in order to open up the Malaysian plantations at Langkat the wooden hulk *Andes* was positioned to Penang.

The effect, against the background of tobacco's different cropping season from tea, coupled with the ongoing lower cargoes of Chinese produce, was dramatic.

It also provided another commodity in which the company might judiciously trade.

The deep sea Far East fleet saw the commissioning of *Jason* (I) and the ten *Laertes* class. The fleet now numbered 23 vessels.

1880 *Achilles* ran aground, fully laden, at Hankow; at John Swire's behest she was towed to port by the China Navigation Company's *Shanghai*.

By February — barely six months after the commencement of the Far Eastern Conference —the results revealing the evidence of John Swire's wisdom. Equally Holts in Liverpool were reassured by the receptive attitude of the shippers and their brokers. Clearly their need for reliable rates on regular sailings was more important to business than unsettling cut throat competition during which no-one gained and many lost. As far as the Ocean Steam Ship Company was concerned the recession of 1879 was behind them and they were able to face the '80's' in a stronger trading position.

By the autumn of the year Ocean's cargo results were 40 per cent up on 1879 — despite an oversupply of tonnage on the China run. Even so Philip Holt observed to Swire that with the recession behind them Holts would have achieved the 40 per cent gain even in a competitive market — a view with which John Swire did not agree.

1881 Two new tobacco steamers entered service; they were *Mercury* and *Ganymede*.

To improve the facilities storage sheds at Belawan-Deli replaced the ageing *Sarah Nicholson* and for the agent there a commodious house-cum-office was built.

During late 1880 John Swire and Alfred Holt became engaged in a somewhat acrimonious correspondence.

The problem for Swire was that Holt ships were slow. They were derived from pre-Suez concepts of low coal burning engines. Blue Funnel passenger fares were two thirds of those charged by their Conference colleagues because — they all agreed — Holt ships were slower. But Holts made extra to voyage profits money from passengers and were satisfied. John Swire urged the building of faster vessels. "Merchants pay for delivery not warehousing" was his view.

Alfred Holt rebuffed him by instancing the then inevitable loss of the 15% earning which they made on their slow-ship passenger rate conference advantage.

But when, wearing the other hat, the Holts asked for lower freight rates because of slower steamers there was, to put it mildly, somewhat of a furore.

Trouble was brewing.

1882 The end of the recession in 1879 was short lived. Now a new slump began which was to last until 1886. In an attempt to influence production, interest rates fell; one effect was that Holt's share of cargoes outbound and inbound actually grew in volume. 1882's results were the best yet; Albert Crompton being appointed the Manager during the year to join Alfred and Philip Holt. Crompton, whose name first appears as a part shareholder in the tobacco fleet vessels with 8/64ths, was a staunch traditionalist and frequently resisted with much force and logic the more liberal views of John Swire. Albert Crompton was also a man who imposed and practised rigid economies and with the Holt brothers adopted the careful role of devil's advocate. His policies had done much to keep the company slim in terms of land

based overheads and these now paid off because there now followed a period of depressed annual returns which lasted without a break until 1893. The only comfort the Holts could draw was that their competitors suffered equally with them from the extremely low freight rates that prevailed for a decade.

It was made worse on the Far East route because of the habit of other owners to dump vessels on the Pacific berth in times of depression.

1882 As a part of the development of maritime trading, as opposed to their pure shipping activities, the company set up a Cargo Insurance Adjustment Fund. By this scheme they were able, on certain cargoes, to assume some of the risk themselves thereby enabling their port agents to charge and obtain higher rates by virtue of the lower insurance premiums.

In the tobacco trade the picture continued to be rosy and the company's tobacco accounts revealed annual average profits of £25,000.

But competition was to arrive in 1883 with its usual effect upon monopolistically inclined situations.

In the interim however, Holts, in partnership with their Singapore agents built the *Hecuba* with which to enter the Bangkok rice exporting business. Rates were nothing near as good as tobacco mainly because of the presence of a multitude of Chinese and several German owners. *Hecuba* however carried passengers at a time when few berths were available and this revenue, offsetting the low freight rates, was profitable. The vessel is recorded as making a profit (on the new accountancy system) of £10,000 per annum. The Holt share of this being 46/64ths.

1882 Apr: John Swire resigned as Chairman of the Far East Shipping conference. The attitude of Holts was his reason. Their slower ships were claimed to require lower freightage rates as well as lower passenger rates. But when Thomas Skinner and McGregor Gow asked for the same rates for their own slower ships Holts refused. In parallel the Conference commission (then called primage) was set at 5%. In Liverpool Holts paid 10% and refused to change to the agreed level. Because, they said, their slower ships required an inducement to shippers. Despite all of this the need to maintain some sort of control predominated and, albeit unhappily, the Conference survived. It was recognised as a necessary evil and the truth of this is that Conferences have persisted widely to this day in most common carriage industries (including aviation).

In the autumn of the year new Far East competition loomed. A company to be known as 'The China Shippers Mutual Steam Navigation Company' was announced to act as a self contained Conference to be owned and controlled by the shippers not the carriers. Subscription for the shares was invited. Holts regarded the new organisation with scepticism. Operating ships was, in itself, damnably difficult. To do so and keep shareholding merchants happy was nigh on an impossibility.

1883 The Holt family, particularly George and Philip were involved in the firm of Lamport & Holt.

Regular weekly sailings to Singapore and China were introduced. Inward cargoes were mainly rice, rubber, tea and tobacco.

In this year Blue Funnel purchased the Lamport & Holt ship *Memnon* which was mainly based at Singapore for feeder ship duties.

1884 Apr 21: *Oopack*, China Mutual's first ship arrived at Hong Kong, 41 days out from London. Dents were their agents in Hankow and Shanghai. Norris & Joyner in London. Surprisingly to Holts a profit was recorded in the company's first year and a 5% dividend

became payable on a profit of £7,700. This being followed in 1885 with another 5% paid from a better profit of £12,600.

The China Mutual's Board also showed their strength by announcing that the dividend would rise in future to 8%. All of this being against the background of recession and a depression in shipping that was affecting the Blue Funnel Line. All this saw the commencement of a prolonged and stoutly fought competitive struggle between the members of the Far East Conference, with Holts as main activators and China Mutual.

1885 It is interesting to note that Holts were generally sticklers for the niceties of business. For example when Theodore Bogaardt purchased the small local steamer *Pyah Pekhet* 'on the company's behalf' before approval was given by Liverpool Holts refused to ratify the purchase as such but offered to buy 33/64ths. This Bogaardt declined but he, in turn, accepted a loan of half the purchase price.

Using the same processes of loans, applicable to 33/64ths of the profits, Bogaardt extended his Singapore feeder services to an ever widening range of East Indian ports.

The vessels which Bogaardt owned under this system were to include *Banjermassin*, *Calypso*, *Devonhurst*, *Flintshire* and *Kongsee*. Not one of them was Holt owned, but all of them were Blue funnellers and each contributed to the growth of Singapore as a trading city and to the port becoming Holts main collecting base.

One aspect of the Singapore base was its effect on the Far Eastern Conference. Feeder services were omitted from Conference terms and conditions with the odd result that some of Holt's feeder cargoes ended up in the holds of non-Blue Funnel vessels. Their Conference con-freres being firmly of the opinion that owner's feeder profit must arise from the voyage (the voyage profits of old) and not upon the feeder's potential to load deep sea carriers at a profit.

The traditional flow of Chinese emigrants from Swatow to either Singapore or Bangkok continued but now instead of being carried mainly in Chinese vessels, mainly junks, over half of the total were using the faster and larger ships of the Holt-Mansfield-Bogaardt partnership which operated as the Singapore-Bangkok Line.

The Ocean Steam Ship Company certainly had a controlling interest in the venture and even loaned funds to build the ships but wisely they realised that local traders, as represented by Messrs. Mansfield, Bogaardt and Crompton, would have infinitely more grasp of local conditions than would any group of managers based in Liverpool.

To quote the Board minutes: 'Mr. Bogaardt who (with Mansfield) represents the Company's interests at Singapore has considerable shares in all three steamers and may be trusted to do the best with them that can be done. This has been a main inducement to the managers to enter on this business'.

Hebe, the first of two sister ships (the other was *Calypso*) for the tobacco trade entered service at Singapore. *Telamon* (I), *Titan* (I) and *Palamed* (I) were commissioned for the Far East Ocean SS Co.'s fleet.

The year also saw the arrival of the three trim cargo passenger liners *Medusa*, *Hecate* and *Hydra* for the Singapore-Bangkok service; both were 33/64ths being shared with Theodore Bogaardt, Mansfield and Crompton.

Teucer, inward bound with a full cargo of Sumatran tobacco was lost off Ushant.

1886 *Palinurus* (I) *Prometheus* and *Dardanus* of the Laertes class were completed; they entered service at a time when the China Shippers Mutual S N Co. were enfilading the Holt preserves by part loading at Glasgow, then Liverpool and finally London. Until now Liverpool and its industrial heartland had been Holt territory. The only saving grace was that China Mutual had agreed, reluctantly, to load at Conference rates. At this time Holts owned 28 ships.

1887 Killick Martin were appointed London outward cargo agents. They were to hold the appointment until 1945. Up to 1887 Liverpool and Birkenhead had been the loading berths with London as a unloading port prior to calls at continental ports such as Rotterdam, Amsterdam and Hamburg. The ships then proceeded round the north of Scotland to Glasgow and Liverpool.

For this Swires acted as inbound agents only.

The London appointment came about as a result of a fundamental change in outward cargo requirements. Holt ships were carrying increasing amounts of machinery, steel pipes and girders plus boilers and quantities of shaped steel plating for the construction of storage tanks. Railway construction metals was also on the increase.

Feb 16: Blue Funnel ships commenced loading at Glasgow in retaliation and in opposition to China Mutual.

Apr: China Mutual now refused to recognise Conference freight rates and joined with Gellatly, Hankey & Sewell's Mogul Line to operate their own Far East Conference – at rates below those currently in force. The situation was worsened by the parity with P&O rates – excluding passenger.

July: Ocean SS and Glen (McGregor, Gow) offered Shipping Agents a voyage profit rebate system which was similar in concept to the scheme that had led to the formation of China Shippers Mutual S N Co. A rate war was to follow.

Sept 26: China Mutual matched the Ocean/Glen rates and conditions.

1887 *Sappho* was built for Far East feeder services based upon Singapore. Holt's also acquired a remarkable little ship – *Will o' the Wisp*. Built in 1883 and registered in Hull she nevertheless was based at Yokohama to operate feeder services out of the many small Japanese ports which then lacked interior roadways to the bigger cities. This concept was unsuccessful and Walter Mansfield secured her in 1886 for similar small port services along the undeveloped Malaysian East cost with ownership passing to Alfred Holt & Co. – not Ocean SS Co – in 1887.

In a career spanning 52 years this tiny steamer passed through the hands of 18 owners. Her mythical name, new to the East, translated into a phrase which is said still to exist as 'Shegum-Shego' to describe a peripatetic coaster.

1888 In the dispute with China Mutual John Swire was asked to mediate. His proposal was starkly simple – China Mutual should participate in an outward and homeward Conference. There was to be no undercutting inbound to undermine the United Kingdom (and European) cargo rates. Also, to prevent unbalancing the pooling effect, rotational sailings China Mutual and Mogul should not exceed their existing one sailing per month. This was refused although within China Mutual there were sharp Board room differences of opinion; John Swire's solution had the merit of the economic sense that always came from this sagacious trader.

Ulysses (II) of the *Laertes* class was delivered; she was given a steel hull and triple expansion engines. Her performance did not impress Holts and the next four ships reverted to compound engines.

In shipping terms the Blue Funnel vessels began to become dated because the well proven design of the past was no longer sufficient.

Jan 11: *Priam* (I) was lost.

1889 *Hydra* was placed in in the Singapore-Bangkok service. The Far East trade war continued with freight rates falling. In Jan 1888 heavy goods stood at £2.80 per ton. By Aug 1889 they had fallen to £1.35 with tea actually as low as £1. As part of their reaction to the situation the Ocean SS managers. Alfred and Philip Holt and Albert Crompton had

commenced routing ships directly out to Japan and home via Australia (with voyage profit reductions due to extra steaming distances).

The crisis had created within the India Building a realisation that trade virtually dependent upon Shanghai as the turn-round port was no longer in Blue Funnel's best interests. Cautious diversification was seen to be a necessity although, with so much at stake, finding a settlement with China Mutual remained the prime objective.

To meet the demand mentioned in 1887 it was decided to release a part of the firm's Reserve Investments. The sum of £400,000 was earmarked for the building of eight ships in two groups of four. The first to be in service by late 1890 and the second quartet in 1892. Passenger accommodation was to be excluded because of the growth in size and capacity of the mail liners owned by P&O.

There was a degree of opposition from the shareholders — those involved preferred four ships only. The Holt management put, as the alternative option, the closing down of the company and the distribution of the proceeds. This, however, mobilised the silent majority and the scheme went ahead.

With the arrival of the first four new ships: *Myrmidon* (I), *Teucer* (II) *Priam* (II) and *Polyphemus* (I), the fleet stood at 30 vessels. Services to Australia were commenced by means of a joint venture with the West Australian S.N.Co. (Charles Bethell & Co.) from Singapore to Fremantle. Through freight rates from Liverpool to Australia were introduced. Prior to 1889 the West Australia S.N. Co's ships connected with P&O's services at Singapore. Now Holts, through the good offices of John Swire, became the sole agents for the service to Western Australia. Holt's placed *Saladin* in service with West Australian's *Australind*.

1890 The third of the cyclical trade depressions began and once again was to last for six years.

These general recessions were more land based than seaborne and despite their effect on employment in the manufacturing spheres did little to curtail the steady growth of larger and more efficient steamships. Holts followed their policy of ordering new tonnage when prices and loan interest rates were low.

Myrmidon (I), *Teucer* (II), *Polyphemus* (I) and *Priam* (II) were all delivered.
Ulysses lost.

Changes in the inward cargo from China were now the cause for a careful re-appraisal. China tea was being displaced by Indian and Ceylonese brands. In fact during the 1890 tea season only three full cargoes of tea were loaded and Holts carried one of them. In place of tea came rice, sago, sugar, timber and wool. These commodities were also loaded at ports different from the tea wharves of the traditional locations of the past.

1891 There was some degree of satisfaction in Liverpool because the new Blue Funnel ships had been designed for the carriage of bulk and awkward cargoes and this capability commenced to attract a new style of freight at virtually the same moment as the Lancashire and Yorkshire textile exports started to decline. Some of the outward cargoes were, in fact, mill machinery with which to equip China's own home textile industry.

During the year the subsidiary company *Nederlandsche Stoomboot Maatschappij 'Oceaan'* (N.S.M.O.) was founded in conjunction with the Amsterdam firm of J. B. Meyer. Originally founded in 1851 by H. W. Meyer as sailing ship owners, the name changed to J. B. Meyer with the decisions to go in to steam.

The service inaugurated by N.S.M.O. had terminal ports at Amsterdam and Batavia. Blue Funnel was now in a position to compete with the Dutch *Rotterdam Lloyd* and *Netherland Lloyd* who together had in 1880 formed the Dutch East Indies operator *Koninklijke Paketvaart Maatschappij* (K.P.M.) — The Royal Packet Company.

These Dutch feeder services were a competitive threat to Holt's Singapore entreport

connections. Furthermore they were diverting trade to Dutch ports. To counter this and to compete Blue Funnel formed, in 1891, a Singapore based subsidiary the *East Indian Ocean Steam Ship* Company (E.I.O.S.S.) with a capital of £98,000. The new company absorbed the Bogaardt vessels plus the local services steamers owned by Alfred Holt. Although operating from Singapore control was exercised from Liverpool by reason of the holding by the parent concern of a majority of the issued share capital. The ships were even registered at Liverpool.

Competition in the East Indies became intense.

The competing *China Mutual S.N.Co.* finally gave up its struggle against the Conference terms and joined the Homeward Conference by accepting its conditions. Like Blue Funnel China Mutual was becoming increasingly aware of the continental European competition. For one thing the growth in cargo capacity which came from Europe was inexorably driving down the freightage rates. Only the growth in annual freight carryings supported Blue Funnel's profits. Even in England the increasing trade out of Manchester was having an effect.

1892 Blue Funnel earned £27,500 from 70 voyages undertaken during the year.

To their acute discomfort China Mutual's results revealed an earning of £45,000 from a mere 21 sailings. The shareholders who had opposed the size of the recent eight ship programme seemed to have been justified but some of the new vessels coming on stream were not yet contributing to the voyage profit account.

Nevertheless a need to revitalise the aggressiveness of the management commenced to gain ground.

One bright spot was the reaching of an agreement with the Dutch mail companies in the Java trade. This stopped the gathering price cutting war and reinstated commercial realism into what could easily have become cut throat competition. Unfortunately the compromise did not include the K.P.M. subsidiary whose rates still undercut those of E.I.O.S.S.

The small steamer *Maha Vajirunhis*, operated by Haacke & Co, but in reality built and paid for by Alfred Holt (although the records do not show the ship as being a Blue Funneller) became the centre piece of the struggle. K.P.M's brilliant local Director, Op Ten Noort recognised that Holt's would not continue their Padang-Penang-Singapore service indefinitely at a loss. He was right and Holts sold *Maha Vajirunis* to K.P.M who continued to work her for Haacke.

1893 China Mutual came to a compromise with Holts on the outward bound cargo rates but still resisted actual Outward Conference membership.

During the year (January 1st—December 31st) net profits rose from the previous £27,500 to £50,000.

1894 The discovery of gold in Western Australia led to a general increase in shipping. This resulted in the introduction of the jointly owned steamer *Sultan*. The service became Singapore-Batavia-Darwin-Cossack-Onslow-Gascogne-Geraldton-Fremantle.

Back in Europe the terms of the outward Conference were finally agreed and China Mutual's management played a more willing part in their implementation. Profits for the year doubled to £114,700. This was not because of any dramatic changes in the freight rates for the volume carried. It arose from a fall in the price of coal, a reduction in the Suez Canal dues, which came from a change in the method of calculating tonnage, plus a batch of internal re-organisations and cost cutting economies at the India Buildings. This latter action included a 15% reduction in salaries — which brought Blue Funnel more or less in line with others in the industry at Liverpool.

1895 At the annual general meeting three new managers were appointed: Richard Durning Holt, George Holt, Junior and Maurice Llewelyn Davies. One other innovation was the proposal to pay them a salary — a thing unheard of until now; mainly because the original managers (Alfred Holt, Philip Holt and Albert Crompton) held such considerable investments in the company that the annual dividends were held to be sufficient incentive to do well. Under the stimulus of the new blood a period of expansion commenced. Profits for the year rose to £123,000.

1896 British and foreign tonnage in and out of Singapore reached 3,919,000 tons. There was also a marked degree of over capacity and, as one would expect, freight rates fell. This can be seen in the year's results which fell back to £59,100.

1897 To help combat the overcapacity problem the Straits Homeward Conference was re-instated.

1898 Blue Funnel purchased the West Australian S.N. Co's half share in the *Sultan* consequent upon the introduction by the Australians of their *Karrakatta*. This gave each partner two steamers each for the Singapore-Fremantle service.

1900 The company's profits reached their highest yet peak at £302,880. This represented a twelvefold increase in only eight years. At the turn of the century a fleet of 41 ships carried the Holt colours.

1901 A monthly service was inaugurated from Glasgow to Australia. The route was out via the Cape of Good Hope and inwards via the Suez Canal. *Orestes* (III) took the first sailing on February 2nd. One aspect was the avoidance of the need to tranship at Singapore. The service had the side effect of by-passing the work of the East Indian Ocean S.S.Co.

1902 The Ocean S.S.Co. added the word 'Limited' to its title. But more importantly the year saw the acquisition of the competing *China Mutual Steam Navigation Company* which had been formed in 1882. A fleet of 13 steamers grossing 76,100 tons was taken over. One new service was inherited with the fleet — it was from China across the Pacific to the Juan de Fuca and Puget Sound ports of Canada and the United States. Vancouver, Seattle and Portland being amongst them.

1903 Mansfields became a limited company with Holts as the major shareholders. The group's new offices at Singapore became known as Blue Funnel Corner — although the correct name was Ocean Building.

1908 Three passenger ships were ordered for the Australian service.

1910 The inauguration of a first class passenger service to Australia commenced with the completion of *Aeneas* (I), *Ascanius* (II) and *Anchises* (III) (actually delivered in 1911). The premier sailing was taken by *Aeneas* on November 8th.

1911 When Alfred Holt died in this year the combined fleets stood at 62 vessels. His nephews Richard Holt and Lawrence Holt continued the business together with Alfred's son George. Richard Holt acted as the senior partner and motivator until his retirement in 1941.

1913 *Nestor* (III) and *Ulysses* (IV) were delivered for the Australian service — making a total of five ships on the route. Liverpool by now had also replaced Fishguard as the passenger embarkation port. The two new ships were the largest on the Australian berth — but not for long. White Star introduced their elegant *Ceramic* in July.
Interestingly Blue Funnel placed during the year orders with Workman Clark & Co, Belfast, for two 19,000 ton Australia passenger ships but with the intervention of the war these ships were never built.

1914 The ships owned by the Straits S.S.Co. stood at 17 vessels as Holts became the largest shareholder.
August 4: Great Britain entered the First World War. Blue Funnel owned 83 exceptionally fine ships of which 71 saw Government service. 18 were sunk by enemy action and a further twelve were seriously damaged.

1915 To replace war losses Royden's Indra Line of seven ships was purchased. They, too, provided an entry into the New York — Far East Conference which was retained. This new route, coupled with the transpacific service of China Mutual was consolidated into the 'Round the World' route.

1917 June saw the purchase of Greenshields, Cowie & Co's 'Knight Line' consisting of four steamers.

1919 The post war reconstruction of the group called for the building of 28 new vessels of which 4 were designed to carry a substantial number of passengers.

1920 May 29 *Aeneas* (I) resumed the Australian services which were intermittent until *Nestor* (III), *Ulysses* (IV), *Ascanius* (II) and *Anchises* (III) returned to the service.

1922 Mansfield's took over the managership of the Straits S.S.Co. and the staff of both concerns was merged.

1923 After the war the demand for passenger berths to the Far East was such that Blue Funnel built the four *Sarpedon* class ships and transferred *Aeneas* from the Australia route. This enabled a four-weekly service to Singapore, China and Japan to be maintained.

1924 Against the background of reduced passenger trading on the Australian service Holt's five passenger ships were entered into a joint service with the White Star Line; the aim being to control and eliminate surplus capacity. The first sailing of the joint service was taken by *Ascanius* on March 4.

1926 The Australian joint service was joined by the Aberdeen Line and with their advent a fortnightly sailing was achieved. Nevertheless it was quickly realised that there were now too many vessels employed and *Aeneas* (I) was transferred to the Far East route. The decline in trade continued and lasted until the end of the coming Great Depression.

1928 The Singapore-Western Australia service was now maintained by Blue Funnel's *Centaur* (II) in consort with the West Australian S.N.Co's *Gascoyne* and *Minderoo.*

1935 The Glen Line — comprising the Glen and Shire Lines — was acquired out of the collapse of the Royal Mail Group:
During the year a controlling interest was taken in the Straits S.S.Co. This greatly improved Blue Funnel's capabilities in the handling of the smaller amounts of cargo to and from the many small ports in the Straits area.

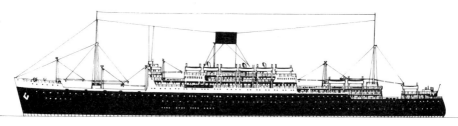

JASON
The profile of the proposed 20,000 ton liner was unmistakably 'Blue Funnel'

1939 Shaw Savill & Albion had taken over the previous services and ships of the White Star Line and had continued the joint service with Blue Funnel. However the advent of *Dominion Monarch* so unbalanced the pool that Holts withdrew and thereafter their ships sailed independently. Within months the exigencies of war reduced the service to one ship —and that was the Blue Funnel *Nestor* (III). Holts considered building a 20,000 ton answer to *Dominion Monarch* which was overtaken by war. *Jason* would have been her name.
The outbreak of the second World War saw, once more, the switching of virtually all of the fleet into Government service of one sort or another. As in the previous conflict the company was to suffer grievous losses.

1940 Jan 21: *Protesilaus* (I) was mined in the Bristol Channel.
Feb 17: *Pyrrhus* (II) fell to a torpedo off Cape Finisterre.
June 17: *Teiresias* (I) was bombed and sunk off St Nazaire.
July 2: *Aeneas* (I) sank after prolonged air attack of Start Point, Devon.
Nov 11: *Automedon*. At daylight in the Indian Ocean the armed merchant cruiser *Atlantis*, Capt. Bernhard Rogge, first encountered *Automedon* (I) at a range of 18 miles in a plate glass sea. The two ships converged until, at 4,600 yards, *Atlantis* swung to starboard, cleared for action and fired a warning shell over his enemy. The Blue Funneller, for Rogge recognised the elegantly distinctive silhouette when it was ten miles away, began immediately to radio for assistance. *Atlantis* at once opened fire. *Automedon* managed only to send 'RRR Automedon 0416N' before the transmission was jammed.
After twelve prior similar actions the gunfire of *Atlantis* was extremely accurate; in fact the very first shells demolished the bridge. Capt. W. B. Ewan and everyone there was killed. The following three salvoes scored eleven hits before *Atlantis* fell silent. Aboard *Automedon*,

still steaming at full speed, a man appeared at the stern gun intent upon opening fire. Three more salvoes plummeted into *Automedon*, killing the gunner.

The Holt ship now stopped. When the boarding party from *Atlantis* gained the wallowing vessel they were met by a shambles of destruction with all the ship's papers, except those in the safe, destroyed. Opening the hatches revealed a cargo worth millions to the Allied war effort. *Automedon* was voyaging from Liverpool, via Durban, to Penang, Singapore, Hong Kong and Shanghai. The cargo, all crated, consisted of aircraft, motor cars, machinery spares, bicycles, microscopes, service uniforms, steel and copper sheets, cameras, sewing machines plus whisky, beer, cigarettes and food supplies. There were also 120 mail bags.

Bernhard Rogge knew that he was lying in a relatively busy shipping lane and that any ship coming up on the two stationary vessels would recognise the situation in time to send out a radio message before *Atlantis* could act to prevent it. He therefore allowed only three hours for the transfer to *Atlantis* of the crew (31 British — of whom 2 died of wounds — 56 Chinese and three passengers, of which one was a woman), all their possessions, all the frozen meat and food, the ship's papers plus the mail bags. The Britons showed their appreciation of Rogge's gesture over their personal effects by assisting with the transfer of the food but with nothing else — except that they showed the enemy where 550 cases of whisky were stowed in number three hold! Later 2½ million Chesterfield cigarettes were helpfully located.

Rogge next became aware that the 56 Chinese contained twenty or so survivors of Lawther & Latta's *Anglo-Saxon* which had been sunk in the North Atlantic. These men were now on their way home to Hong Kong. Their phlegmatic stoicism was impressive. While the transshipment continued the ship's papers were prised from the safe. The death of all those on the bridge had prevented the destruction of the secret documents. Thus the Germans gained possession of Admiralty Sailing Instructions, the Merchant Navy code, deciphering tables 7, 8 and 9. Later, when the mail bags were examined two sacks were found to be marked 'Safe Hand. British Master Only'. To the astonishment of Capt. Rogge these proved to be mail to the Commander-in-Chief, Far East and included Cabinet papers on a suggested defence of the Far East plus a review of the European situation at that time. Details were also found of minefields, new fleet cipher tables plus a number of secret service documents in code. The range of the contents of these two mail sacks was so comprehensive that the Japanese, later, believed them to be fakes put aboard merchant ships for the purpose of misleading the enemy . . .

The engineers of *Atlantis* next reported that *Automedon's* steering gear had been wrecked by shells. The concept of towing her clear of the shipping lanes had to be abandoned. Accordingly time bombs were put aboard and at 15.07 hours the thirteenth victim of *Atlantis* sank by the stern.

By coincidence that same night, using the *Automedon's* decodes, the W/T office picked up an exchange of signals between another Holt ship, *Helenus* (I) and Colombo. Both were alarmed at the 'RRR' signal, meaning raider followed by silence. *Atlantis* took a bearing on the signals and established that *Helenus* was on a parallel course with the German ship. Fortunately for *Helenus* Capt Rogge was not awakened until dawn and, by then, *Helenus* was too far away to chase.

Rogge's involvement with Blue Funnel ships does not quite end at this point.

When, at 08.09 on November 22 1941 the British cruiser Devonshire detected *Atlantis* between Ascension and Freetown in the South Atlantic the German ship, herself, sent out the 'RRR' raider alert followed by the name *Polyphemus*. Aboard *Devonshire* Capt. R. D. Oliver knew that the correct procedure was now 'RRR' followed by the code letters of the day. Keeping *Atlantis* at a safe distance he checked. *Polyphemus* (III) had been at Balboa on Sept. 21 1941. It could well be her. He checked again with his C-in-C. 'Is *Polyphemus* genuine?' and the reply was 'No, repeat No.' In the interim Captain Oliver flew the scouting Walrus aircraft over the suspect vessel with the query 'Is the stern cruiser or counter?'. Back came the fatal reply 'Cruiser'. At 09.35 *Devonshire* opened fire. *Atlantis* sank at 10.16 by scuttling charges as the crew abandoned ship.

Sept 4: *Titan* (II) was sunk in the North Atlantic. She was followed in the same ocean by the loss of *Eurymedon* (II) on Sept 25.

Nov 3: *Patroclus* (III) was sunk, the eighth in the year.

1941 The toll of ships continued:

Jan 8: *Clytoneus* (I) was lost to bombing off north west Ireland.

Jan 14: *Eumaeus* (II) torpedoed off Freetown.

Jan 24: *Meriones* lost by bombs off the east coast of England.

Jan 29: *Eurylochus* fell to *Kormoran* off Freetown.

Feb 28: *Anchises* (III) bombed off north west Ireland.

Mar 11: *Memnon* (IV) torpedoed off West Africa.

April 21: *Calchas* (II) torpedoed off West Africa.

May 7: *Ixion* (II) lost to a submarine in the North Atlantic.

Dec 26: *Tantalus* (II) was sunk by Japanese bombers in Manila Bay.

During this year Richard Holt reluctantly retired.

1942 In the whole of the company's history nothing can ever have occurred to match the devastation of 1942. The very listing of the losses alone reveals the fearful punishment meted out by the enemy:

Jan 11: *Cyclops* (II), torpedoed off the east coast of the U.S.A.

Feb 6: *Talthybius* (I) was sunk in dock at Singapore; she however lived to return, eventually, to be managed by her late owners.

March 3: *Helenus* (I) was torpedoed off West Africa.

Apr 5: *Hector* (IV) fell to Japanese bombs at Colombo, Ceylon.

Apr 6: *Autolycus* (II) shelled by Japanese cruisers in the Indian Ocean, Bay of Bengal.

Apr 6: *Dardanus* (III) shelled to a standstill and then torpedoed by Japanese warships in the Bay of Bengal.

Apr 10: *Ulysses* (IV) torpedoed off Palm Beach, Florida.

May 3: *Laertes* (III) By U-boat in the North Atlantic.

May 17: *Peisander* (I) fell prey to the U-boat activities off the coast of the U.S.A. being torpedoed off Nantucket.

May 26: *Polyphemus* (III), lost by torpedo in the North Atlantic.

May 28: *Mentor* (I) went to a U-boat off Key West.

Aug 10: *Medon* (II) torpedoed in the South Atlantic by an Italian submarine.

Aug 12: *Deucalion* (III), lost by bombs and aerial torpedoes during the Malta convoys.

Sept 5: *Myrmidon* (III) Another loss by torpedo off Freetown.

Oct 11: *Agapenor* (I) Also torpedoed off West Africa.

Oct 27: *Stentor* (III) Torpedoed off North West Africa.

Nov 13: *Maron* (I) Lost in the Mediterranean by torpedo attack.

Nov 27: *Polydorus* (I) Torpedoed off the coast of Africa.

In all a total of eighteen ships.

1943 The Battle of the Atlantic was being waged with increasing vigour and the Allies were moving to the offensive. This can, to a degree, be seen in the decrease in Blue Funnel casualties after the devastation of 1942. Only four valuable ships were lost:

Feb 3: *Rhexenor* (I) Torpedoed on the North Atlantic.

Feb 5: *Dolius* (I) Again a North Atlantic torpedo attack victim.

May 14: *Centaur* (II) Torpedoed by a Japanese submarine off the east coast of Australia when in full hospital ship rig.

Dec 19: *Phemius* (II) Torpedoed off West Africa.

1944 The decline in losses continued to the profound relief of the owners.

Jan 16: *Perseus* (II) Fell to a torpedo near to Madras.

Aug 31: *Troilus* (III) became the final sad casualty when she, too, was torpedoed in the Indian Ocean.

In all 41 ships were lost totalling 321,673 gross tons and no fewer than 324 lives were lost. Proudly the company can say that not one lifeboat which left a sinking ship failed to reach port safely.

1945 During the period 1939—45 the fleet had scarcely been added to by new building to the owner's specifications. *Priam* (IV) and *Telemachus* (IV) being the only two.

Two of the fast 'Empire Rawlinson' type were now acquired and completed to Holt specifications; they were *Rhexenor* (II) and *Stentor* (IV).

McGregor, Gow & Holland (the Glen Line) became Holt's London agents as outward cargo brokers in place of Killick Martin & Co. who had held the appointment since 1887.

1946 Plans to rebuild the depleted fleet were laid but as as an interim measure a number of American Liberty and Victory ships which Holts had managed for the Ministry of War Transport were now purchased. Sturdy vessels which gave splendid service, they were, nevertheless, a far cry from the ships which flew the flag of 'Alfred Holt's Navy'.

In August of the year Mrs Lawrence Holt launched the first of the *Anchises* class, *Calchas*, the first of 21 virtually similar sister ships. Designated Mark A 1 the remainder of the series was to be spread over 7 years.

Blue Funnel had its own cadet training establishment — 'Aulis'. This was now transferred back to Liverpool and enlarged.

1953 June 30: Lawrence Durning Holt retired. He was also a director of Caledon S.B. & E. Co, the builders of many Blue Funnel ships, the Glen Line, Elder Dempster Lines Holdings and another builder of Holt ships Scotts S.B. & E. Co.

Lawrence Holt was succeeded by Sir John Richard Hobhouse who had been a partner since 1920.

1956 Passenger calls at Cape Town were ended and the Australian service was routed via the Suez Canal and Aden.

1965 Elder Dempster Lines had come under the effective control of Richard Holt and L. H. Cripps back in 1932. When Elder Dempster Lines Holdings was formed in 1936 the Ocean S.S.Co became the largest ordinary shareholder. There then followed a seven year agreement whereby Holts were to be the managers of the Elder Dempster fleet. This agreement terminated in 1943 and, because of the war, was not renewed. Elder Dempster de facto ran itself.

In 1953 the name was changed to Liner Holdings Ltd and it was this company which was taken over by Ocean S.S.Co in 1965 when they became the sole ordinary shareholder. They already held 674,750 shares and the acquisition of the remainder gave them 2,214,111 shares.

One immediate effect was the integration of the two fleets and the commencement of a good deal of interchange to meet needs.

In the same year Overseas Containers Ltd was formed in which Ocean had a 49% holding. This enterprise was the beginning of the end of the traditional Blue Funneller.

1966 Ocean S.S.Co made an offer of £4.19 for each £1 share of the China Navigation Co; the intention being that the company should henceforth be owned equally by John Swire and Holts with Swires remaining as managers.

1967 April 25 It was announced that Elder Dempster Lines would be integrated into the group. Two new companies were formed:
Ocean Management Service Ltd and Ocean Fleets Ltd, the latter to operate all the seagoing vessels.
The famous name of Alfred Holt & Co disappeared; in its place the shipping side was divided into two divisions: Blue Funnel Line Ltd and Elder Dempster Lines Ltd. The ships owned were transferred accordingly.
The closure of the Suez Canal during the Third Arab-Israeli War — better known as the Six Days War — trapped *Melampus* (II) and *Agapenor* (II) in the Great Bitter Lake. (See *Melampus* (289) for details). Care and maintenance of these ships was undertaken by a rotation of crews who served aboard for one month.

1969 Aug: Attempts to abandon *Melampus* and *Agapenor* to the Liverpool & London War Risks Insurance Association failed because the ships were held to be still under the control of the owners. Thereafter it was arranged that the vessels would be looked after by the Czechoslovakian ship *Lednice*. By January 1973 the ships were officially in the hands of the Underwriters.

1971 Ocean Inchcape Ltd (O.I.L) was founded jointly by Ocean Fleets Ltd and the Inchcape Group. OIL operated offshore supply and services world wide under contract to the oil companies, drilling contractors, oil rig operators, exploration firms as well as oil, gas and underwater exploration organisations.

1972 The firm of William Cory & Son Ltd was acquired.
Ocean S.S.Co. changed its name to Ocean Transport and Trading Co. Ltd. There became six divisions:

1) Liner Shipping.	To operate the conventional services of Blue Funnel, Elder Dempster and Glen. Basically these were the non-containerised ships.
2) Specialised Shipping.	Operated by Ocean Titan Ltd and as a partner in the Atlantic Bulkers and Scanscot consortiums. This division included Cory Ship Towage.
3) Ship Procurement.	As its name indicates procurement, design and conversions fell to this division. It is also involved in overseeing Ocean's involvement in Liquified Gas carriage.
4) Ship Management.	Which includes repair, engineering and design services for the company's deep sea fleets plus the five vessels owned by Overseas Containers.
5) Distribution.	This division comprises mainly William Cory & Son's fuel and merchandising services known as Ocean Cory. It also includes McGregor Swire Air Services (M.S.A.S.). The freight forwarding plus the specialist shipbuilders James W. Cook & Co. (Wivenhoe) Ltd.
6) South East Asia.	This division includes the Straits S.S.Co. in which there is a 35.2% holding plus all the group's interests in the area.

1973 Nov: *Centaur* (II) was purchased from Blue Funnel in a contract worth around £15 million by the Straits S.S.Co. The deal included all the share capital of Mansfields, the managers of the Straits S.S.Co. The cost was met by Straits issuing to Ocean 14,455,000 shares in the company thereby raising Holts holding in Straits from 35.2% to 64.47%. The owners of *Centaur* became Blue Funnel S.E.A. (Private) Ltd.

1974 A joint service with the Ben line was introduced; named Ben Ocean.
Also the Barber Blue Sea Line was formed to operate between the U.S.A. and the Far East. The other partners were the Barber Line of Oslo, an offshoot of Wilhelm Wilhelmsen, and the Swedish East Asiatic Co. of Gothenburg.

1976 Blue Funnel's Jeddah services were transferred on to a Roll-on, Roll-off basis. A 'Tarros' type vessel *Captain Paddon* was chartered for the route.
Ocean's 50% holding in the China Navigation Co, acquired in 1966 was sold to John Swire & Co.

1977 *Queensgarth* the last vessel owned by Cory Maritime Ltd was sold and the company wound up.
Nov 24: A joint service U.K.-Jeddah-Aqaba was formed with P&O's Strath Services Division. Operating twice monthly from Ellesmere Port the sailings were taken by *R.S. Jason* and *R. S. Ixion*.

1978 The ships of the 'P' class of 1966—7 were disposed of. Although only 12 years old the rate of change towards containerisation had been so swift that the ships had become outdated. In their place vessels with a container capacity of 600 were necessary and the 'P' class ships could only accommodate 150. Their new owners were able to use them satisfactorily on non-containerised routes.
In all Ocean Fleets disposed of 18 of the older and less productive cargo vessels. The reduction in the number of ships led to the release of 860 staff.   *AID - OFF!!*
The frequency of sailings, on some routes, had to be reduced.

1981 *Centaur* (III) made her last voyage before being chartered to Curnow's St. Helena Shipping Co. To replace her on the Singapore cruising berth Peter Deilmann's *Berlin*, built in 1980, has been chartered by the Straits S.S.Co. and renamed *Princess Mahsuri*.

1983 The 40% Inchcape holding in Ocean Inchcape Ltd (O.I.L.) was acquired.

1983 The 58% holding in Straits Steamship Pte Ltd was sold for £88 million; a 40% stake in Ocean Inchcape Ltd (O.I.L.) was acquired.

1986 In April Ocean's holding in Overseas Container Line was sold to P&O; in return they sold to Ocean their holding in Panocean Storage & Transport to give a net surplus of £78 million.
A £300 million take over bid by IEP (UK) failed.
One interesting sidelight was the choosing of Ocean Fleets to oversee the £19 million refitting, at Devonport, of the Royal yacht *Britannia*.

1987 The six deep sea vessels of the fleet were transferred to the Isle of Man off-shore register.

1988 India Buildings, where the Company was founded in 1865, was sold. Two floors being retained on long-lease. The remaining six ships of Ocean Fleets being: On charter: *Apapa Palm* (322) to C.A.V.N. *Melampus* (321) to N.Y.K. On Elder Dempster UKWAL service: *Memnon* (320) and *Menelaus* (319). On Barber Blue Sea: *Barber Hector* (330) and *Barber Perseus* (329). None serve on the original Blue Funnel berths although this vigorous Group continues to expand its land-based activities world wide.

Livery

Funnels 1847—1984: Powder blue with black top, normally a shade deeper than the rectangle formed by the width of the funnel. Steam pipes and donkey boiler uptakes similar.

Masts 1847—1984: Chocolate brown. From *Gunung Djati* onwards passenger ships and modern masts stepped out of the bridge were white.

Hulls 1847—1984: Black. *Gunung Djati* and *Centaur* (III), white with powder blue band; 1932—1936: some ships (viz: *Agamemnon* (III) class) were given grey hulls but the change was shortlived; 1979—1984: *Barber Priam* class have orange buff hulls; 1977: *Nestor* (V) had a grey green hull for a short period.

Derrick Posts 1847—1984: Mast colour. Tankers and bulk carriers, white; 1899—1903: White on *Idomeneus* (II) class and *Ajax* (II) class, derricks brown; 1947: *Calchas* (III) introduced white posts on the bridge deck abaft the funnel; 1958—1983: Passenger ships had an all white livery.

Deck Cranes 1972: White.

Waterline 1865—1984: The upper strake (approx 6 ft (1.83 m); Flesh pink. Lower plating: dark wine red. (see 186, *Sarpedon* drawing); 1972: Tankers and bulk carriers have normal red colour. The vessels with grey hulls in the thirties had green boot-topping. *Barber Priam* class: Black.

Ventilators 1847—1865: Black, blue interiors; 1865—1984: Mast vents brown. Funnel clusters: black; 1932—1984: Bridge deck vents became progressively white followed by fcsle, bridge deck and poop vents becoming white. Interiors remained blue.

Decks 1847—1939: Iron and steel decks were bitumen black or dark grey. Around planked decks black or mast brown was used; 1939—1984: dark grey green appeared on steel decking; 1972: Bulkers, viz: *Hector* (VI): bright red-brown but *Achilles* (VI) class had flesh pink decks with pale grey hatches. *Nestor* (V): Pale grey-green.

Routes

1852—1853 Whitehaven—Cardiff.

1853—1855 Liverpool—Bordeaux.

1857—1864 Liverpool—West Indies.

1865—1869 Liverpool—Mauritius—Penang—Singapore—Hong Kong—Shanghai.

1869—1980 Liverpool—Suez Canal—Penang—Singapore—Hong Kong—Shanghai—Japanese Ports.

1880—1899 Singapore—Belawan Deli and Singapore—Penang with calls at intermediate quays.

1894—1973 Singapore—Batavia—Darwin—Derby—Cossack—Onslow—Gascoyne—Geraldton—Fremantle.

1901—1956 Glasgow—Liverpool—Cape Town—Australian ports.

1902—1984 Chinese ports—Vancouver—Seattle—North Pacific coast ports—San Diego. (China Mutual route).

1910—1913 Liverpool—Fishguard (passenger embarkation)—Australia.

1915—1978 New York—Panama—Far East ports (Indra Line service). This later developed into the Round the World Service (see *Helenus* (136) for a detailed steaming log).

[handwritten: PORT SWEETENHAM]

1973—1978 Fremantle—Sunda Strait—Singapore—Malacca Strait—Klang—Georgetown (Penang)—Singapore—Christmas Island—Fremantle.

1979—1981 Fremantle—Singapore—Manila—Hong Kong—Fremantle.

[handwritten: KWANGSI AND KWEICHOW MUST SINGAPORE FREEMANTLE AUCKLAND — AFTER '79 → AUCKLAND]

Other Blue Funnel activities:

Seasonal: Pilgrimage traffic Indonesia, Malaysia and Singapore to Jeddah.

Roll-on Roll-off: Ellesmere Port — Jeddah. In 1978 this was transferred to O.C.L. ships. Blue Funnel routes were virtually always Liner services, as opposed to tramping or chartering out. But the ports of call both in Europe and the Far East were always at the behest of trade. Thus Holt ships were to be seen in many locations which were ports of call rather than preset itinerary destinations. Nevertheless during the history of Blue Funnel the area of trade remained firmly based upon the Far East.

Only in 1972, with the advent of the Tanker and Bulk Carrier fleets were the Ocean Fleet ships to be seen outside of their original area of trade. The present fleet is 'fixed' in the open market to trade as trade demands.

BLUE FUNNEL LINE

Fleet Index

Achilles (I)	10	Argo	333	Charon (II)	217
Achilles (II)	89	Ascanius (I)	41	Charon (III)	315
Achilles (III)	168	Ascanius (II)	148	Charon	340
Achilles (IV)	229	Ascanius (III)	238	Ching Wo	96
Achilles (V)	283	Askalon	5	Ching Wo	CM3
Achilles (VI)	305	Asphalion (I)	197	Circle	152
Adrastus (I)	182	Asphalion (II)	229	Cleator	2
Adrastus (II)	243	Astyanax (I)	123	Clytoneus (I)	213
Aenaes (I)	147	Astyanax (II)	230	Clytoneus (II)	231
Aenaes (II)	227	Atalanta	91	Clytoneus (III)	314
Aenaes (III)	324	Atreaus (I)	129	Crusader	7
Agamemnon (I)	8	Atreus (II)	239	Cyclops (I)	32
Agamemnon (II)	87	Autolycus (I)	145	Cyclops (II)	119
Agamemnon (III)	207	Autolycus (II)	181	Cyclops (III)	232
Agamemnon (IV)	306	Autolycus (III)	233	Cyclops (IV)	313
Agapenor (I)	137	Automedon (I)	180		
Agapenor (II)	227	Automedon (II)	235	Danae	260
Ajax (I)	9	Automedon (III)	232	Dardanus (I)	39
Ajax (II)	88			Dardanus (II)	72
Ajax (III)	211	Banjermassin	336	Dardanus (III)	175
Ajax (IV)	284	Barber Hector	330	Dardanus (IV)	261
Ajax (V)	309	Barber Memnon	320	Dardanus (V)	283
Alcinous (I)	85	Barber Menelaus	319	Dardanus (VI)	302
Alcinous (II)	198	Barber Menestheus	322	Demodocus (I)	131
Alcinous (III)	240	Barber Priam	328	Demodocus (II)	279
Alcinous (IV)	226	Beagle	66	Deucalion (I)	20
Anchises (I)	23	Bellerophon (I)	33	Deucalion (II)	90
Anchises (II)	77	Bellerophon (II)	116	Deucalion (III)	209
Anchises (III)	149	Bellerophon (III)	237	Deucalion (IV)	262
Anchises (IV)	226			Deucalion (V)	284
Anchises (V)	308	Cadmus	240	Devonhurst	337
Andes	42	Calchas (I)	83	Diomed (I)	11
Antenor (I)	21	Calchas (II)	170	Diomed (II)	73
Antenor (II)	81	Calchas (III)	225	Diomed (III)	143
Antenor (III)	189	Calypso	47	Diomed (IV)	171
Antenor (IV)	282	Centaur (I)	76	Diomed (V)	280
Antenor (V)	307	Centaur (II)	196	Dolius (I)	192
Antilochus (I)	118	Centaur (III)	292	Dolius (II)	263
Antilochus (II)	234	Cerberus	68	Dolius (III)	281
		Charon (I)	111		

BLUE FUNNEL LINE

Dumbarton Youth 1
Dymas (I) 264
Dymas (II) 282

Elpenor (I) 144
Elpenor (II) 244
Eumaeus (I) 133
Eumaeus (II) 176
Eumaeus (III) 252
Eumaeus (IV) 242
Euryades (I) 161
Euryades (II) 182
Euryades (III) 252
Eurybates (I) 159
Eurybates (II) 206
Eurydamus 156
Eurylochus 162
Eurymachus 158
Eurymedon (I) 157
Eurymedon (II) 193
Eurymedon (III) 253
Euryplus (I) 160
Euryplus (II) 254

Fantee 43

Ganymede 29
Glaucus (I) 19
Glaucus (II) 79
Glaucus (III) 177
Glaucus (IV) 221
Glaucus (V) 250
Glaucus (VI) 245
Gorgon (I) 112
Gorgon (II) 216
Gunung Djati 291

Hebe 46
Hecate 53
Hector (I) 15
Hector (II) 28
Hector (III) 74
Hector (IV) 188
Hector (V) 274
Hector (VI) 312
Hecuba (I) 51
Hecuba (II) 185
Helenus (I) 136
Helenus (II) 272
Helenus (III) 311
Hydra 54
Hyson 105
Hyson CM11

Idomeneus (I) 82
Idomeneus (II) 204
Idomeneus (III) 236
Ixion (I) 62
Ixion (II) 151
Ixion (III) 275

Jason (I) 35
Jason (II) 95
Jason (proposed liner) 28
Jason (III) 218
Jason (IV) 273

Kaisow 98
Kaisow CM4
Keemun 106
Keemun CM6
Kintuck 100
Knight Companion 167
Knight of the Garter 164
Knight of the Thistle 165
Knight Templar 166
Kongsee 335

Laertes (I) 31
Laertes (II) 114
Laertes (III) 146
Laertes (IV) 236
Laertes (V) 316
Laomedon (I) 132
Laomedon (II) 241
Lycaon (I) 135
Lycaon (II) 245
Lycaon (III) 317

Machaon (I) 84
Machaon (II) 174
Machaon (III) 287
Maha Vajirunhis 339
Maron (I) 212
Maron (II) 248
Maron (III) 290
Maron (IV) 325
Medon (I) 191
Medon (II) 224
Medusa (I) 52
Medusa (II) 153
Melampus (I) 195
Melampus (II) 289
Melampus (III) 321
Memnon (I) 45
Memnon (II) 110
Memnon (III) 124
Memnon (IV) 210
Memnon (V) 250
Memnon (VI) 288
Memnon (VII) 320
Menelaus (I) 17
Menelaus (II) 75
Menelaus (III) 173
Menelaus (IV) 285
Menelaus (V) 319
Menestheus (I) 208
Menestheus (II) 286
Menestheus (III) 322
Mentor (I) 139
Mentor (II) 249
Mentor (III) 326
Mercury 44
Meriones 178
Moyune 101
Moyune CM5
Myrmidon (I) 58
Myrmidon (II) 122
Myrmidon (III) 214
Myrmidon (IV) 251
Myrmidon (V) 327

Neleus (I) 128
Neleus (II) 277
Nestor (I) 12
Nestor (II) 67
Nestor (III) 154
Nestor (IV) 276
Nestor (V) 318
Ningchow 107
Ningchow CM2
Normanby 338

Oanfa (I) 109
Oanfa (II) 108
Oolong CM10
Oopack 97
Oopack CM1
Orestes (I) 24
Orestes (II) 25
Orestes (III) 70
Orestes (IV) 203
Orestes (V) 276

Pak Ling 99
Pak Ling CM7
Palamed (I) 36
Palamed (II) 80
Palinurus 37
Patroclus (I) 18
Patroclus (II) 80
Patroclus (III) 187
Patroclus (IV) 267
Patroclus (V) 298

Peisander (I)	201	Pyrrhus (II)	140	Teiresias (I)	141
Peisander (II)	294	Pyrrhus (III)	266	Teiresias (II)	270
Peleus (I)	92			Telamon (I)	49
Peleus (II)	265	Ranee	334	Telamon (II)	115
Perseus (I)	126	Rhesus (I)	130	Telamon (III)	271
Perseus (II)	172	Rhesus (II)	248	Telemachus (I)	34
Perseus (III)	268	Rhexenor (I)	179	Telemachus (II)	94
Perseus (IV)	299	Rhexenor (II)	222	Telemachus (III)	220
Phemius (I)	134	Rhexenor (III)	290	Telemachus (IV)	221
Phemius (II)	183	Rhipeus	109	Telemachus (V)	270
Phemius (III)	198	R.S. Ixion	331	Teucer (I)	26
Phemius (IV)	219	R.S. Jason	332	Teucer (II)	59
Phemius (V)	300			Teucer (III)	117
Philoctetes (I)	169			Teucer (IV)	271
Philoctetes (II)	267	Saladin (I)	3	Theseus (I)	127
Phrontis (I)	200	Saladin (II)	57	Theseus (II)	278
Phrontis (II)	297	Sarah Nicholson	30	Titan (I)	50
Ping Suey	104	Sappho	48	Titan (II)	120
Ping Suey	CM8	Sarpedon (I)	14	Titan (III)	259
Plantagenet	4	Sarpedon (II)	27	Titan (IV)	303
Plumleaf	323	Sarpedon (III)	71	Troilus (I)	138
Polydorus (I)	194	Sarpedon (IV)	186	Troilus (II)	142
Polydorus (II)	246	Sarpedon (V)	211	Troilus (III)	184
Polydorus (III)	240	Sarpedon (VI)	301	Troilus (IV)	255
Polyphemus (I)	61	Stentor (I)	22	Troilus (V)	310
Polyphemus (II)	125	Stentor (II)	86	Tydeus (I)	93
Polyphemus (III)	215	Stentor (III)	199	Tydeus (II)	256
Polyphemus (IV)	247	Stentor (IV)	223	Tyndareus	163
Polyphemus (V)	229	Stentor (V)	288		
Priam (I)	13	Sultan	69	Ulysses (I)	16
Priam (II)	60			Ulysses (II)	40
Priam (III)	113	Talisman	6	Ulysses (III)	64
Priam (IV)	219	Talthybius (I)	150	Ulysses (IV)	155
Priam (V)	293	Talthybius (II)	257	Ulysses (V)	269
Prometheus (I)	38	Talthybius (III)	246		
Prometheus (II)	78	Tantalus (I)	63	Will o' the Wisp	55
Prometheus (III)	202	Tantalus (II)	190		
Prometheus (IV)	296	Tantalus (III)	258	Xanthus	205
Protesilaus (I)	121	Tantalus (IV)	247		
Protesilaus (II)	295	Tantalus (V)	304	Yang Tsze	103
Pyrrhus (I)	65	Teenkai	102		

Illustrated fleet list

DUMBARTON YOUTH

1 DUMBARTON YOUTH

B 1847 William Denny & Brothers, Dumbarton, River Clyde. **T:** 239 g, 187 n.
D 126 ft (38.4 m) oa. 113.9 ft (34.71 m) × 21.9 ft (6.67 m) × 12.8 ft (3.9 m).
E Sgl scr, 2 cyl simple expansion, direct acting with condenser. 44 HP, 8 kts. 1 square boiler. Engine by Caird & Co., Greenock.
H Iron, one dk.

1847 Apr 1: Ordered as a collier by a Mr Whyte, cost £6,820. Her sister ship, named *Mazeppa* was registered as owned by Henry Smith.
1852 Purchased for £4,250 and shown as being owned equally by Thomas Ainsworth and George Holt, with Alfred Holt acting as Agent and also as Superintendent Engineer. Employed initially between Whitehaven and Cardiff, probably continuing her previous work, but shortly afterwards *Dumbarton Youth* was placed on the Liverpool—Bordeaux route.
18?? Sold to Horsfall & Co.

2 CLEATOR

B 1854 Cato & Miller, Brunswick Dock, Liverpool. **T:** 391 g, 341 n.
D 183.9 ft (56.05 m) × 24.3 ft (7.41 m) × 14.3 ft (4.36 m).
E Sgl scr, simple, 2 cyl; 40HP, 8 kts. By Rothwell & Co, Bolton.
H Iron, 1 dk. Cargo: Iron ore or coal.

1854 The capital to purchase this ship was loaned by the Ainsworth family of Cleator, after which the ship was named. Ownership was however that of Alfred and Philip Holt.
1855 During the construction the Crimean War commenced. *Cleator* was then chartered to the French Government for the duration at 62s 6p per gross ton per month. When completed the vessel served in the Mediterranean carrying stores and mules to either Istanbul or the Crimea.

1864 Alfred Holt's own design of compound tandem engine was installed. In addition 2 locomotive type boilers were fitted capable of working at the, then, high steam pressure of 60 lbs per square inch. Without this capability compounding was ineffective because the residual pressure for the low pressure cylinder was insufficient to be of any practical use. *Cleator's* steam pressure was three times that of normal ships of the day.

1869 *Cleator* became the first Holt vessel to transit the Suez Canal. During the year she was lengthened. **T**: 391 g.

1872 Sold to John Dill Ross; renamed *Alastor*. Used for trading out of Labuan.

1892 Broken up.

3 SALADIN

Details as *Cleator* (2) except: **T**: 535 g.

1855 Built with the intention of being placed on charter like her sister ship, however the Crimean War ended before this was achieved. The ship was therefore placed on the Liverpool—West Indies run with a passage time of 18 days to Jamaica. Despite the heavy competition that existed voyage profits were recorded. This, together with similar returns from *Cleator* caused Alfred Holt to pay much more attention to the sea; he turned his back on railway engineering.

1865 Operated by Lamport & Holt's Liverpool, Brazil and River Plate S.N.Co.

1872 Sold to J. Martin & Co, Liverpool: same name.

1882 Broken up.

PLANTAGENET, ASKALON, TALISMAN & CRUSADER
(Note: drawing is of sister ship *Etna*)

4 PLANTAGENET

B 1857 Scott & Co, Greenock. **T**: 695 g.
D 202 ft (61.57 m).
E Sgl scr, 2 cyl simple direct acting; Stm P 20 lbs; 9 kts. By builder.
H Iron, 1 dk; 2 masts.

1857 Built for Alfred and Philip Holt plus 'one or two friends'. Placed on the West Indies service.

1864 Sold the West India & Pacific S.S.Co.
Further career not traced.

5 ASKALON

B 1857 Scott & Co, Greenock. **T**: 975 g.
D 228 ft (69.49 m).
E Sgl scr, simple, 2 cyl. By builder.
H Iron, 1 dk.
1857 Built for the West Indies service.
1864 Sold to the West India & Pacific S.S.Co.
Further career no traced.

6 TALISMAN

B 1857 Scott & Co, Greenock. **T**: 738 g.
D 202 ft (61.57 m).
E Sgl scr, 2 cyl. 9 kts. By builder.

1857 Built for the West Indies routes and operated like the remainder of the fleet on a single ship company basis.
1864 Sold to the West India & Pacific S.S.Co.
1873 Jan 21: Foundered in the North Atlantic.

7 CRUSADER

B 1857 Scott & Co, Greenock. **T**: 901 g.
D 221.3 ft (67.4 m) × 30.4 ft (9.26 m) × 17.7 ft (5.39 m).
E Sgl scr, simple, 2 cyl, 8½ kts. 100 HP. By builder.
H Iron, 1 dk.

1857 Built for the West Indies services.
1864 Sold to the West India & Pacific S.S.Co.
1871 Lost off the West Indies.

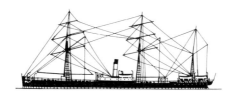

AGAMEMNON (I), AJAX (I) and ACHILLES (I)

8 AGAMEMNON (I)

B 1865 Scott & Co, Greenock. **T**: 2,280 g, 1,550 n.
D 309.5 ft (93.9 m) × 38.8 ft (11.8 m) × 28.3 ft (8.64 m).
E Sgl scr, compound tandem driving a single crank shaft counterblanced with a half flywheel; 2 cyl; 945 IHP. 2 double ended locomotive type boilers: Stm P: 69 lb; 10 kts.
Designed by Alfred Holt and constructed by the builder. Fuel consumption: 20 tons of coal per day was averaged on the maiden voyage of 12,350 miles (19,875 km).
H Iron, 2 dks. In these three pioneer ships the traditional position of the rudder and propeller were reversed. The rudder was located in the deadwood of the stern with the screw protruding beyond it. This experiment was not successful, mainly because of the lack of propeller thrust on the rudder plate which made steering much more sluggish.
Boilers. Those installed in the three ships, plus several ensuing ships, were 24ft (7.31 m) long and 14 ft (4.27 m) in diameter with 6 furnaces which fed a single combustion chamber traversed by 3 Galloway water tubes. The designed steam pressure was 69 lbs compared with 10 lbs in contemporary steamers. The boiler design was a by-product of Alfred Holt's railway engineering days when he was working with locomotives of the London & North Western Railway Company which used steam at 120lbs pressure. The Board of Trade limit for the selfsame boiler aboard ship was Holt's 69 lb per sq. inch. The reason for the discrepancy was that salt water was then in use at sea with resultant caking. Fires were drawn regularly for descaling but even so explosions were not uncommon and a number of ships were lost from this cause.

1864 Laid down as part of a 3 ship order worth £156,000. *Agamemon* was the initial ship for the Ocean Steam Ship Co.

1865 April 19: Maiden voyage Liverpool—Mauritius (first port of call)—Penang—Singapore—Hong Kong—Shanghai. Captain Isaac Middleton. The voyage time was 77 days. On the homeward journey additional calls were made, including Foochow. Freight rates were £6 + 10% per ton of 40 cubic feet (3.71 cu m) outbound and £6.25 + 10% inbound.

1869 The cargo loaded at Hankow off the tea crop was, at 2,516,000 lbs, the largest yet loaded in a single ship. The freight of £28,087 was also a record.

1897 Transferred to the Dutch flag subsidiary Nederland Stoomboot Maatschappij 'Oceaan'; same name.

1899 Broken up in Italy after a service life of 35 years with the same original 'experimental' machinary. A truly remarkable vessel.

9 AJAX (I)

Details as *Agamemnon (8)*.

1865 Entered service to the Far East.

1868 Sank at Shanghai. The propeller shaft had been disconected from the crank while an overhaul and engine running test was carried out. The receding tide 'unscrewed' the shaft out of the ship with the result that the vessel settled in shallow water with her superstructure above the high water level. Alfred Holt recognised this as a design fault and thereafter Holt ships were given a water tight gland in the shaft tunnel (together with a flange) that prevented any chance of recurrence.

1897 Transferred to N.S.M. 'Oceaan'; same name.

1900 Scrapped at Genoa. The ship was initially intended for further trading but was not worth the cost of re-boilering.

10 ACHILLES (I)

Details as *Agamemnon* (8) except:
B 1866. Cost £45,500.

1866 Dec: When the ship reached Shanghai on Christmas eve the appointed agents Bruell & Co informed the captain that they were unable to offer any homeward bound cargo. However the newly established firm of Butterfield & Swire interceded with a part cargo of shirtings consigned to Lancashire. This enabled *Achilles* to make a profitable start to her journey. Alfred Holt, moreover, was much impressed with the initiative of Butterfield & Swire. Another factor was that their trade was in textiles and silks in addition to tea. This provided a wider scope for freight than that of Bruell & Co. Holt therefore appointed Butterfield & Swire as agents at Shanghai thereby beginning a most valuable and longlasting relationship which was to have an immense effect upon the fortunes of the Blue Funnel Line.

1891 Transferred to N.S.M. 'Oceaan'.

1898 Broken up at Genoa.

DIOMED (I), NESTOR (I), PRIAM (I), SARPEDON (I), HECTOR (I), ULYSSES (I) and MENELAUS (I)

11 DIOMED (I)

B 1868 Andrew Leslie & Co, Hebburn-on-Tyne. **T:** 1,848 g, 1,201 n.

D 291.5 ft (88.85 m) × 34.5 ft (10.51 m) × 28.3 ft (8.64 m).
E Sgl scr compound tandem; 2 cyl; 170 NHP; 10 kts. Stm P: 60 lb. By R. Stephenson & Co, Newcastle.
H Iron, 1 dk.

1867 Ordered from Scott & Co, Greenock, who went into temporary bankcruptcy later in the year. When, out of necessity, the building plans for the unstarted ship were transferred to Leslie's yard the hull was redesigned by the two men to provide for a wider beam. This was because of Alfred Holt's recognition that the initial trio of ships were overpowered for the route needs. In addition to the hull changed the compound engine was reduced in power by some 20%.
1868 Entered service.
1894 Sold to the Japanese firm of Yamamoto Tosuke, Osaka. Renamed *Genzan Maru*. Given a plain black funnel like seemingly all Japanese vessels of the era.
1903 Oct 8: Wrecked at Nemouro, on the very western most tip of Hokkaido.

12 NESTOR (I)

Sister of *Diomed* (11) except:
T: 1,869 g, 1,414 n.
D 313.6 ft (95.58 m) × 32.8 ft (9.98 m) × 27.9 ft (8.49 m).

1868 Completed for Far East service.
1894 Sold to Japanese owners; renamed *Daisan Mayoshima Maru*. Renamed again in the same year; became *Mayayoshi Maru No 3*. Owned by Fukunaga Shoshiki Kobe.
1894 Nov 9: Lost by fire during Russo-Japanese War at Si-yuen-chang while transporting troops.

13 PRIAM(I)

Details as *Diomed* (11) except:
B 1870 Scott & Co. Greenock. **T:** 2,039 g, 1,572 n.
D 313.6 ft (95.58 m) × 32.8 ft (10 m) × 27.9 ft (8.50 m).
E By Greenock Foundry Co.

1870 Entered service.
1889 Jan 11: wrecked on Sisgarsas Island, near to Corunna, Spain. En-route Liverpool— Hong Kong.

14 SARPEDON (I)

Details as *Diomed* (11) except:
B 1871. **T:** 1,949 g, 1,519 n.
D 310.7 ft (94.69 m) × 33.5 ft (10.21 m) × 25.5 ft (7.77 m). **E** 250 NHP.

1870 Laid down.
1871 Completed for the Far East service.
1876 Sept 4: Sank of Ushant, inward bound for London from Shanghai, after a collision with the Belgian steamer *Julia David*, owned by David Verberst & Co, Antwerp. A prolonged court case ensued which initially found in favour of the Belgian vessel but the case was reopened following allegations by the steward, named Meyer, that the witnesses had committed perjury. As a result Alfred Holt was able to prove the allegations and the decision of the court was reversed in favour of *Sarpedon's* captain. (see chronology).

15 **HECTOR** (I)

Details as *Diomed* (11) except:
B 1871. **T**: 1,956 g, 1,523 n.
D 312.1 ft (95.15 m).

1871 Entered service.
1875 Oct 4: Lost aground on a reef outside Amoy harbour when inward bound from Shanghai. The vessel and her cargo was valued at £36,000. This was the company's first total loss.

16 **ULYSSES** (I)

Details as *Diomed* (11) except:
B 1871. **T**: 1,949 g, 1,519 n.

1871 Completed. During the whole life of the ship she was thought of as unlucky. During her first voyage she grounded heavily in the Red Sea. After salvage it was found that the repairs necessitated a return to Liverpool and the voyage had, therefore, to be abandoned. This resulted in a heavy financial loss.
1872 As the ship entered Shanghai roadstead she shed her propeller and drifted ashore, happily without serious consequences.
1887 Aug. 16: On her outward leg out of London the vessel ran aground on Jubal Island in the Gulf of Suez. She carried a general cargo destined for Penang.
Oct: The ship was written off as a total loss.

17 **MENELAUS** (I)

Sister of *Diomed* (11) except:
B 1871. **T**: 1,956 g, 1,523 n.
D 312.2 ft (95.15 m). **E** 580 IHP.

1871 Completed.
1891 Transferred to the Dutch subsidiary N.S.M. 'Oceaan'.
1894 Broken up at Briton Ferry.

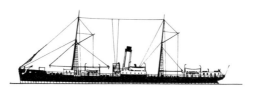

PATROCLUS (I), GLAUCUS (I), ANTENOR (I) and DEUCALION (I)

18 **PATROCLUS** (I)

B 1872 Andrew Leslie & Co, Hebburn-on-Tyne. **T**: 2,074 g, 1,604 n.
D 328.6 ft (100.15 m) × 32.6 ft (9.93 m) × 25.3 ft (7.72 m).
E Sgl scr 2 cyl compound tandem, 214 NHP, 700 IHP, 10 kts. By R. Stephenson & Co, Newcastle.
H Steel. 2 dks. **P** Nil.

1872 Delivered.
1882 Re-boilered.
1892 Transferred to the Dutch flag subsidiary N.S.M. 'Oceaan' in order to permit trading to the Dutch East Indies.

1895 Sold to Minamishima Masuku, Tokio. Renamed *Shiganoura Maru*. Later owned by Nagata Sanjuro; same name.
1924 Broken up in Japan.

19 GLAUCUS (I)

Sister of *Patroclus* (18) except:
B 1871. Entered service.

1891 Transferred to Dutch flag: N.S.M. 'Oceaan'. Same name.
1898 Sold to Japan; renamed *Jintsu Maru*.
1898 June 28: Wrecked at Shimoda, near Nagoya on Honshu.

20 DEUCALION (I)

Sister of *Patroclus* (18) except:
B 1872.

1872 Delivered.
1891 Transferred to N.S.M. 'Oceaan'.
1896 Transferred to the Blue Funnel subsidiary East Indian Ocean SS Co, same name. *Deucalion* was the only deep sea trader of that concern and was used principally on longer routes as far north as the Philippines.
1899 Acquired, with the remainder of the East Indian Ocean SS Co's fleet by Norddeutscher Lloyd, then managed by A. O. Meyer. The ship was registered as owned by Bremen Lloyd. Renamed *Sandaken*.
1903 Sold to Tung Kee & Co, Shanghai. Became *Tai Ping*.
1907 After the end of the Sino-Japanese war the ship was taken over by the Russians. In 1908 she was renamed *Ermack* by Ellwanger Bros. of Vladivostok.
1911 Owned by Kusnetsov Bros, Vladivostock.
1913 March. Broken up at Shanghai.

21 ANTENOR (I)

Sister of *Patroclus* (18) except:
B 1872. **T:** 2,162 g, 1,241 n.
1872 Delivered.
1884 Re-boilered.
1891 Transferred to N.S.M. 'Oceaan'; Dutch flag.
1893 Sold to Baba Dokiu, Tokio; became *Tateyama Maru*. Later owned by Baba Michihisa, Higashi, Iwase, Japan.
1921 Sold to Inukami Keigoro, Nishinomaya. Same name.
1929 Broken up in Japan. 57 years of service.

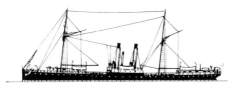

STENTOR (I), ANCHISES (I), ORESTES (I), ORESTES (II) and TEUCER (I)

22 STENTOR (I)

B 1875 Scott & Co, Greenock. **T:** 2,025 g, 1,278 n.
D 314.1 ft (95.73 m) × 35.2 ft (10.73 m) × 26 ft (7.92 m).
E Sgl scr 2 cyl comp. tandem, 700 IHP, 10 kts. By Greenock Foundry, Greenock.

H Iron. 2 dks. Bridge deck 49 ft (14.9 m).

1875 Completed.
1891 To the Dutch subsidiary N.S.M. 'Oceaan'; same name.
1896 Sold to E. Nathan, Singapore; Renamed *Charterhouse.*
1900 Went to Lin Ho Puah, Singapore; same name.
1906 Sept 30: On passage Haihow—Hong Kong foundered during a typhoon off Hai-Nan. All aboard were lost.

23 ANCHISES (I)

Sister of *Stentor* (22) except:
T: 2,021 g, 1,304 n.
When the ship entered service she was square rigged on the foremast; one sail.

1875 Completed.
1891 Transferred to the Dutch N.S.M. 'Oceaan'; same name.
1895 July: Reverted to the British flag; same name.
1896 Sold to Ung Lee Koo, Penang, without change of name. British flag. June 26: Wrecked near to Rangoon en-route for Singapore.

24 ORESTES (I)

Sister *Stentor* (22) except:
T: 2,057 g, 1,323 n. **D** 316.5 ft (96.47 m).

1875 Delivered.
1876 March 7: Lost off Galle, Ceylon, en-route Liverpool—Penang.

25 ORESTES (II)

Sister of *Stentor* (22) except:
B 1872. **T**: 2,057 g, 1,323 n.
D 316.5 ft (96.47 m).

1877 This ship was a replacement for *Orestes* (I).
1894 Sold to Japan.
May: wrecked during the delivery voyage still bearing the name *Orestes*.

26 TEUCER (I)

Sister of *Stentor* (22) except:
B 1877. **T**: 2,057 g, 1,303 n.
D 316.5 ft (96.47 m). **H** Steel.

1877 Completed. The first steel hull.
1885 May 30: Wrecked off Ushant en-route Singapore—Amsterdam.

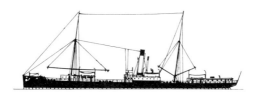

SARPEDON (II) and HECTOR (II)

27 SARPEDON (II)

B 1877 Andrew Leslie & Co, Hebburn-on-Tyne. **T**: 2,036 g, 1,592 n.

D 310 ft (94.49 m) × 34.2 ft (10.41 m) × 25.3 ft (7.71 m).
E Sgl scr compound inverted 2 cyl, 188 NHP; 10 kts. By R. Stephenson & Co, Newcastle.
H Iron. 2 dks.

1877 Entered service.
1893 Transferred to N.S.M. 'Oceaan'; same name.
1894 Became *Tamahime Maru*. Gomei Kwaisha Umenura Tasaka Kwaisoten, Tokio.
1896 Oct. 4: Wrecked on the coast of Japan.

28 HECTOR (II)

Sister to *Sarpedon* (27) except:
T: 2,111 g, 1,570 n.
D 316.8 ft (96.5 m) × 33.5 ft (10.21 m) × 24.7 ft (7.53 m).

1877 Completed.
1891 Transferred to N.S.M. 'Oceaan'; same name.
1894 Sold to Japan; renamed *Moji Maru*, owned by Nippon Yusen KK.
1910 Acquired by Kamiya Dembei, Yokohama. Same name.
1918 Owned by Gomei Kaisha ida Shoten, Yokohama.
1924 Owned by Mojimaru Goshi Kaisya, Kobe.
1930 Broken up in Japan at Fuchu.

29 GANYMEDE

B 1879 Scott & Co, Greenock. **T:** 405 g, 236 n.
D 166.5 ft (50.75 m) × 28 ft (8.53 m) × 10.8 ft (3.29 m).
E Sgl scr, simple, 1 cyl, 80 RHP, 8 kts. By builder.
H Iron, 1 dk.

1879 Ordered. Cost £11,000.
1880 The construction of this ship followed the decision of Holt's to enter into the Sumatra-
-Singapore tobacco business. *Ganymede* served between Belawan Deli (then Deli) and
Singapore.
1894 Transferred to N.S.M. 'Oceaan'; same name.
1900 Sold.
1907 Hulked at Belawan Deli.

SARAH NICHOLSON

30 SARAH NICHOLSON

B 1865 Nicholson & Co, Annan, Scotland. **T:** 934 g, 934 n.
D 194.7 ft (59.34 m) × 32.7 ft (9.97 m) × 22.6 ft (6.89 m).
E Sailing ship. **H** iron, 1 dk.

1865 Commissioned as a sailing barque for Nicholson & Co, Dumfries.
1880 Acquired by Alfred Holt and converted into a tobacco storage hulk at Singapore.
Towed to her station at Deli. She remained anchored in the harbour until Holts built their
own wharf and tobacco wharehouses in 1881.
Note: Drawing is of 'a tobacco store ship' at Deli. The name is not given but since *'Andes'*
(32) was stationed at Penang it is assumed that the illustration is of *Sarah Nicholson*.

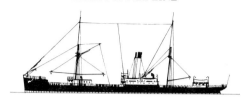

LAERTES (I), CYCLOPS (I) and BELLEROPHON (I)

31 LAERTES (I)

B 1879 Scott & Co, Greenock. **T:** 2,097 g, 1,482 n.
D 320.5 ft (97.69 m) × 34.3 ft (10.41 m) × 26 ft (7.92 m).
E Sgl scr, compound, 2 cyl, 188 NHP, 10 kts. By Greenock Foundry Co, Greenock.
H Iron. 1dk. **P** 35.

1879 The lead ship in a class of ten vessels which still maintained the basic characteristics of the early Holt ships. The smaller powered engine was used to propel a better designed hull with the consequence that they were larger cargo carriers. The redoutable John Swire felt that these ships were not as modern in their concept as some of the competition.
1894 Transferred to N.S.M. 'Oceaan'; same name.
1901 Reverted to Ocean S.S.Co, Liverpool.
1903 Sold to Li Shek Pang of Hong Kong; retained the name *Laertes*. Owned by Hung Hing S.S.Co.
1917 Dec. 15: Lost by collision in the Malacca Strait. She was sailing in ballast from Rangoon to Singapore.

32 CYCLOPS (I)

Sister of *Laertes* (31) except:
B 1880. **T:** 2,064 g, 1,499 n.
D 321.4 ft (97.97 m).

1880 April: Completed.
1894 Transferred to N.S.M 'Oceaan'; same name.
1902 Sold to Uruguay; renamed *Iberia*, R. Rup and Giulfo of Montevideo.
1904 May: Scrapped at Montevideo.

33 BELLEROPHON (I)

Sister of *Laertes* (31) except:
B 1880. **T:** 2,154 g, 1,318 n.
D 320 ft (97.54 m).
E By Builder.

1880 Entered service.
1893 Flew the Dutch flag of N.S.M. 'Oceaan'; same name.
1898 Sold to Manakani Toshiro, Uraga; same name. A very rare exception to the 'Maru' suffix.
1900 Became *Nitto Maru* of T. Okasaki, Kobe.
1915 Apr 4: Wrecked en-route Otaru–Nagoya at Tamagawa on the north coast of Honshu.

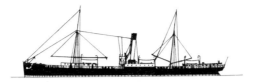

TELEMACHUS (I), JASON (I), PALAMED (I), PALINURUS (I), PROMETHEUS (I), DARDANUS (I) and ULYSSES (I)

34 TELEMACHUS (I)

Sister of *Laertes* (31) except:
B 1880 Andrew Leslie & Co, Hebburn **T**: 2,186 g, 1,340 n.
D 320.9 ft (97.79 m).
E By R. Stephenson & Co. Newcastle.

1880 Completed.
1894 Transferred to N.S.M. 'Oceaan'.
1899 Reverted to Ocean S.S.Co.
1902 Sold to Li Shek Pang, Hong Kong, purchaser of *Laertes*. As with her sister retained her original name.
1908 When sold to Lai Hing SS Co she still traded without a change of name.
1936 Sold for further trading by Lai Hing SS Co but found to be unfit for service and broken up at Hong Kong.

35 JASON (I)

Sister of *Laertes* (31) except:
B 1880 Andrew Leslie & Co, Newcastle. **T**: 2,187 g, 1,336 n.
D 320.9 ft (97.81 m) × 34.6 ft (10.54 m).
E By R. Stephenson, Newcastle.

1880 Completed.
1894 To the Dutch subsidiary N.S.M. 'Oceaan'. Same name.
1903 Renamed *Ugo Maru*, Akita Kisen K.K, Hakodate.
1913 Owned by Okazaki K. K. K. Kobe, same name.
1920 Became *Nichiun Maru*, owned by Mitsubayashi Naosuke, Amagasaki.
1922 Broke up in Japan.

36 PALAMED (I)

Sister of *Laertes* (31) except:
B 1885 Andrew Leslie & Co, Newcastle. **T**: 2,479 g, 1,537 n.
D 320.2 ft (97.6 m) × 36.5 ft (11.12 m).
E By R. Stephenson, Newcastle.

1885 Entered service.
1897 Sold to Oakai Kikusaburo, Kobe; renamed *Kwan-On Maru No 15*.
1913 Became *Nichinan Maru*, Busai Kisen K.K, Kobe.
1928 Jan 5: Wrecked on the coast of Korea.

37 PALINURUS

Sister of *Laertes* (31) except:
B Hawthorn Leslie & Co, Newcastle. **T**: 2,523 g, 1,564 n.

D 326.7 ft (99.5 m) × 36.1 ft (11 m) × 26.4 ft (8.05 m).
E By R. Stephenson & Co, Newcastle.
H 2 dks.

1886 Entered service to the Far East.
1896 Transferred to the Dutch N.S.M. 'Oceaan'; same name.
1897 Reverted to the Ocean S.S.Co service and the British flag.
1897 Made one voyage out with cargo to Japan and there sold to Oakai Kikusaburo of Kobe and renamed *Kwan-On Maru No. 20.*
1913 Renamed *Nippoku Maru* (Okazaki K.K.K, Kobe).
1920 Owned by Goho Shokai K.K, Susami.
1923 Became *Nippoku Maru* owned by Seito Kaiun K.K, Nishinomiya.
1923 Broken up in Japan.

38 **PROMETHEUS** (I)

Sister of *Laertes* (31) except:
B 1886. **T**: 2,376 g.
D 320.2 ft (97.59 m) × 36.3 ft (11.06 m).

1886 Delivered.
1894 To Dutch N.S.M. 'Oceaan'; same name.
1894 Sold to Japan; Renamed *Ushina Maru*, Nippon Yusen Kaisha, Tokio. Spelling later adjusted to *Ujina Maru*. Taken over by Japanese Government for use as a Russo-Japanese War troopship.
1895 May 10: Wrecked on the East coast of Japan in the Gulf of Tai Lin Wau.

39 **DARDANUS** (I)

Sister of *Laertes* (31) except:
B Hawtorn Leslie & Co, Newcastle. **T**: 2,502 g, 1,551 n.
D 326.8 ft (99.6 m) × 10.88 ft (10.88 m) × 26.3 ft (8.02 m).
E By R. Stephenson & Co, Newcastle.
H 2 dks.

1886 Delivered.
1894 Renamed *Otaru Maru* by Nippon Yusen Kabusiki Kaisya,Tokio.
1903 May 3: Sunk as a block ship at Port Arthur.

40 **ULYSSES** (II)

Sister of *Laertes* (31) except:
B 1886. **T**: 2,140 g, 1,372 n.
D 320.8 ft (97.78 m) × 36.3 ft (11.06 m) × 25.8 ft (7.86 m).
E Sgl scr triple expansion; 1604 IHP; 10 kts. By builder.
H Steel 2 dks.

1886 The first triple expansion ship in the fleet. Clearly Holt's were not satisfied with the performance of the vessel because they reverted to compound tandem.
1890 April 21: Wrecked, en-route Shanghai—Yokohama, near to Tanabe, Japan.

41 **ASCANIUS** (I)

B 1880 Cochrane & Co, Birkenhead. **T**: 107 g, 74 n.
D 74 ft (22.56 m) × 18.1 ft (5.51 m) × 7.5 ft (2.29 m).
E Sgl scr, simple, 1 cyl direct acting, 9 kts. By builder.

H Iron, 1 dk with a poop on the half deck for crew accommodation.

1880 A tug built for tobacco barge towing duties at Singapore. Towed *Sarah Nicholson* (30) to her base at Deli.

1890 Sold to Ah Hi, Saigon; same name. Remained in service until the first world war.

42 ANDES

B 1859 Willaimson & Co, Harrington. **T**: 328 g, 328 n.
D 123 ft (37. 4m) × 25.6 ft (7.8 m) × 17 ft (5.18 m).
H Wood, 1 dk.

1859 Sailing Barque.
1880 Acquired and converted into a tobacco and general storage hulk stationed at Penang.

43 FANTEE

B 1879 Alex. Stephen & Sons, Linthouse. **T**: 167 g, 98 n.
D 120.2 ft (36.63 m) × 18 ft (5.49 m) × 8.4 ft (2.53 m).
E Tw scr compound inverted, 2 × 2 cyl; Stm P 70 lb; 50 HP; 9 kts.
H Steel, 1 dk; Quarterdeck 35 ft (10.67 m).

1879 Sailed out to her Singapore berth by Captain Highton.
1890 A metal smelter had been built on Pulan Braui a waterless islet in Singapore harbour. There already existed a derelict dry dock and *Fantee* was installed there without her engines or superstructure other than the quarterdeck accommodation. She was then filled with water and used as the supply for the smelting works being served by water lighters from the port.
1894 Sold to W. Kinsey, Singapore; used as a store hulk.
1899 Scrapped.

44 MERCURY

B 1892 Bowdler, Chaffer & Co, Liverpool. **T**: 303 g, 189 n.
D 138.6 ft (42.24 m) × 21.7 ft (6.6 m) × 12 ft (3.66 m).
E Sgl scr, comp. inverted, 2 cyls, 70 HP, 9 kts. By J. Taylor, Birkenhead.
H Iron, 1 dk.

1872 Built for the Oceanic S.S. Co. This is not the White Star Line whose title was Oceanic Steam Navigation Company.
1881 Acquired by Holt's and based at Singapore for service as a tobacco fleet feeder ship.
1900 Sold to the Tanjong Pagar Dock Co, Singapore and used as a stores ship.

MEMNON (I)

45 MEMNON (I)

B 1861 Scott & Co, Greenock. **T**: 1,290 g, 825 n.
D 253. 6 ft (77.9 m) × 32.6 ft (9.94 m) × 23 ft (7.01 m).
E Sgl scr comp direct drive, 2 cyl; 150 NHP; 9 kts. By Fawcett, Preston & Co, Liverpool.
H Iron, 1 dk and poop.

1861 Built as *Memnon* for Lamport & Holt's Liverpool, Brazil & River Plate S.N.Co. At the time of her construction the engine was a 2 cyl simple direct drive by the builder.
1872 Re-engined as above.
1883 Purchased by the Ocean S.S.Co; same name. Far East feeder vessel.
1888 Re-boilered.
1893 Transferred to the East India Ocean S.S.Co, owned by Alfred Holt & Company.
1899 Hulked at Singapore.

HEBE, CALYPSO and SAPPHO

46 HEBE

B 1885 Scott & Co, Greenock. **T:** 545 g, 346 n.
D 190 ft (57.91 m) × 30.7 ft (9.32 m) × 11.6 ft (3.51 m).
E Sgl scr comp, 2 cyl, 90 RHP; 9 kts. By builder.
H Iron, 1 dk. F 26 ft (7.92 m). P 26 ft (7.92 m).

1885 Joined the tobacco fleet.
1910 Sold to R. C. Willis & Partners, Singapore. Same name.
1912 Acquired by the Straits S.S. Co, Singapore. A concern that was substantially owned by Holts.
1922 Scrapped.

47 CALYPSO

Sister of *Hebe* (46) except:
B 1889. **T:** 544 g, 339 n.

1889 Built for the tobacco fleet.
1912 Acquired by Straits S.S.Co, Singapore.
1929 Broken up at Singapore.

48 SAPPHO

Sister of *Hebe* (46) except:
B 1887. **T:** 532 g, 328 n.
H Poop 31 ft (9.45 m).

1887 Entered the tobacco fleet.
1890 Sold to the Straits Steamship Company on its foundation and comprised one of the original five ships which they owned. In the history of the Straits company the *Sappho* is recorded as being subscribed to the new concern by Theodore Bogaardt. This may indicate that the ship was a joint venture vessel.
1899 Went aground on Palau Oudon adjacent to the lighthouse, the ship was refloated with the assistance of a tug. The Mate's certificate was suspended for negligence.
1923 Sold to the Menam Pilot's Association, Bangkok and used as a floating pilot station being anchored at the bar of the River Menam.
1928 Broken up.

BLUE FUNNEL LINE

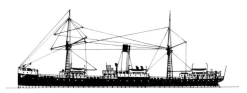

TELAMON (I) and TITAN (I)

49 TELAMON (I)

B 1885 Scott & Co, Greenock. T: 2,292 g, 1,632 n.
D 320 ft (97.54 m) × 36.3 ft (11.05 m) × 25.8ft (7.86 m).
E Sgl scr, comp. inverted; 2 cyl; 188 NHP; 10 kts. By builder.
H Iron, 1 dk. F: 31 ft (9.45 m). B: 50 ft (15.24 m).

1885 Delivered.
1897 to N.S.M. 'Oceaan'; same name.
1902 Broken up at Genoa.

50 TITAN (I)

Sister of *Telamon* (49) except:
T: 2,283 g, 1,621 n.
D 320.2 ft (97.59 m).

1885 Completed.
1895 to N.S.M. 'Oceaan'; same name.
1902 Scrapped at Genoa.

51 HECUBA (I)

B 1882 Scott & Co, Greenock. T: 918 g, 590 n.
D 233.4 ft (71.12 m) × 32.6 ft (9.93 m) × 15.8 ft (4.8 m).
E Sgl scr comp. inverted, 2 cyl; 98 RHP; 10 kts.
H Iron; F: 29 ft (8.84 m). Schooner rig.
P 1st and deck.

1882 Built for the Bangkok—Singapore rice trade. Cost £22,000. Owned Ocean 46/64. Mansfield 18/64. Bogaardt 18/64. Transferred to the East India Ocean S.S.Co.
1899 Sold with the East India fleet to Norddeutscher Lloyd, Bremen. Renamed *Kudat*.
1905 Became *Matsushima Maru* of Hokuriku Kisen Goshi Kaisya, Osaka.
1916 Out of service.

52 MEDUSA

B 1885 W. H. Potter & Sons, Liverpool. T: 967 g, 609 n.
D 237.4 ft (72.36 m) × 34.2 ft (10.42 m) × 15.4 ft (4.69 m).
E Sgl scr, comp. inverted, 2 cyl; 88 RHP; 9 kts. By Fawcett, Preston & Co, Liverpool.
H Iron, 1 dk; F: 40 ft (12.19 m). B: 58 ft (17.68 m). P: 27 ft (8.23 m).
P 25 1st plus deck.

1885 Built in Queen's Dock, Baffin St, Liverpool for the tobacco trade to replace *Calypso*. Owned Ocean 33/64, Bogaardt 8/64, Mansfield 15/64 and Crompton 8/64. Cost £15,500. Transferred to the East India S.S.Co.
1899 Sold with the fleet to A. D. Meyer, Norddeutscher Lloyd, Bremen. Renamed *Kelantan*; used on the same services into Singapore.
1903 Sold to Y. Kaji, Kobe. Became *Jingi Maru No 3*. Later the ownership is shown as Y. Fujiyama, Kobe.
1921 Scrapped.

53 HECATE

Sister of *Medusa* (51) except:
T: 968 g, 609 n.

1885 Entered the Bangkok–Singapore tobacco and coastal service. Cost £15,750. With the same shared ownership as her sister ship. Transferred to East India Ocean S.S.Co.
1899 Passed into the hands of Norddeutscher Lloyd, Bremen; renamed *Patani* (I).
1904 Sold to Japan; Became *Ikuta Maru No 2*.
1908 Owned by Hokuyo Kisen K.K., Nana-O; renamed *Hokuyo Maru*. Later shown as owned by Yamamoto Atuzo of Nana-O.
1924 Broken up.

54 HYDRA

Sister of *Medusa* (51) except:
B 1889. **T**: 990 g, 619 n.
D 237.3 ft (72.33 m).

1889 Entered the Swatow–Singapore–Bankok service. Cost £18,123. Ownership Ocean 36/64, Bogaardt 10/64, Mansfield 10/64 and Crompton 10/64. Owned by the East India Ocean S.S.Co.
1899 Sold to Norddeutscher Lloyd, Bremen. Renamed *Kedah*.
1905 Acquired by Y. Fujiyama, Nishinomiya; became *Sekkai Maru*.
1918 Broken up.

WILL O' THE WISP

55 WILL O' THE WISP

B 1883 Norfolk & Co, Hull. **T**: 283 g, 148 n.
D 120.4 ft (36.7 m) × 22.2 ft (6.77 m) × 10 ft (3.05 m).
E Sgl scr, comp, 2 cyl, 45 RHP, 8 kts. By Wood Bros, Sowerby Bridge.
H Iron, 1 dk. **F**: 18 ft (5.49 m). **B**: 30 ft (9.14 m). **Q**: 29 ft (8.84 m).

1883 June: Built for W. S. Davison, Yokohama. Registered at Hull.
1886 Sold to Walter Mansfield & Co, Singapore. Registered as owned by A. P. Adams, one of the directors.
1887 Sold to Alfred Holt & Co, Liverpool.
1890 Transferred to the Straits S.S.Co. at its formation.
1896 Passed into the hands of Tan Poh Tong, Singapore.
1898 Sold to Tan Hok Hay as owner master, Singapore.
1899 To Lim Kee Joo, Singapore.
1900 Acquired by Ng Nguan Teng, Singapore.
1906 Owned by Sug Toon Ghee, Singapore.
1908 Owned by K. A. Somasuntheran Chitty, Singapore.
1909 Transferred to Wee Brothers S.S.Co, Singapore.
1917 Sold to Hong Kong owners Wong Poh Keung. Resold during the year to H. A. Lamont, Hong Kong.
1918 Passed to Wee Seng Bee S.S.Co, Hong Kong and then, during the year, to A. L. Alves in the same port.
1923 Returned to Singapore; owned by Wee Teow Beng.
1924 Teo Hu Lai purchased the ship.
1935 Sold to Heap Eng Moh S.S.Co, Singapore but broken up at the year's end, having served for 52 years without change of name.

FLINTSHIRE

56 **FLINTSHIRE**

B 1872 London & Glasgow Co, Glasgow. **T:** 1,565 g, 1,017 n.
D 270.7 ft (82.51 m) × 32.8 ft (9.99 m) × 28.8 ft (8.78 m).
E Sgl scr, comp. 2 cyl. Stm P 70 lb. 9 kts. By builder.
H Iron. 2dks.

1872 July: Built for Jenkin's Shire Line of Cardiff.
1882 Reboilered.
1888 Sold to Lim Tiang Hee, Singapore. Same name.
1889 Acquired by the Ocean S.S.Co, Liverpool for their services out of Singapore and based there.
1891 Transferred to East India Ocean S.S.Co for local feeder services.
1892 Transferred to N.S.M. 'Oceaan' without change of name.
1895 Reverted to East India Ocean S.S.Co.
1896 Sold to Okazaki Tokichi, Kobe; renamed *Yayeyama Maru*.
1898 Dec 12: Lost by collision at Nagasaki.

57 **SALADIN** (II)

B 1890 Thomas Royden & Co, Liverpool. **T:** 1,874 g, 1,140 n.
D 254.6 ft (77.57 m) × 38.2 ft (11.63 m) × 24 ft (7.31 m).
E Sgl scr, comp. inverted, 2 cyl; 159 NHP, 10 kts. By Fawcett, Preston, Liverpool.
H Iron, 2 dks and spar dk. **F:** 30 ft (9.14 m).
P 45 plus day deck.

1890 Built for the Singapore—Batavia—Fremantle service. Owned by Alfred Holt & Co. but operated under an agreement with the West Australia S.N.Co. Registered at Fremantle.
1905 Sold to Japan; became *Kotohira Maru No 3* of Kawasaki Yoshitaro, Kobe, later sold to Kentaro Kawachi, Kobe.
1926 Scrapped in Japan.

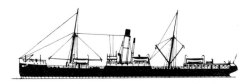

MYRMIDON (I), TEUCER (II), POLYPHEMUS (I) and PRIAM (II)

58 **MYRMIDON** (I)

B 1890 Scott & Co, Greenock. **T:** 2,868 g, 1,591 n.
D 336.1 ft (102.44 m) × 38.5 ft (11.73 m) × 27 ft (8.23 m).
E Sgl scr, comp, 2 cyl; 248 NHP; 10 kts; By builder.
H Steel, 2 dks. **F:** 46 ft (14.02 m). **B:** 50 ft (15.24 m). **P:** 16ft (4.88 m).
P 12 carried in cabins aft together with that of the master. 500 deck pilgrims and 200 'tween deck passengers.

1890 The first of a class of four. Cost £52,320. They were wet ships due to the lack of bulwarks and had higher than normal coamings in order to keep accommodation dry. In the tropics cooling for passengers was by means of hand operated punkahs.

1899 Transferred to N.S.M. 'Oceaan'; same name.

1904 Sold to Tatsuma Shokwi K.K, Naruo; renamed *Tatsu Maru*.

1911 Renamed *Tencho Maru*, Tatsuma Kisen K.K, Nishinomaya.

1920 Became *Hai Tien*, Chinese flag.

1927 Renamed *Ho Ping*, owned by Tsieging Chin of Chefoo.

1929 Broken up at Hong Kong.

59 TEUCER (II)

Sister of *Myrmidon* (58) except:

T: 2,846 g, 1,741 n.

1890 Completed at a cost of £48,500.

1890 Transferred to the Dutch flag subsidiary N.S.M. 'Oceaan'; same name.

1903 Reverted to Ocean S.S.Co's ownership.

1906 Sold to K. Matsugata, Kobe. Renamed *Chusa Maru*. The name was the Japanese equivalent of *Teucer*.

1907 Aug 9: wrecked near to Toto on the coast of Japan.

60 PRIAM (II)

Sister of *Myrmidon* (58) except:

T: 2,846 g, 1,799 n.

1890 Delivered; cost £48,668.

1899 Passed over to the Dutch N.S.M. 'Oceaan'; same name.

1903 Sold to K. Kishimoto, Hamadera. Later this company was re-styled Kishimoto Kisen K.K, Nishinomaya. Renamed *Shingu Maru*.

1914 Owned by Nippon Kosen Gyogyo K.K, Foetsyo.

1938 Under the revised system of spelling the ship became *Singu Maru*. Owned by Nippon Suisan K.K.

1942 Owned by Sansin Kisen K.K., Hutyo.

1944 May 3: Bombed, set on fire and sunk by U.S. air attack south west of Formosa.

61 POLYPHEMUS (I)

Sister of *Myrmidon* (58) except:

T: 2,868 g, 1,813 n.

1890 Built at a cost of £53,364 for the Far East services but also shown as being able to undertake the Mecca pilgrimage services from Singapore. This entailed additional water and sanitary facilities together with cooking services at the break of the fcsle and poop. This ship also carried the then fleets only stewardess.

1898 To the Dutch 'Oceaan' company; same name.

1904 Became *Tatsu Maru No 2*, owned by Tatsuma Shokwi K.K, Naruo.

1911 Renamed *Chikyu Maru*, same owners.

1916 Jan 31: Wrecked on the coast of Korea at Joshin.

BLUE FUNNEL LINE

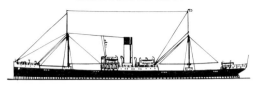

IXION (I), TANTALUS (I), ULYSSES (III) and PYRRHUS (I)

62 **IXION** (I)

B 1892 Scott & Co, Greenock. **T**: 3,572 g, 2,272 n.
D 354.9 ft (108.8 m) × 42.8 ft (13.03 m) × 26.7 ft (8.13 m).
E Sgl scr, tpl exp, 3 cyl; 282 NHP; 10 kts. By builder.
H Steel, 2 dks. F: 42 ft (15.85 m). B: 68 ft (20.73 m). P: 32 ft (9.75 m).
P 12.

1892 Lead vessel in a class of 4; cost £51,000.
1902 Transferred to N.S.M. 'Oceaan'; same name.
1911 Oct 2: Lost by fire off Enggano, Indonesia, en-route Java—Amsterdam. The first loss for 21 years.

63 **TANTALUS** (I)

Sister of *Ixion* (62) except:
T: 3,621 g, 2,282 n.

1892 Completed; cost £51,500.
1904 To N.S.M. 'Oceaan'; same name.
1922 Sold to Leonard R. Muller, Hamburg and renamed *Florian Geyer*.
1924 Broken up at Hamburg.

64 **ULYSSES** (III)

Sister of Ixion (62) except:
T: 3,261 g, 2,282 n.

1892 Cost £52,185.
1912 Sold to Japan; renamed *Daisai Maru*.
1917 Transferred to French Government ownership as a war loss replacement became *St Medard*.
1920 Became *General Moiner*.
1921 Reverted to *St Medard* owned by Société Maritime Française, La Rochelle.
1924 Broken up at Ardrossan.

65 **PYRRHUS** (I)

Sister of *Ixion* (62) except:
T: 3,261 g, 2,282 n.

1892 Entered service; cost £52,180.
1907 To N.S.M. 'Oceaan'; same name.
1914 Sold to Japan; renamed *Shingo Maru*.
1916 Sold to Madrigal & Co, Manila. Became *Macaria*.
1917 Taken over by the United States as a transport; renamed *Villemer*.
1917 Nov 7: Torpedoed by *UC-38* east of Crete.

BEAGLE

66 BEAGLE

B 1892 Blackwood & Gordon, Port Glasgow. **T:** 147 g, 100 n.
D 110.5 ft (33.68 m) × 20.2 ft (6.25 m) × 6.9 ft (2.06 m).
E Tw scr comp, 2 × 2 cyl, 35 RHP each, 8 kts; By builder.
H Steel, 1 dk. F: 12 ft (3.66 m). Q: 19 ft (5.79 m). P: 10 ft (5.79 m).

1892 Steam lighter based at Cossack, W. Australia.
1908 Sold to Italians.
1909 Owned Government of Siam.

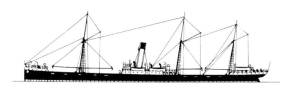

NESTOR (II)

67 NESTOR (II)

B 1889 Schlesinger, Davies & Co, Newcastle. **T:** 3,767 g, 2,417 n.
D 370.5 ft (112.9 M) × 42.2 ft (12.8 m) × 27.2 ft (8.28 m)
E Sgl scr tpl exp; 3 cycl, 413 NHP, 10 kts; By builder.
H Steel, 2 dks. 3 masts. F: 41 ft (12.5 m). B: 98 ft (29.87 m). P: 56 ft (17.1 m).

1889 Built as *Sullamut*, Hajee Jasoob Poorbhoy, Bombay. Became *Queen of India*, Beyts, Craig & Co.
1894 Acquired by Ocean S.S.Co; renamed *Nestor*. Refurbished at a cost of £37,000.
1911 Sold to Italy. Became *Teresa* then *Assunzione*.
1917 June 15: Torpedoed and sunk in the Mediterranean.

68 CERBERUS

B 1894 Workman Clark & Co, Belfast. **T:** 1,754 g, 1,123n.
D 257.3 ft (78.42 m) × 41.1 ft (12.53 m) × 20.9 ft (6.37 m).
E Sgl scr, tpl exp, 3 cyl; 148 NHP; 10 kts; by builder.
H Steel, 2 dks. F: 24 ft (7.31 m). B: 26 ft (7.92 m).
P 24 plus deck.

1894 Built for Alfred Holt & Co. Operated by East India S.S.Co.
1899 Sold to Norddeutscher Lloyd, Bremen for service in East Indian waters. Renamed *Singora*. The ship is first recorded as *Singgora* but corrected in the following edition of Lloyds register.
1910 Sold to Y. Hachiuma, Nishinomaya; renamed *Tamon Maru No 1*.
1925 Became *Kiku Maru* of Shizaki Yokichi, Kobe.
1931 Broken up in Japan.

69 SULTAN

B 1894 Workman Clark, Belfast. **T:** 2,063g, 1,270.
D 258.5 ft (78.79 m) × 38 ft (11.58 m) × 13.9 ft (4.24 m).
E Sgl scr, tpl exp, 3 cyl; 206 NHP; 10 kts. By builder.
H Steel, 1 dk and spar dk. B: 52 ft (15.85 m). P: 57 ft (17.37 m).
P 48.

1894 Apr: Jointly owned by Ocean S.S.Co. and the West Australian S.N. Co. for the Singapore—Batavia—Fremantle route.
1898 Wholly owned by Holts.
1909 Became *Kayo Maru* of Oaki Goshi Kaisya, Yokohama.
1929 Laid up at Yokohama.
1930—31 Broken up locally.

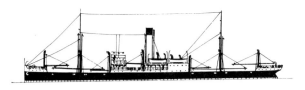

ORESTES (III), SARPEDON (III), DARDANUS (II),
DIOMED (II), HECTOR (III) and MENELAUS (II)

70 ORESTES (III)

B 1894 Scott & Co, Greenock. **T:** 4,653 g, 2,992 n.
D 392.3 ft (119.58 m) × 47.1 ft (14.35 m) ×26.4 ft (8.05 m).
E Sgl scr tpl exp, 3 cyl, 2,600 IHP, 350 NHP. 10 kts. By builder.
H Steel, 2 dks. F: 49 ft (14.93 m). B: 106 ft (32.31 m). P: 32 ft (9.75 m). Crew: 52.

1894 The first ship in a class of 6 and the company's largest ship to date. Cost £51,786. It is worth noting that building prices remained fairly constant even though the ships themselves increased in size, tonnage and, above all, carrying capacity.
1901 Took the first Liverpool—Australia service.
1925 Sold to Italian breakers.

71 SARPEDON (III)

Sister of *Orestes* (70) except:
B Workman Clark, Belfast. **T:** 4,663 g, 3,023 n.
D 391.5 ft (119.3 m).
E By builder.

1894 Completed. Cost £52,010.
1914 Passed to the Dutch flag N.S.M. 'Oceaan'; same name.
1915 Reverted to the British flag to replace wartime losses.
1918 Nov 7: Missed by a torpedo in the Mediterranean. This was the final German attack on a Blue Funnel vessel in the first World War.
1923 Acquired by Leonard R. Muller, Hamburg. Renamed *Gotz von Berlichingen*.
1925 Broken up at Hamburg.

72 DARDANUS (II)

Sister of *Orestes* (70) except:
T: 4,653 g, 2,992 n.

D 392.0 ft (119.48 m). P: 44ft (13.41 m)

1894 Delivered. Cost £52,030.
1911 To Dutch flag, N.S.M. 'Oceaan'; same name.
1923 Sold to Germany renamed *Fingal*, Paulsen & Ivers, Kiel.
1926 Sold to Italy renamed *Fortunato Secondo*. I.N.S.A Genoa.
1927 Broken up at Genoa.

73 **DIOMED** (II)

Sister of *Orestes* (70) except:
B 1895. **T:** 4,672 g, 3,005 n.
D 392 ft (119.48 m).
H P 44 ft (13.41 m).

1895 Completed. Cost £53,401.
1915 Aug 22: Torpedoed 57 miles of the Scilly Isles. Captain J. Myles and 2 others were killed on the bridge, and others were lost while abandoning ship in heavy seas.

74 **HECTOR** (III)

Sister of *Orestes* (70) except:
B 1895 Workman Clark Belfast. **T:** 4,660 g, 3,006 n.
D 391.5 ft (119.25 m).
H F: 47 ft (14.33 m). B: 108 ft (39.92 m). P: 34 ft (10.36 m).

1895 Entered service.
1915 Served as a balloon ship during the Dardenelles campaign.
1923 Sold for breaking up by Schiffswerke Unterelbe, Wilhelmshaven.

75 **MENELAUS** (II)

Sister of *Orestes* (70) except:
B 1895. **T:** 4,672 g, 3,006 n.
D 392 ft (119.48 m).
H P: 44 ft (13.41 m).

1895 Delivered. Cost £53,532.
1916 Sold to British Admiralty; used as balloon ship renamed *Davo*.
1923 Broken up at Genoa.

76 **CENTAUR** (I)

B 1895 Workman Clark, Belfast. **T:** 1,900 g, 1,223 n.
D 278 ft (84.73 m) × 41.1 ft (12.53 m) × 20.8 ft (6.34 m).
E Sgl scr tpl exp 3 cyls 148 NHP, 10 kts by builder.
H Steel 2 dks, F: 28 ft (8.53 m), B: 38 ft (11.58 m).

1895 Built for Holt's East India SS Co. Virtually a sister to *Cerberus* (68).
1899 Sold to Norddeutscher Lloyd; renamed *Korat*.
1911 Sold to Japan; renamed *Daito Maru*.
1918 Out of service.

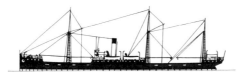

ANCHISES (II)

77 ANCHISES (II)

B 1888 Wigham Richardson, Newcastle-upon-Tyne. **T**: 2,718 g, 1,841 n.
D 325 ft (99.06 m) × 40 ft (12.19 m) × 25.9 ft (7.87).
E Sgl scr tpl exp, 3 cyls, 400 HP Stm P 150; 10 kts. By T. Richardson, Hartlepool.
H Steel, 2 dks. F: 43 ft (13.11 m). B: 90 ft (25.43 m). P: 37 ft (11.28 m).
P 40 in berths located on the poop.

1888 Built for Lund's Blue Anchor Line as *Wilcannia*, one of the five *Hubbuck* class.
1897 Sold to Alfred Holt when a new *Wilcannia* was ordered but on condition that the name was changed. Renamed *Anchises*. Used mainly as a reserve ship on the Indonesian and West Austrialian services.
1898 Transferred to N.S.M 'Oceaan'; same name.
1906 Reverted to Ocean S.S.Co.
1910 Broken up at Briton Ferry.

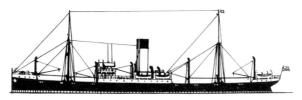

PROMETHEUS (II), PATROCLUS (II)/PALAMED (II),
GLAUCUS (II) and ANTENOR (II)

78 PROMETHEUS (II)

B 1896 Scott & Co., Greenock. **T**: 5,570 g, 3,583 n.
D 422 ft (128.63 m) × 49 ft (14.93 m) × 38.3 ft (11.67 m).
E Sgl scr tpl exp 4,000 IHP 520 NHP, 10 kts. By builder.
H Steel 2 dks. F: 46 ft (14.02 m), B: 115 ft (35.05 m), P: 38 ft (11.58 m)

1896 First of a class of 4 which exceeded 5,000 grt and 400 ft (121.92 m) in length. Cost £62,558.
1924 Sold to Italy renamed *Delia*, I.N.S.A. (Industrie Navali Soc. Anon), Genoa.
1925 Broken up in Italy.

79 GLAUCUS (II)

Sister of *Prometheus* (78) except:
B Workman Clark, Belfast. **T**: 5,509 g, 3,548 n.
D 423.1 ft (128.96 m) × 49.2 ft (14.99 m).
1896 Completed. Cost £62,801.
1918 June 3: Torpedoed off Sicily 20 miles west of Cape Granitola.

80 **PATROCLUS** *(II)*/**PALAMED** (II)

Details as *Prometheus* (78) except:
B 1896 Workman Clark, Belfast. **T**: 5,509 g, 3,548 n.
D 422 ft (128.63 m) × 49.4 ft (15.06 m) × 28.6 ft (8.71 m).
E By builder.
H F: 43 ft (13.11 m). B: 121 ft (36.88 m). P: 39 ft (11.89 m).
P 12.

1896 Completed.
1914 To Dutch flag N.S.M. 'Oceaan'; same name.
1923 Renamed *Palamed* (II) due to the advent of *Patroclus* (III).
1924 Dec: Sold to Atlantide S.A. per Imprese Marittima, Genoa; Renamed *Australia*.
1929 Broken up at Genoa.

81 **ANTENOR** (II)

Sister of *Prometheus* (79) except:
B 1896 Workman Clark, Belfast. **T**: 5,531 g, 3,563 n.
E By builder.

1896 Delivered. Cost £62,796.
1914 Transferred to the Dutch N.S.M. 'Oceaan'; same name, but later returned to the parent company.
1918 Feb 9: Torpedoed in the Mediterranean but was helped into port.
1925 March: sold and renamed *Fortunato*. I.N.S.A. (Industrie Navali S.A.). Genoa.
1926 Broken up in Italy.

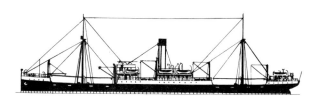

IDOMENEUS (I), CALCHAS (I), MACHAON (I)
ALCINOUS (I), STENTOR (II), AGAMEMNON (II)
AJAX (II), ACHILLES (II) and DEUCALION (II)

82 **IDOMENEUS** (I)

B 1899 Scott & Co, Greenock. **T**: 6,764 g, 4,299 n.
D 441.8 ft (134.65 m) × 52.6 ft (16.03 m) ×30.3 ft (9.25 m).
E Sgl scr Tpl exp 521 NHP, 4,000 IHP, 10 kts; By builder.
H Steel 2 dks. F: 58 ft (17.68 m). B: 154 ft (46.94 m). P: 50 ft (15.24 m).

1899 The first of a class of nine vessels which were the first to exceed 6,000 grt thereby becoming the largest vessels yet owned. Despite the increase in carrying capacity the hull design and engine improvements provided the same cost per nautical mile as their predecessor class.
1917 Sept 15: Torpedoed and beached off the west coast of Scotland.
1922 To the Dutch N.S.M. 'Oceaan'; same name.
1925 Sold to Ditta L Pittaluga Vapori, Genoa. Renamed *Aurania*.
1933 Broken up at Genoa.

83 CALCHAS (I)

Sister of *Idomeneus* (82) except:
T: 6,748 g, 4,279 n.

1899 Entered service. Cost £83,983.
1917 May 11: Torpedoed off Tearaght Island, Ireland. No lives lost.

84 MACHAON (I)

Sister of *Idomeneus* (82) except:
T: 6,738 g, 4,277 n.

1899 Completed.
1918 Feb 27: Torpedoed off Cani Rocks, Tunisia.

85 ALCINOUS (I)

Sister of *Idomeneus* (82) except:
T: 6,743 g, 4,278 n.

1918 Mar 31: Reached port after being torpedoed in the English Channel.
1918 Sept 2: Drove off an attacking submarine by means of accurate gun fire.
1925 Sold to Ditta L Pittaluga Vapori, Genoa; renamed *Carmania*.
1928 Became *Silvania*, same owner.
1932 Broken up at Genoa.

86 STENTOR (II)

Sister of *Idomeneus* (82) except:
B Workman Clark, Belfast. **T**: 6,773 g, 4,308 n.
D 442.4 ft (134.84 m) × 52.8 ft (16.09 m) × 30.6 ft (9.33 m).
E D. Rollo & Sons, Liverpool.
H F: 55 ft (16.76 m). B: 156 ft (47.55 m). P: 49 ft (14.93 m).

1899 Delivered.
1922 To Dutch flag N.S.M. 'Oceaan'; same name.
1926 Jan: Sold to Madrigal & Co, Manila, Philippines; renamed *Don José*.
1929 Broken up at Singapore.

87 AGAMEMNON (II)

Sister of *Idomeneus* (82) except:
B 1900. **T**: 7,011 g, 4,462 n.
D 442.1 ft (134.75 m).
H F: 58 ft (17.68 m). B: 154 ft (46.94 m). P: 50 ft (15.24 m).

1900 Delivered.
1917 July 16: A submarine surfaced and gave chase with gunfire but was unable to catch *Agamemnon*.
1927 Dec: Sold to Soc. Anon. Commerciale Italo-Chilena, renamed *Impero*.
1932 Jan: Broken up at Genoa.

88 AJAX (II)

Sister of *Idomeneus* (82) except:
B 1900. **T**: 7,043 g, 4,484 n.

D 442.5 ft (134.85 m).

1900 Entered service.
1902 June 1: grounded on Jeddah Reef; filled with water but salvaged.
1915 Oct 10: Rescued by a destroyer when under submarine gunfire in the Mediterranean.
1930 Broken up in Japan.

89 ACHILLES (II)

Sister of *Idomeneus* (82) except:
B 1900. **T:** 7,043 g, 4,484 n.
D 442 ft (134.85 m).

1900 Entered service. Cost £89.142.
1915 April: Employed on Admiralty service between Alexandria and the Dardanelles carrying Indian troops. Came under fire from the Turkish shore batteries; 2 killed. Next used as a wounded reception ship. Later *Achilles* rescued 49 survivors from the torpedoed troopship *Royal Edward*, sunk on Aug. 13 in the Aegean with the loss of 132 lives.
1916 March 31: Torpedoed off Ushant by U-44. 5 lost.

90 DEUCALION (II)

Details as *Idomeneus* (82) except:
B 1900. **T:** 7,030 g, 4,476 n.
D 443 ft (135.03 m).

1900 Built.
1930 Jan: Sold to Ditta L Pittaluga Vapori, Genoa. Renamed *Aquitania*.
1933 Broken up at Genoa.

ATALANTA

91 ATLANTA

B 1899 Kwong Tak Cheong, Hong Kong. **T:** 107 g, 37 n.
D 86 ft (26.21 m) × 17.1 ft (5.23 m) × 8.6 ft (2.68 m).
E Sgl scr, comp 2 cyl; 37 RHP, 7 kts. By Kwong Hep Loong, Hong Kong.
H Wood. 1 dk.

1899 Built for harbour tender service at Hong Kong.
1902 Acquired by Holts for similar duties. Owned by Ocean S.S.Co.
1924 Dismantled. Used as a barge locally. Finally laid up as a hulk; rotted.

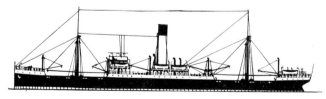

PELEUS (I), TYDEUS (I), TELEMACHUS (II) and JASON (II)

92 PELEUS (I)

B 1901 Workman Clark, Belfast. **T:** 7,441 g, 4,800 n.
D 454.7 ft (138.58 m) × 54.1 ft (16.49 m) × 32.3 ft (9.86 m).

E Sgl scr, Tpl exp; 533 NHP; 10 kts. By builder.
H Steel, 2 dks. F: 57 ft (17.37 m). B: 160 ft (48.77 m). P: 53 ft (16.15 m).
P 12.
Note the fractional rake to the funnel.

1901 Entered service. The commencement of yet another class of larger ships.
1931 Apr: Sold to Madrigal & Co, Manila; renamed *Perseus.*
1933 Broken up in Japan.

93 **TYDEUS** (I)

Details as *Peleus* (92) except:
H B: 219 ft (66.75 m).

1901 Completed.
1931 Jan: Broken up by Smith & Houston, Port Glasgow.

94 **TELEMACHUS** (I)

Details as *Peleus* (92) except:
B Workman Clark, Belfast. **T**: 7,450 g, 4,802 n.

1902 Delivered.
1910 May 7: When 464 miles west of Minikoi Island a small boat was seen in which there was one man alive and another dead. It turned out that the survivor, Joshua Green, with two others, had set out from their home to cross from one Seychelle island to another but had lost sight of land. A steamer had stopped, provisioned them and set them on the correct course for home. Once again they had become lost. One man's body had been put overboard but Green had become too weak to deal with the other. When picked up Green was 900 miles from home and had been adrift for four months.
1932 Sold to Ditta Luigi Pittaluga Vapori, Genoa; became *Tasmania.*
1933 Broken up in Italy.

95 **JASON** (II)

Sister of *Peleus* (92) except:
B 1902 Workman Clark, Belfast. **T**: 7,450 g.

1902 Entered service.
1931 Broken up in Japan.

96 **CHING WO**

B 1894 Workman Clark, Belfast. **T**: 3,883 g, 2,517 n.
D 370 ft (112.78 m) × 45.3 ft (13.82 m) × 27 ft (8.23 m).
E Sgl scr, tpl exp, 3 cyls, 398 NHP; 2 sgl ended boilers 180 lb. 10 kts. By builder.
H Steel. 2 dks. F: 42 ft (12.8 m). B: 73 ft (22.25 m). P: 26 ft (7.92 m).

1894 Sept: Completed for the China Mutual S.N.Co, Liverpool.
1902 Taken over with the fleet by Alfred Holt. Owner's name not changed.
1911 Became *Unkai Maru No 2*, Uchida Kisen K.K. Tarumi, Japan.
1920 Sold to the French Government; renamed *Indochine.*
1923 Scrapped.

97 OOPACK

Details as *Ching Wo* (96).

1894 Completed in October for China Mutual S.N.Co, Liverpool.
1902 Fleet taken over by Alfred Holt; same name and same owner.
1918 Oct 4: At 2.30 am the ship was twice torpedoed, the first struck No 1 hold and the second No 2 hold. The ship was 110 miles east of Malta. *Oopack*, Captain D. T. Williams, had left Milo, Greece, on October 2 in a seven ship 7 knot convoy for Malta, 479 miles away. The escort was H.M.S. *Snapdragon*. During the evening of the 4th a submarine was seen shadowing the convoy. It was *UB 68*, commanded by Lt-Cmdr Karl Doenitz, later to be Hitler's ultimate successor. After the attack *Snapdragon* chased the submarine which surfaced close to her. As the crew came on deck to man their guns the first shell from *Snapdragon* demolished the conning tower and the helpless *UB 68* surrendered. Thus it came about that the crew of both *Oopack* and *UB 68* were survivors aboard the same ship. Doenitz believed that he had sunk two ships. Captain Williams told him that it was only one. As the *Snapdragon* entered Malta the survivors lined the decks. Doenitz ordered his men to take their caps off and then they shouted 'Hoch der Kaiser' (Up the Kaiser).
Oopack was the last Blue Funnel World War I loss.

98 KAISOW

Details as *Ching Wo* (96) except:
B 1895 D & W Henderson, Glasgow. **T:** 3,921 g, 2,529 n.
E By builder.
H F: 44 ft (13.41 m). P: 25 ft (7.62 m).

1895 Built for the China Mutual S.N.Co, Liverpool.
1902 Fleet taken over by Holts without change of name or ownership.
1911 Sold to Japan. Became *Shintsu Maru*, Kanamori Gomei Kaisha, Amagasaki.
1919 Renamed *Toyo Maru*.
1921 Acquired by Denmark; renamed *Alssund*, A/D Gylfe, managed by T. C. Christensen, Copenhagen.
1923 Broken up.

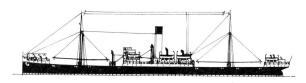

PAK LING, KINTUCK, MOYUNE, TEENKAI

99 PAK LING (II)

B 1895 Workman Clark, Belfast. **T:** 4,614 g, 2,875 n.
D 410 ft (124.97 m) × 48.1 ft (14.66 m) × 27.4 ft (8.36 m).
E Sgl scr, Tpl exp; 3 cyls; 600 NHP. 2 dbl ended boilers 180 lb. By builder.
H Steel. 2 dks. F: 47 ft (14.33 m). B: 108 ft (32.92 m). P: 45 ft (13.72 m).

1895 Built for China Mutual S.N.Co, Liverpool.
1902 Fleet taken over by Alfred Holt; same name and owner.
1920 July 6: Went ashore in fog on Button Island, Bonham Straits, 100 miles south of Shanghai. July 13: Refloated chiefly by aid of the tug *St Dominic*, owned by the Shanghai Tug & Lighterage Co. Repaired at Shanghai.
1923 Broken up by Schiffswerke Unterelbe A.G., Wilhemshaven.

100 KINTUCK

Details as *Pak Ling* (99) except:
T: 4,447 g, 2,881 n.

1895 Built for the China Mutual S.N.Co, Liverpool.
1902 Taken over by Blue Funnel with the rest of the fleet. Same name.
1916 Dec 2: Attacked off southwest Ireland. Drove off the submarine by accurate gunfire.
1917 June 13: Again attacked by submarine gunfire but escaped in bad light.
1917 Dec 2: *Kintuck* was torpedoed and this time sank off Godrevy Lighthouse, Cornwall.

101 MOYUNE

Details as *Pak Ling* (99) except:
T: 4,646 g, 3,016 n.
B D & W Henderson, Glasgow.
E By builder. 3 sgl ended boilers.

1895 Completed for the China Mutual S.N.Co, Liverpool.
1902 Taken over by Blue Funnel; same name and owner.
1918 Apr 12: Torpedoed and sunk south-east of Cape Palos, near Cartagena, Spain.

102 TEENKAI

Details as *Pak Ling* (99) except:
T: 4,642 g, 3,016 n.
B D & W Henderson, Glasgow.
E By builder. 3 sgl ended boilders.

1895 Oct: Built for the China Mutual S.N.Co, Liverpool.
1902 Taken over by Holts.
1922 Sold to Germany; renamed *Gerfrid*, "Globus" Rheederei A.G, Bremen.
1927 Acquired by Pereira Carneiro & Cia, Rio de Janeiro, Brazil; renamed *Merity*.
193? Broken up.

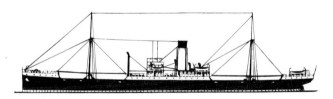

YANG TSZE, PING SUEY (I) and HYSON

103 YANG-TSZE

B 1899 Workman Clark, Belfast. **T**: 6,457 g, 4,149 n.
D 450 ft (137.16 m) × 53.1 ft (16.2 m) × 31 ft (9.45 m).
E Sgl scr, Tpl exp, 3 cyls; 620 NHP. 2 dbl ended boilers, 180 lb. By builder.
H Steel, 2 dks. F: 45 ft (13.72 m). B: 145 ft (144.19 m). P: 36 ft (10.97 m).
P 12.

1899 Mar: Built for the China Mutual S.N.Co, Liverpool. The first of a trio.
1902 Taken over with the remainder of the fleet by Blue Funnel.
1918 Apr 25: Missed by torpedo attack west of Gibraltar.
1927 Sold to Madrigal & Co, Manila; renamed *Macaria* (II).
1933 Broken up in Japan.

104 PING SUEY (I)

Details as *Yang-Tsze* (103) except:
T: 6,458 g, 4,150 n.

1899 Built for the China Mutual S.N.Co, Liverpool.
1902 Taken over by Alfred Holt. Same name and owners.
1916 June 24: Went ashore on Dassen Island, Cape of Good Hope. Crew existed on Penguin eggs until rescued.
1917 May: Patching up completed, salved and sold to Italy 'as lies'. Repaired. Sold to Lloyd de Pacifico, Savona. Renamed *Attalita*.
1918 Apr 25: Missed by torpedo attack west of Gibraltar.
1932 Aug: Broken up at Genoa.

105 HYSON

Details as *Yang-Tsze* (103) except:
T: 6,608 g, 4,232 n.
B D & W Henderson & Co, Glasgow.
E By builder.

1899 Built for the China Mutual S.N.Co, Liverpool.
1902 Taken over with the fleet by Holt's. Same name and owner.
1917 May 29: Chased by U-boat in the English Channel.
1926 Aug: Sold to Italy; renamed *Maria Rosa*, E. Bozzo and L. Mortola, Genoa.
1932 May: Broken up at Spezia.

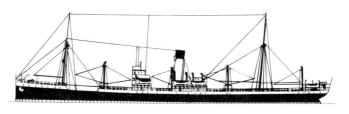

KEEMUN (II), NINGCHOW and OANFA (II)

106 KEEMUN (I)

B 1902 Workman Clark, Belfast. T: 9,067 g, 5,727 n.
D 482 ft (146.91 m) × 58.2 ft (17.73 m) × 32.8 ft (9.96 m).
E Tw scr Tpl exp, 2 × 3 cyls each, 801 NHP; 3 dbl ended boilers 200 lb. 10 kts. By builder.
H Steel, 2 dks. F: 79 ft (24.08 m). B & P 338 ft (103.02 m).
P 12. 1,200 deck pilgrims.

1902 Building for China Mutual S.N.Co, Liverpool when taken over by Holt's.
1918 June 13: Attacked by submarine gunfire in the Atlantic. *Keemun* drove off the U-boat with accurate gunnery.
1933 Broken up in Japan.

107 NINGCHOW

Details as *Keemun* (106) except:
T: 8,813 g, 5,716 n.
B D & W Henderson Glasgow.

1902 Built for China Mutual S.N.Co, and taken over by Alfred Holt.
1932 Nov 4: Arrived at Spezia, Italy, for scrapping.

108 OANFA (II)

Details as *Keemun* (106) except:
T: 7,602 g, 4,867 n.
B 1903 D & W Henderson, Glasgow.

1903 Jan: Built for China Mutual S.N.Co, Liverpool now a Holt subsidiary. With the arrival of this ship *Oanfa* (I) was renamed *Rhipeus* (108).
1931 Sold to Japan for scrap.
1932 Broken up.

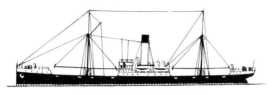

OANFA (I)/RHIPEUS (I)

109 OANFA (I)/RHIPEUS

B 1888 Aitken & Mansel, Glasgow. **T**: 3,061 g, 1,950 n.
D 325.5 ft (99.19 m) × 47.2 ft (14.38 m) × 22.5 ft (6.84 m).
E Sgl scr, tpl exp, 3 cyls. 293 NHP. 10 kts. 2 sgl ended boilers 180 lb. By J & J Thomson, Glasgow.
H Steel. 1 dk. F: 48 ft (14.63 m). B: 98 ft (29.87 m). P: 23 ft (7.01 m).

1888 Built for the China Shippers Company as *Oanfa*.
1893 Became one of the China Mutual S.N.Co's fleet.
1900 Acquired by N.S.M. 'Oceaan' and renamed *Rhipeus* under the Dutch flag. This was two years before the fleet as a whole came under the Blue Funnel flag.
1910 Sold to Italy; renamed *Ginolia*, N. G. Pittaluga, Genoa.
1911 May: Broken up at Genoa.
Note: Other China Mutual vessels owned by them prior to the takeover are listed at the end of this fleet list.

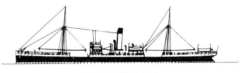

MEMNON (II)

110 MEMNON (II)

B 1888 Hawthorn Leslie, Newcastle. **T**: 2,458 g, 1,560 n.
D 320 ft (97.54 m) × 40.3 ft (12.27 m) × 22.6 ft (6.86 m).
E Sgl scr Tpl exp 3 cyls, 361 NHP. Stm P 170; 10 kts. By Blair & Co, Stockton-on-Tees.
H Steel, 2 dks. F: 89 ft (27.13 n). B: 88 ft (26.82 m). P: 83 ft (25.3 m).

1888 Built as the *Gulf of Guinea*, Gulf Line (D. MacDougall manager), Greenock. Her sister ship was the *Gulf of Martaban*. This firm was later named the Greenock Steam Ship Company.
1899 Dec: Acquired by Holt's; renamed *Memnon*.
1900 To N.S.M. 'Oceaan', same name. Dutch flag.
1905 Renamed *Togo Maru No 1*, K. Watanabe, Hakodate. Name later reduced to *Togo Maru*.
1907 Sold.
1923 July 20: Wrecked off Mokpo, Korea.

111 CHARON (I)

B 1903 Caledon S.B.Co, Dundee. **T:** 2,682 g, 1,661 n.
D 306.1 ft (93.29 m) × 45.2 ft (13.77 m) × 19.6 ft (5.94 m).
E Sgl scr, Tpl exp, 3 cyls, 233 NHP, 12 kts. By builder.
H Steel, 2 dks. F: 35 ft (10.67 m). B: 124 ft (37.79 m). P: 47 ft (14.33 m).
P 60 1st.

1903 Built for the Singapore—Batavia—Freemantle service jointly with the West Australian Steam Nav. Co. *Charon* flew the house flags of both concerns.
1925 Sold to Chinese owners; renamed *Yuan Lee*, Yuang Heng S.S.Co.
1935 Renamed *King Lee*, same owner. Became *Wing Fook*, owned by Kwang Tung Product Sales Bureau, Canton.
1942 No trace.

112 GORGON (I)

B 1908 Scotts S.B. & E Co, Greenock. **T:** 2,885 g, 1,734 n.
D 300 ft (91.44 m) × 42 ft (12.8 m) × 26.6 ft (8.08 m).
E Sgl scr, Tpl exp; 189 NHP, 12 kts. By builder.
H Steel, 2 dks; F: 36 ft (10.97 m); B: 104 ft (31.7 m); P: 40 ft (12.19 m).
P 60 1st.

1908 Built for the same joint service as *Charon* (111). Owned by Ocean S.S.Co.
1928 Sold to Cheong Hing S.S.Co, Hong Kong; renamed *Lyeemoon*.
1941 In Japanese hands, became a war loss.

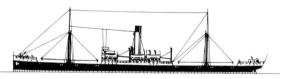

PRIAM (III), LAERTES (II) and TELEMON (II)

113 PRIAM (III)

B 1904 R & W Hawthorn Leslie & Co, Newcastle. **T:** 4,543 g, 2,905 n.
D 382.7 ft (116.64 m) × 47.2 ft (14.38 m) × 28.2 ft (8.58 m).
E Sgl scr, Tpl exp, 3 cyls; 350 NHP, 10 kts. By N.E. Marine Eng. Co, Newcastle.
H Steel, 2 dks; F: 42 ft (12.8 m); B: 117 ft (35.66 m); P: 39 ft (11.89 m).

1904 Delivered to the Ocean S.S.Co. From this time onwards Holt ships were owned by either the Ocean or China Mutual concerns. There were a few exceptions.
1931 Broken up in Japan.

114 LAERTES (II)

Details as *Priam* (113) except:
T: 4,541 g, 2,904 n.

1904 Entered Ocean S.S.Co. service.
1915 Feb 10: Escaped an attack by U-boat torpedo and gunfire attack off the Dutch coast.
1917 Aug 1st: Torpedoed and lost of Prawle Point. 14 lost.

115 TELAMON (II)

Details as *Priam* (II) except:
B Workman Clark, Belfast. **T:** 4,509 g, 2,843 n.
D 383.3 ft (116.8 m) × 47.2 ft (14.38 m).
1904 Entered service with Ocean S.S.Co.
1933 Sold to Douglas & Ramsey and then broken up by Smith & Houston, Port Glasgow.

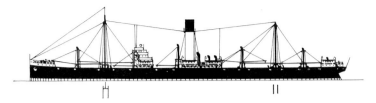

BELLEROPHON (II), TEUCER (III), ANTILOCHUS (I) CYCLOPS (II), TITAN (II) and PROTESILAUS

116 BELLEROPHON (II)

B 1906 Workman Clark, Belfast. **T:** 8,954 g, 5,744 n.
D 485.3 ft (147.88 m) × 58.3 ft (17.78 m) × 31 ft (9.45 m).
E Tw scr Tpl exp, 2 × 3 cyls, 585 NHP, Stm P: 200 lb by 2 dbl ended Scotch boilers, 14 kts.
Consumed 90 tons of coal per day. By builder.
H Steel, 3 dks; F: 35 ft (10.67 m); 7 holds, 9 hatches; 18 × 2 ton derricks, 8 × 10 ton
derricks; Cargo 616,000 cu ft (17,433 cu m) g; Fuel 1,400 tons coal.
P 12.
1906 The first of the renowned 'goal post' masted ships and Holt's largest vessel to date.
Owned by the Ocean S.S.Co. she took up service on the China Mutual route: Glasgow—
Liverpool—Singapore—China—Japan—Vancouver—Seattle route which had been acquired
by the 1902 purchase of China Mutual. *Bellerophon's* hull lines were exceptionally sea
kindly although her decks were regarded as being cluttered. She, alone of the sisters had steel
decks. The remainder were wood cladded.
1914 Aug: Taken over as a British Expeditionary Force troop ship and horse carrier out of
Liverpool for France.
1927 Feb: Loaded troops, horses and supplies at Birkenhead for Hong Kong and Shanghai
during the 'China Affair'. She carried 750 horses and their troopers. The *Bellerophon* made
full speed all the way stopping only to refuel for 12 hours at Port Said. The two other ships
with her were P&O's *Karmala* and Aberdeen line's *Herminius*.
1948 Apr 18: Arrived at Barrow-in-Furness for scrapping at the BISCO (British Iron &
Steel Corporation) yard of Thos. W. Ward.

117 TEUCER (III)

Details as *Bellerophon* (116) except:
B 1906 Hawthorn Leslie & Co, Newcastle. **T:** 9,017 g, 5,805 n.
E By N.E. Marine, Newcastle.

1906 Entered service with the Ocean S.S.Co. This vessel actually went into commission just
ahead of *Bellerophon* and was always the fastest of the four. Her voyage times indicated an
average speed of 13.01 kts.
1915 Dec: Outpaced a surfaced U-boat in the Mediterranean.
1948 Jan 10: Arrived at Troon for scrapping by W. H. Arnott Young & Co.

118 ANTILOCHUS (I)

Details as *Bellerophon* (II) except:
B 1906 Hawthorn Leslie & Co, Newcastle. **T:** 9,011 g, 5,796 n.
E By builder.

1906 Delivered to the Ocean S.S.Co.
1915 Sept 10: Fought off, by gunfire, a U-boat in the Mediterranean.
1942 May 29: Rescued the survivors of *Mentor* (139) off Florida.
1948 Sold to BISCO and allocated to Thos. W. Ward for breaking up.
Apr 11: Arrived for scrapping at Briton Ferry.

119 **CYCLOPS** (II)

Details as *Bellerophon* (116) except:
B D. & W. Henderson & Co, Glasgow. **T**: 8,998 g, 5,748 n.
D 485 ft (147.83 m).
E By builder.

1906 Entered service for the Ocean S.S.Co.
1917 Feb 11: Chased by a submarine off southern Ireland.
Apr 11: Missed by a torpedo west of the Scillies.
1942 Jan 11: Torpedoed off the coast of New England by U-123. The ship was 200 miles off Cape Sable. 46 passengers and 41 crew lost. For many years *Cyclops* was commanded by Capt. W. Cosker who was known as 'God Bless You Cosker' because of his invariable habit of ending every radio message with those words.

120 **TITAN** (II)

Sister of *Bellerophon* (116) except:
B 1906 D. & W. Henderson & Co, Glasgow. **T**: 8,954 g, 5,720 n.
E By builder.

1906 Delivered to the Ocean S.S.Co.
1940 Sept 3/4: Torpedoed at midnight by U-47 north west of Rockall en-route London—Sydney in ballast. Six lost.

121 **PROTESILAUS** (I)

Sister of *Bellerophon* (116) except:
B 1910 Hawthorn Leslie & Co, Newcastle. **T**: 9,547 g, 6,116 n.
D 484.9 ft (147.8 m) × 60.4 ft (18.41 m) × 39.5 ft (12.04 m).
E By N.E. Marine, Newcastle.
1910 Completed.
1940 Jan 21: Mined in the British Channel off Swansea. Towed into port but found to be beyond economical repair.
1942 Broken up by Thos. W. Ward at Briton Ferry. The goal post masts in this vessel were Rugby post 'H' style.

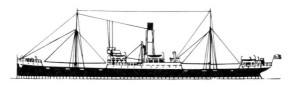

MYRMIDON (II), ASTYANAX (I), MEMNON (III) POLYPHEMUS (II)

122 **MYRMIDON** (II)

B 1905 Armstrong Whitworth & Co, Newcastle. **T**: 4,965 g, 3,063 n.
D 391.5 ft (119.33 m) × 49.2 ft (14.99 m) × 28.8 ft (8.76 m).
E Tpl exp, 3 cyls, 339 NHP, 10 kts. By N.E. Marine Eng. Co, Newcastle.
H Steel, 2 dks; F: 43 ft (13.11 m); B: 110 ft (33.53 m); P: 41 ft (12.5 m).

1905 Completed for China Mutual S.N.Co.
1917 Sept 7: Torpedoed in the Mediterranean, beached in sinking condition and then salvaged.
1930 Feb: Sold to Italy. Renamed *Rubicone*, Marittima Ravenate S.A., Ravenna. No house or lifeboat on the poop and lifeboats abreast funnel removed.
1959 Broken up at Split.

123 ASTYANAX (I)

Details as *Myrmidon* (122) except:
B Scotts S.B.& E Co, Greenock. **T**: 4,872 g, 3,021 n.
D 392.3 ft (119.56 m).
E By builder.

1906 Delivered.
1916 Dec 9: Chased by a submarine off southern Ireland. Escaped.
1917 May 9: Again escaped a submarine; this time off south west Ireland.
1930 Sold as a hulk at Singapore; renamed *Oscar II*.

124 MEMNON (III)

Sister of *Myrmidon* (122) except:
B Scotts S.B.& E Co, Glasgow. **T**: 4,870 g, 3,019 n.
D 392.1 ft (119.51 m).
E By builder.

1906 Completed for China Mutual S.N.Co.
1930 June: Broken up at Kobe.

125 POLYPHEMUS (II)

Sister of *Myrmidon* (122) except:
B 1906. **T**: 4,807 g, 3,019 n.
D 392 ft (119.48 m).

1906 Completed for China Mutual S.N.Co.
1917 July 20: Missed by torpedo off the south west of Scotland. An attack the following day from the shadowing U-boat also missed as *Polyphemus* was able to comb the torpedo and used her speed to escape before the follower could surface and use its gun.
1923 Fitted to burn oil.
1930 May: Broken up at Kobe.

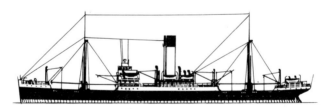

PERSEUS (I), THESEUS (I), NELEUS (I), ATREUS (I), RHESUS (I)
DEMODOCUS (I), LAOMEDON (I), EUMAEUS (I), PHEMIUS (I), LYCAON (I),
HELENUS (I), AGAPENOR (I), TROILUS (I), MENTOR (I), PYRRHUS (II),
TEIRESIAS (I), TROILUS (II), DIOMED (III) and ELPENOR (I)

126 PERSEUS (I)

B 1908 Workman Clark, Belfast. **T**: 6,728 g, 4,299 n, 8,600 dwt.
D 443 ft (135.03 m) × 52.9 ft (16.13 m) × 32 ft (9.75 m).
E Sgl scr, Tpl exp, 3 cyls. 4,600 IHP, 532 NHP; 11 kts. By builder.
H 2 dks; **F**: 54 ft (14.64 m); **B**: 162 ft (49.38 m); **P**: 50 ft (15.24 m); 6 holds.
P 12. Carried 'tween deck pilgrims Singapore—Jeddah seasonally.

1908 Built for the Ocean S.S.Co.
1915 Mar 29: Escaped U-boat gunfire attack 40 miles west of the Scillies.
1917 Feb 21: Sunk by a mine laid by the German raider *Wolf* off Colombo, Ceylon.

127 THESEUS (I)

Details as *Perseus* (126) except:
T: 6,723 g, 4,297 n.

1908 Delivered to the Ocean S.S.Co.
1947 Sold to BISCO and allocated to Thos W. Ward for breaking up;
Sept 16: Went aground in the River Ribble en-route to the scrap yard.
Nov 10: Refloated and towed into Preston for dismantling.

128 NELEUS (I)

Details as *Perseus* (126) except:
T: 6,685 g, 4,260 n.

1911 Completed for the China Mutual S.N.Co.
1948 Oct: Sold to BISCO for scrap. Allocated to Thos W. Ward.
Nov 1: Arrived at Preston for breaking up.

129 ATREUS (I)

Sister to *Perseus* (126) except:
B 1911 Scotts S.B & E. Co, Greenock. T: 6,699 g, 4,291 n.
D 443.5 ft (135.15 m).

1911 Entered China Mutual S.N.Co's service.
1949 Oct 3: Sold to BISCO and broken up at Rosyth.

130 RHESUS (I)

Details as *Perseus* (126) except:
B 1911 Scott's S.B & E. Co., Greenock. T: 6,719 g, 4,280 n.
D 443.5 ft (135.18 m) × 52.8 ft (16.09 m).
E By builder.
H F: 52 ft (15.85 m).

1911 Delivered to China Mutual S.N.Co.
1917 July 14: Missed by torpedo attack off south west Ireland.
1950 July 8: Sold for breaking up.

131 DEMODOCUS (I)

Sister to *Perseus* (126) except:
B 1912 Workman Clark, Belfast. T: 6,689 g, 4,269 n.

1912 June: Completed for China Mutual S.N.Co. As built the ship had a house and lifeboats at the bridge deck after derrick pair.
1917 Taken over by the Liner Requisition Scheme.
1918 March 23: Torpedoed in the Mediterranean. 5 killed. Towed to port.
1932 Transferred to the Australian service.
1949 Jan: Towed *Lycaon* (135), which had lost her propeller, 850 miles to Cape Town. This provided a legal nicety. *Demodocus* had lost 20 days voyage time and had consumed an extra 1,154 tons of coal. She therefore claimed against *Lycaon* for the loss of profit (£128 per day) plus general salvage. The Court of Admiralty awarded £12,500 to the owners, £350 to the Captain and £2,400 for division among the crew.
1951 Sold for £51,000 to Ditta Luigi Pittaluga Vapori and renamed *Ircania*.
1956 Acquired by P. Tomei, Genoa; became *Miriam*.
1958 Oct 10: Arrived at Trieste for breaking up.

132 LAOMEDON (I)

Sister of *Perseus* (126) except:
B 1912. **T**: 6,693 g, 4,268 n.

1912 Delivered to China Mutual S.N.Co.
1916 Apr 2: Used stern gun to fight off an U-boat attack in the Mediterranean.
1949 Dec 22: Sold to BISCO and broken up at Faslane by Shipbreaking Industries Ltd.

133 EUMAEUS (I)

Details as *Perseus* (126) except:
B 1913. **T**: 6,696 g, 4,266 n.

1913 Delivered to Ocean S.S.Co.
1917 Feb 6: Stood by the mined *Tyndareus* (163) off Cape Town.
1918 Feb 26: Torpedoed 24 miles N.N.E. off Ile de Vierge.

134 PHEMIUS (I)

Details as *Perseus* (126) except:
B 1913. **T**: 6,699 g, 4,268 n.

1913 Completed for the Ocean S.S.Co.
1917 June 4: Torpedoed of Eagle Island, Ireland.
This completed the first 9 of this class of ship. A second series, slightly longer and larger, then followed some of which were straight replacements for war losses.

135 LYCAON (I)

B 1913 Hawthorn Leslie & Co, Newcastle. **T**: 7,552 g, 4,814 n.
D 455.3 ft (138.78 m) × 56.3 ft (17.16 m) × 32.5 ft (9.91 m).
E Sgl scr, Tpl exp, 3 cyls. 11 kts. By N.E. Marine Eng. Co, Newcastle.
H Steel 2 dks; F: 60 ft (18.29 m); B: 162 ft (49.38 m); P: 53 ft (16.15 m).

1913 Built for China Mutual S.N.Co.
1949 Jan: Lost propeller in the Indian Ocean; Towed to Cape Town by *Demodocus* (131).
1951 Transferred to the Glen Line. Renamed *Gleniffer*.
1952 July 7: Broken up at Faslane.

136 HELENUS (I)

Sister of *Lycaon* (135) except:
B 1913 Scott's S.B.& E. Co, Greenock. **T**: 7,555 g, 4,810 n.
E By builder.

1913 Completed for the Ocean S.S.Co.
1917 Dec 1: Torpedoed in the English Channel. Towed into port.
1918 June 30: Missed by a torpedo in the North Sea.
1918 Aug 22: Attacked by gunfire from a pursuing U-boat but *Helenus* fired back and succeeded in out pacing the enemy.
1940 See the *Automedon* 1940 Nov 11 entry.
1942 Mar 3: Torpedoed off Freetown, Sierra Leone, by U-68. 5 lost.

HELENUS

By courtesy of Mr Peter B. Cowling, who was an apprentice on Voyage 45, the steaming log is given in full. It is a useful insight into a typical Blue Funnel itinerary.

Port		Date	Time Taken	Days Out	Port		Date	Time Taken	Days Out
Liverpool	L	Apr 18	—	1	Tjilitjap	A	. . 20	2 days	125
Belfast	A	. . 19	10 hrs	2		L	. . 21		126
	L	. . 19		2	Probolinggo	A	Aug 24	3 days	129
New York	A	. . 30	10 days	14		L	. . 24		129
	L	May 14		29	Sourabaya	A	. . 25	19 hrs	130
Philadelphia	A	. . 15	19 hrs	30		L	. . 26		131
	L	. . 20		35	Samarang	A	. . 27	18 hrs	132
New York	A	. . 21	18 hrs	36		L	. . 27		132
	L	. . 28		43	Tegal	A	. . 27	6 hrs	132
Norfolk	A	. . 29	19 hrs	44		L	. . 27		132
	L	. . 30		45	Pamanukan	A	. . 28	10 hrs	133
Savannah	A	Jun 1	2 days	47		L	. . 28		133
	L	. . 1		47	Telok Betang	A	. . 29	8 hrs	134
Colon	A	. . 7	6 days	53		L	. . 30		135
	L	. . 7		53	Batavia	A	. . 30	10 hrs	135
Balboa	A	. . 77	8 hrs			L	Sep 2		138
		Transit of the Panama Canal			Padang	A	. . 4	2 days	140
						L	. . 5		141
San Pedro	A	Jun 17	10 days	63	Colombo	A	. . 11	6 days	147
	L	. . 19		65		L	. . 11		147
Manila	A	Jul 11	22 days	87	Aden	A	. . 19	8 days	155
		No ship sighted trans-Pacific				L	. . 19		155
	L	Jul 11		87	Port Sudan	A	. . 22	3 days	158
Hong Kong	A	. . 13	2 days	89		L	. .		158
	L	. . 13		89	Suez	A	. . 25	3 days	161
Shanghai	A	. . 16	3 days	92		L	. . 25		161
	L	. . 20		96			Transit Suez Canal		
Moji	A	. . 22	2 days	98	Port Said	A	. . 26	15 hrs	162
	L	. . 27		101		L	. . 26		162
Dairen	A	. . 30	3 days	104	Marseilles	A	Oct 1	6 days	168
	L	Aug 5		110		L	. . 2		169
Tsingtao	A	. . 6	1 day	111	London	A	. . 10	8 days	177
	L	. . 7		112		L	. . 10		177
Macassar	A	. . 17	10 days	122	Amsterdam	A	. . 11	16 hrs	178
	L	. . 18		123		L	. . 15		182
					Liverpool	A	. . 18	3 days	185

During the voyage outlined above 25 Blue Funnel ships were encountered either in port or passed at sea.

137 AGAPENOR (I)

Sister of *Lycaon* (135) except:
B 1914 Scott's S.B.& E. Co, Greenock. **T**: 7,587 g, 4,798 n.
E By builder.

1942 Oct 11: Torpedoed off Freetown, Sierra Leone, by U-87. Her Captain, P. W. Savery, had survived the sinking of *Helenus* (135). He was again picked up but 7 crewmen were killed.

138 TROILUS (I)

Sister of *Lycaon* (135) except:
B 1913. **T**: 7,562 g.

1913 Built for the Ocean S.S.Co.
1914 Oct 19: Sunk by the German cruiser *Emden* east of Minikoi Island, Indian Ocean.

139 MENTOR (I)

Sister of *Lycaon* (135) except:
B 1914 Scotts S.B.& E. Co, Greenock. **T**: 7,585 g, 4,798 n.
E By builder.
H B: 165 ft (50.29 m).

1914 Completed for the Ocean S.S.Co.
1942 May 28: Torpedoed off Key West Florida by U-106. *Mentor*, Captain A. Pope, was carrying war materials from New Orleans to Bombay, via Cape Town when the torpedo struck her on the port side of the engine room which was wrecked and flooded. Four engineers and three Chinese crew were killed. A second torpedo almost cut the ship in half. The survivors were picked up by *Antilochus* (118).

140 PYRRHUS (II)

Sister of *Lycaon* (135) except:
B 1914 Workman Clark, Belfast. **T**: 7,615 g, 4,823 n.
D 455.5 ft (138.84 m) × 56.5 ft (17.22 m).
E By builder.
H F: 59 ft (18.20 m).

1914 Built for Ocean S.S.Co.
1940 Feb 17: Torpedoed off Cape Finisterre by U-37 enroute Clyde—Manila. *Pyrrhus* was about 100 miles N.W. of Corunna when hit. The ship broke in two; the fore part floated for two days but the after section sank immediately with the loss of 8 of her crew of 85.

141 TEIRESIAS (I)

Sister of *Lycaon* (135) except:
B 1914 Hawthorn Leslie, Newcastle. **T**: 7,606 g, 4,822 n.
E By North East Marine.

1914 Built for Ocean S.S.Co.
1915 June 30: Damaged by mine in the Small Bitter Lake, Suez Canal.
1940 June 17: Bombed and sunk of St. Nazaire enroute Avonmouth—Quiberon Bay. The first bomb flooded the engine room and stokehold. It also produced a crack across the main deck and down the port side to the waterline. Captain J. R. Davies ordered the crew to stand by in the boats. Next day the list had worsened to 25° and the ship was groaning while rivets were snapping audibly. Another air attack hit *Teiresius* which capsized and sank in one single movement.

142 **TROILUS** (II)

Sister of *Lycaon* (135) except:
B 1917 Caledon S.B. & E. Co., Dundee. **T:** 7,625 g, 4,832 n.
D 455.5 ft (138.68 m).
E By builder.
H F: 61 ft (18.59 m); B: 164 ft (49.99 m); P: 54 ft (16.46 m).

1917 Built for the Ocean S.S.Co.
1917 Apr 11: Chased by a submarine in the North Sea.
1917 May 2 Torpedoed 140 miles off Malin Head.

143 **DIOMED** (III)

Sister of *Lycaon* except:
B 1917 Scotts S.B. & E. Co, Greenock. **T:** 7,523 g, 4,747 n.
D 455 ft (138.68 m).
E Sgl scr, 2 steam turbines sgl reduction geared. By builder.
H B: 165 ft (50.29 m).

1917 Completed for Ocean S.S.Co.
1918 Aug 21: Shelled and sunk off Nantucket lightship by U-140.

144 **ELPENOR**

Sister of *Lycaon* (135) except:
B 1917 Hawthorn Leslie, Newcastle. **T:** 7,601 g, 4,824 n.
E By North Eastern Marine Engineering Co.

1916 Sept: Launched.
1917 Jan: Completed for China Mutual S.N.Co. This ship had a deck house and boats decked at the after end of the bridge deck out of which was stepped the samson posts.
Feb: Maiden voyage under the Liner Requisition Scheme. Tyne—Mediterranean—Baltimore.
1918 Nov: Used as a troop ship between Liverpool and Dublin.
1922 Collided with the Japanese *Inaba Maru*, Nippon Yusen Kaisha, at Kobe.
1935 Apr: Transferred to the Glen Line; renamed *Glenfinlas.*
1941 Damaged by bombs and machine gun fire in the North Sea.
1942 Nov: During the North African landing, Operation Torch, was damaged by bombs in Bougie harbour.
1947 Apr: Returned to Ocean S.S.Co. Reverted to *Elpenor.*
1950 Renamed *Glenfinlas* when again transferred to Glen.
1952 June 10: Arrived at Blyth for breaking up by Hughes Bolckow.

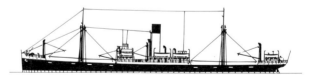

AUTOLYCUS (I) and LAERTES (III)

145 **AUTOLYCUS** (I)

B 1917 Taikoo Dockyard & Engineering Co, Hong Kong. **T:** 5,806 g, 3,664 n.
D 423.8 ft (129.17 m) × 52.3 ft (15.94 m) × 29.9 ft (9.11 m).
E Sgl scr, tpl exp, 3 cyls; 413 NHP, 10 kts. By builder.
H S. 2 dks. F: 42 ft (12.80 m); B: 117 ft (35.66 m); P: 52 ft (15.85 m).
1917 Built for Ocean S.S.Co.
1918 Apr 12: Torpedoed off Cape Palos.

146 **LAERTES** (III)

Sister of Autolycus (145) except:
B 1919. **T**: 5,868 g, 3,647 n.

1919 Built for Ocean S.S.Co.
1922 Transferred to the Dutch flag. N.S.M. 'Oceaan'; same name.
1942 May 3: Torpedoed by U-564 off Cape Canaveral, Florida, enroute New York—Cape Town—Bombay. 18 lives lost.

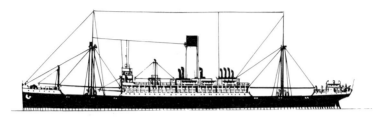

AENEAS (I), ASCANIUS (II) and ANCHISES (III)

147 **AENEAS** (I)

B 1910 Workman Clark, Belfast. **T**: 10,049 g, 6,300 n, 11,600 dwt.
D 509 ft (155.14 m) oa. 493 ft (150.27 m) × 60 ft (18.29 m) × 29 ft (8.84 m).
E Tw scr 2 × quad exp. 2 × x4 cyls 5,700 IHP. 14 kts. By builder.
H S: 3 dks; F: 38 ft (11.58 m); B: 201 ft (61.26 m); P: 46 ft (14.02 m).
Cargo: 374,000 cu ft (10,590.5 cu m) bale plus 74,500 cu ft (2,109.6 cu m) refrigerated. Fuel 1,896 tons coal. 6 holds, 7 hatches. 1 × 45 ton derrick.
P 288 1st.
1910 Aug 23: Launched, yard no. 294. Completed Nov 1.
Nov 18: Maiden voyage Glasgow—Liverpool—Fishguard—Las Palmas—Cape Town—Adelaide—Melbourne—Sydney. Owned by the Ocean S.S.Co. The service was 6 -weekly and took 39 days.
1914 Operated by the Australian Government as a troop ship.
1918 May: Went ashore at Torcor Head, Rathlin Island.
1920 May 29: Returned to the Australian service. Pass 180 1st.
1924 The service became a joint Blue Funnel-White Star venture.
1925 Transferred to the Far East route. Her last Australian sailing was January 10. Joined the Sarpedon (186) class to make a total of 5 ships on the service.
1940 July 2: Enroute London—Glasgow to finish unloading sunk by air attack off Start Point, Plymouth. *Aeneas* was second ship in a line ahead convoy and being the largest vessel she was singled out for attack by machine gun and bomb. The bombs severed the main steam supply and blew out her starboard side. Fires also broke out. Captain D. L. C. Evans ordered her boats away as the ship heeled over and sank.

148 **ASCANIUS** (II)

Details as *Aeneas* (147) except:
T: 10,048 g, 6,777 n.

1910 Oct 29: Launched yard No. 295.
Dec 21: Completed.
Dec 30: Maiden voyage Glasgow—Liverpool—Brisbane.
1914 Served with the Australian Expeditionary Force as a troopship.
1917 Taken over by the Liner Requisition Scheme. Continued her trooping duties but sailing as required.

1920 Aug 21: Resumed Australian services.

1922 Refitted at Palmers Yard, Jarrow.

1926 Pass 180 Ist.

1940 Taken over for use as a troopship.

1944 July 30: Torpedoed but limped safely into Liverpool. Repairs carried out by Cammell Laird.

1945 Used to carry Jewish emigrants Marseilles to Haifa.

1949 Sold to Cia. de Nav. 'Florencia', Genoa, renamed *San Giovannino*. Purchased for a projected Australian service from Italy to carry emigrants but laid up before commencement of the project.

1952 Mar: Broken up at La Spezia. During her lay up the funnel was painted black.

149 ANCHISES (III)

Details as *Aeneas* (147) except:
B 1911. **T:** 10,046 g, 6,380 n.
H F: 63 ft (19.2 m); B: 199 ft (60.66 m); P: 47 ft (14.33 m).

1911 Jan 11: Launched yard No. 296.

Mar 10: Completed for Ocean S.S.Co's Australian service.

1914 Became a troopship.

1918 Sept 23: Attacked in the Atlantic by gunfire from a chasing submarine. *Anchises* drove off the attacker with accurate gunfire.

1922 Sept: Resumed service Glasgow—Liverpool—Brisbane.

1926 Pass: 180 Ist.

1941 Feb 27: Damaged by air attack off the north east coast of Ireland. Power was lost and the ship awaited the arrival of a salvage tug.

Feb 28: The air attack was resumed and *Anchises* finally sank with the loss of 12 lives. She sank only 70 miles short of the Mersey Estuary.

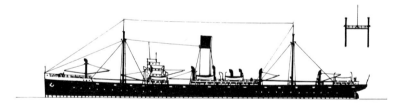

TALTHYBIUS (I) and IXION (II)

150 TALTHYBIUS (II)

B 1912 Scotts S.B. & E. Co, Greenock. **T:** 10,224 g, 6,514 n.
D 506 ft (154.22 m) × 60.3 ft (18.38 m) × 39.5 ft (12.04 m).
E Tw scr tpl exp; 2 × 3 cyls, 586 NHP; 11 kts. By builder.
H S. 3 dks; F: 75 ft (22.86 m).
P 12 1st, 600 steerage.

1911 Nov 7: Launched.

1912 The lead ship in a class of 4; designed for the carriage of large bulk cargoes capable of being unloaded in the roadsteads of ports that were too shallow to take deeper draughts. Owned by Ocean S.S.Co. Liverpool—Far East route.

1941 May 4 and May 8: Hit by bombs at her berth in Liverpool Docks.

1942 Jan 25: Arrived at Singapore from Bombay.

Feb 3: Bombed by the Japanese and set on fire. Moved into the Empire Dock.

Feb 7: The fire was under control but the ship was unseaworthy.
Feb 12: Sunk and abandoned. Salvaged by the invading Japanese and renamed *Taruyasu Maru*.
1945 June 30: Mined off Sado Island, Maizuro Bay. Salvaged after the end of hostilities. Reparied at Hong Kong. Became *Empire Evenlode*, Ministry of War Transport.
1949 Sept 7: Broken up at Briton Ferry.

151 IXION (II)

Details as *Talthybius* (150) except:
T: 10,229 g, 6,527 n.

1912 Oct 29: Launched. Dec: Completed for the Far East service. Owned by China Mutual S.N.Co. Yard No. 442.
1941 May 7: On passage Glasgow—New York torpedoed in convoy 200 miles south west of Reykjavik by U-94. Sank next day. No casualties. *Ixion's* cargo was mainly dollar earning whisky.

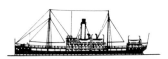

CIRCLE and MEDUSA (II)

152 CIRCE

B 1912 Taikoo Dockyard & Engineering Co, Hong Kong. **T**: 778 g, 314 n.
D 195.7 ft (59.65 m) × 31.6 ft (9.63 m) × 12.4 ft (3.78 m).
E Sgl scr. Tpl exp, 3 cyl, 95 RHP, 10 kts. By builder.
H S. 1 dk and Prom. dk; F: 26 ft (7.92 m); P: 19 ft (5.79 m).
P 24 1st 300 deck.
1912 Built for Ocean S.S.Co. for Singapore feeder services.
1925 Transferred to Straits S.S.Co; same name.
1939 Taken over by the British Admiralty to become H.M.S. *Circe*.
1942 Transferred to the Australian Navy and renamed H.M.A.S. *Medea*.
1946 Sold and broken up at Sydney.

153 MEDUSA

Sister of *Circe* (152) except:
B 1913. **T**: 793 g, 323 n.

1913 Built for Ocean S.S.Co. to serve in conjunction with her sister vessel.
1925 Sold to Straits S.S.Co, same name.
1939 Commissioned by the British Admiralty at H.M.S. *Medusa*.
1942 Transferred to the Australian Navy. Renamed H.M.A.S. *Mercedes*.
1945 Sold for scrapping at Sydney.
These two ships served the whole of their careers together and were known as the 'Heavenly twins'. Even when their naval service was over and it was not economically feasible to re-condition them they were laid up side by side tethered to each other.

NESTOR (III) and ULYSSES (IV)

154 **NESTOR** (III)

B 1913 Workman Clark & Co, Belfast. **T:** 14,501 g, 9,100 n, 16,300 dwt.
D 563.2 ft (171.66 m) × 68.4 ft (20.85 m) × 31.2 ft (9.51 m).
E Tw scr. Tpl exp, 2 × 3 cyls. 6,600 IHP. 13½ kts. 3 dbl and 2 sgl ended boilers, 8 21 in super-hearters. Stm P: 191 lb. Coal 140 tons per day. By builder.
H S 3. dks; F: 67 ft (20.42 m); B: 226 ft (68.88 m) P: 75 ft (22.86 m). Cargo 546,000 cu ft (50,723 cu m) bale and 147,000 cu ft (4,162 cu m) refrigerated.
P 350 1st (Some sources give 275 1st).
Masters: T. Bartlett, R. D. (Daddy) Owen, G. K. Houghton, W. Christie, F. Adcock, J. J. Power, J. H. Blyth and E. W. Powell.

1912 Dec 7: Launched. Yard No. 318. Designed by Henry B. Wortley. Cost £248,250.
1913 May 19: Maiden voyage for Ocean S.S.Co. Liverpool—Brisbane with cargo loading at Glasgow. Calls were made at Cape Town, Adelaide, Melbourne and Sydney.
Sept 19: Arrived back at Liverpool after a voyage time of four months.
1915 Sept: Became a troopship until 1918.
1920 Apr 22: Resumed commercial service Glasgow—Liverpool—Brisbane.
1921 Steam superheaters fitted; engine economy improved. Consumption 110 tons per day.
1926 Pass: 250 1st. Derrick vents painted white.
1935 Passenger accommodation reduced to 175 1st.
1936 With her final rocket managed to get a tow line aboard the Australian United's *Mungana* which was drifting onto the rocks off Cape Jaffa. *Nestor* then towed the disabled ship the 170 miles to Adelaide.
1940 Pass: 250 One class. Requisitioned for government service but retained on the same route. Took children evacuees on the first sailings.
1949 Dec 23: Left on her final sailing to Australia. By comparison with her maiden voyage this last sailing took 5 months and 20 days.
1950 Aug 8: Arrived at Faslane for breaking up by Metal Industries Ltd. having completed 68 round voyages and steaming 2,111,607 miles.
Note position of the funnel siren.

155 **ULYSSES** (IV)

Sister of *Nestor* (154) except:
T: 14,499 g, 9,101 n.
H F: 69 ft (21.03 m); B: 231 ft (70.41 m); P: 74 ft (22.55 m).

1913 July 5 : Launched. Oct 22: Completed for China Mutual S.N.Co. Placed on the Glasgow—Liverpool—Brisbane service.
1915 Became a troopship. Served on the Australia—Suez route with Australian troops.
1917 On the North Atlantic berth carrying American servicemen.
1920 Sept: Resumed commercial service Glasgow—Liverpool—Capetown—Australian ports to Brisbane.
1926 Passenger accommodation reduced to 250 1st.

1928 Her Captain was R. D. Owen, O.B.E. commodore of Blue Funnel who flew the swallow tailed house flag of commodore.
1936 Pass: 175 1st.
1942 Apr 11: Torpedoed 5 miles off Palm Beach, Florida, by U-160. *Ulysses* had been one of the last ships out of Hong Kong prior to the arrival of the Japanese. She sailed to Singapore and at once left for Australia where she loaded a cargo for Liverpool. After crossing the Pacific she traversed the Panama Canal and was heading homewards.
On April 8: She collided during darkness with an oil tanker. The bow damage extended below the water line and speed was reduced to 7 knts, *Ulysses*, Captain J. A. Russell, headed for Newport News, the nearest port. Radio messages warning of submarines were received and at 15.30 hours on April 11 a torpedo struck No. 6 hatch. All the passengers and crew, excepting essential services, including the gunners, abandoned ship. A second torpedo hit her abreast of the funnel and *Ulysses* went down so quickly that the men on board left by life raft. No lives were lost.

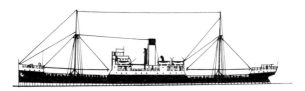

EURYDAMUS, EURYMEDON (I) and EURYMACHUS

156 EURYDAMUS

B 1901 Chas. Connell & Co, Glasgow. **T:** 5,197 g, 3,367 n.
D 410.1 ft (125 m) × 49.3 ft (15.02 m) × 29.6 ft (9.02 m).
E Sgl scr, Tpl exp, 3 cyls, 500 NHP. Stm P: 200 lb. 10 Kts. By D. Rowan Glasgow.
H S: 2 dks; F: 50 ft (15.24 m); B: 146 ft (44.5 m); P: 29 ft (8.84 m).

1901 Oct: Completed for Thos B. Royden & Co as *Indrasamha*.
1915 Acquired by Holts and renamed *Eurydamus*.
1924 Sold to Jugoslavensko Amerikanska Plovidba, Split and renamed *Jugoslavija*.
1934 Broken up at Genoa.

157 EURYMEDON (I)

Sister of *Eurydamus* (156) except:
B 1902. **T:** 5,194 g, 3,361 n.
H F: 52 ft (15.85 m); B: 147 ft (44.81 m); P: 31 ft (9.45 m).

1902 Built as *Indrawadi* for Thos. R Royden & Co, Liverpool for the 'Indra Line'.
1915 Acquired with the fleet of seven ships by Blue Funnel. Renamed *Eurymedon* and allocated to the Ocean S.S.Co.
1922 Sold to A/S Southern Queen, Thore Thoresen, Tonsberg, Norway. Became *Southern Queen*.
1928 Feb 24: Lost in pack ice east of South Orkney. The crew were able to abandon ship onto the ice but the vessel herself was holded and sank. She was taking onboard whale oil from the Thorensen catchers when trapped. 22,700 barrels of whale oil were lost.

Confusion sometimes arises because Royden's *Indrabarah* was purchased by the Admiralty and renamed *Cyclops*. She served as a submarine depot ship during the period 1914–1918.

158 **EURYMACHUS**

Sister of *Eurydamus* (156) except:
B 1906. **T:** 4,995 g, 3,214 n.
D 400.6 ft (122.10 m) × 52.3 ft (15.94 m) × 29.3 ft (8.93 m).
E By Dunsmuir & Jackson, Glasgow.
H F: 47 ft (14.33 m); B: 142 ft (43.28 m); P: 36 ft (10.97 m).

1906 Built as *Inverclyde* for Thos. B. Royden & Co, Liverpool.
1915 Acquired with the fleet. Renamed *Eurymachus*. Owned by Ocean S.S.Co.
1917 June 11: Chased by a U-boat in the Atlantic.
1926 Sold to Jugoslavensko Amerikanska Plovidba, Rijeka. Renamed *Nikola Mihanovic*.
1929 Broken up by Thos. Ward at Inverkeithing.

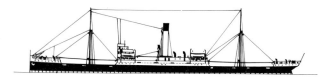

EURYBATES

159 **EURYBATES** (I)

B 1910 Chas. Connell & Co, Glasgow. **T:** 5,529 g, 3, 507 n.
D 430.2 ft (131.12 m) × 50.2 ft (15.3 m) × 30.7 ft (9.35 m).
E Sgl scr, Tpl exp. 3 cyls; 517 NHP. 10 kts. By D. Rowan, Glasgow.
H S: 2 dks; F: 51 ft (15.5 m); B: 146 ft (44.5 m); P: 39 ft (11.88 m).

1910 Built as *Indradeo* for Indra Line of Royden.
1915 Acquired with the remainder of the fleet and renamed *Eurybates*. Owned by Ocean S.S.Co.
1926 Dec: Sold for £30,000 to R & J Thomas, Holyhead. Renamed *Cambrian Peeress*.
1928 Transferred to William Thomas Shipping with R & J Thomas as managers.
1931 Sold to Ben Line (Wm. Thomson & Co.). Became *Bendoran*.
1944 June: Sunk at Arromanches as a blockship to form part of the Mulberry Harbour installation.
1947 Raised and towed to England. Broken up by Hughes Bolckow at Blyth.

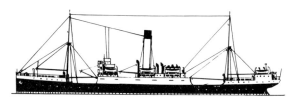

EURYPYLUS (I), EURYADES (I) and EURYLOCHUS

160 **EURYPYLUS** (I)

B 1912 Chas. Connell & Co, Glasgow. **T:** 5,691 g, 3,607 n.
D 430 ft (131.06 m) × 54 ft (16.45 m) × 30.5 ft (9.29 m).
E Sgl scr, tpl exp, 3 cyls, 687 NHP; Stm P: 200 lb. 10 kts. By Dunsmuir and Jackson, Glasgow.
H S: 2 dks; F: 80 ft (24.38 m); B: 148 ft (45.11 m); P: 80 ft (24.38 m).
1912 July: Completed as *Indrakuala* for Thos. B. Royden's Indra Line.
1915 Acquired with the Royden fleet and renamed *Eurypylus* by Ocean S.S.Co.

1938 Sold to Continental Transit Company became *Trade*.
1939 Aug: Purchased by the Board of Trade and renamed *Botavon*.
1942 May 2: Bombed and sunk north west of North Cape, Norway in convoy to Russia.

161 EURYADES (I)

Sister to *Euryplus* (160) except:
B 1913. **T**: 5,713 g, 3,620 n.
H B: 153 ft (46.63 m).

1912 Built as *Indra* for Royden's Indra Line.
1915 Acquired by Holts with the fleet and renamed *Euryades*. Owned by Ocean S.S.Co.
1918 Feb 4: Missed by torpedo in the Irish Channel.
1948 Oct 19: Arrived at Briton Ferry for demolition by Thos. W. Ward.

162 EURYLOCHUS

Sister of *Euryplus* (160) except:
B 1912 London & Glasgow S.B.Co. **T**: 5,723 g, 3,600 n.
D 430.5 ft (131.22 m) × 53.9 ft (16.43 m) × 30.3 ft (9.24 m).
E By builder.
H F: 85 ft (25.9 m); **P**: 79 ft (24.08 m).
Identification: Funnel 10 ft (3.35 m) shorter and no derricks at bridge front.

1912 Built as *Indraghira* for Thos B. Roydon & Co.
1915 Acquired with the remainder of the Indra Line and renamed *Eurylochus*.
1918 July 22: Persued by a surfaced submarine which opened fire. *Eurylochus* out distanced her pursuer in rough seas.
1941 Jan 29: Sunk off Cape Verde Islands by the German Commerce Raider *Kormoran* (Ship 41; ex-*Steiermark*, Hamburg Amerika Line). The raider had sunk *Afric Star* at 16.18 hrs, her third victim. At 19.55 hrs *Eurylochus* was sighted enroute Liverpool—Takoradi. *Kormoran* at once recognised her as a Blue Funneller. "Heave too and no wireless" was sent three times. *Eurylochus*, Captain A. M. Caird, crammed on all speed and commenced to broadcast. *Kormoran* sent up star shells to illuminate her prey and simultaneously opened fire. *Eurylochus* loosed off four rounds before her upper works were wrecked and the ship stopped. The enemy's searchlights showed the crew abandoning ship. When the Germans examined the cargo of their capitive it was found to contain 16 heavy bombers without engines. Captain Theodore Detmets ordered that *Eurylochus* be sunk. Because the ether was full of wireless signals, some quite close by, it was decided to torpedo her. As the missile was fired a lifeboat came into the beam of the searchlight — it was a few of the crew attempting to reboard. Detmets signalled 'Torpedo fired' but this was not heeded and when the torpedo struck *Eurylochus* the lifeboat and the crew in it disappeared. In the attack 38 were killed and 42 made prisoner. The Germans recorded that as *Eurylochus* settled her radio recommenced and sent her name. *Kormoran* opened fire with her AA guns and after hitting the bridge the radio ceased. Two cruisers *Norfolk* and *Devonshire* headed for the spot but the German ship escaped — although she succummbed, on Nov 19 1941, to the Australian cruiser *Sydney* which also sank.

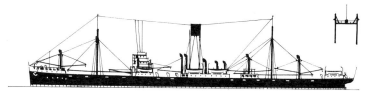

TYNDAREUS

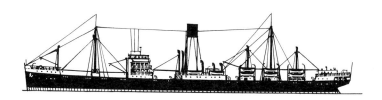

163 TYNDAREUS

B 1915 Scott's S.B. & E. Co, Greenock. **T:** 11,347 g, 7,172 n, 14,000 dwt.
D 507 ft (154.33 m) × 63.2 ft (19.26 m) × 41 ft (12.67 m). Dft: 32.9 ft (9.98 m).
E Tw scr, Tpl exp, 2 × 3 cyls, 622 NHP, 12 kts. By builder.
H S: 3 dks; F: 75 ft (22.86 m); Fuel: 1,600 tons coal at 12 tons per day; Cargo: 776,000 cu ft (21,974 cu m) g.

1915 Dec: Launched.
1916 Completed for the Ocean S.S.Co's Trans-Pacific service.
1917 Feb 6: At 1900 hrs mined off Cape Agulhas. The mines had been laid on January 16 by the raider *Wolf. Tyndareus* had on board the 25th Middlesex Rifle Regiment who took to the boats and rowed to the hospital ship *Oxfordshire* and Blue Funnel's *Eumaeus*. The damaged ship was then towed into Cape Town.
1927 Used, with *Bellerophon*, as a troop and horse transport during the 'China Affair'.
1940 War service as a troop ship and supply vessel.
1949 Converted to Pilgrim carrier at a cost of £126,650.
1950 Placed on the Indonesia—Mecca pilgrimage route with deck and dormitory accommodation for 2,500 pilgrims. Known as the Hadj service. (Drawing 163B) Laid up at Singapore between seasons.
1960 With the acquisition of the pilgrim passenger liner *Gunang Djati Tyndareus* was placed on the disposal list.
Sept 9: Arrived Hong Kong for demolition. 44 years old.

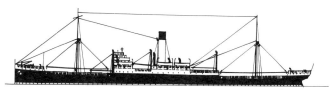

*KNIGHT OF THE GARTER, KNIGHT OF THE THISTLE
and KNIGHT TEMPLAR*

164 KNIGHT OF THE GARTER

B 1902 Chas. Connell & Co, Glasgow. **T:** 6,689 g, 4,277 n.
D 456 ft (138.99 m) × 55.2 ft (16.82 m) × 30.7 ft (9.36 m).
E Sgl scr, tpl exp, 552 NHP, Stm P: 200 lb, 11 kts. By D. Rowan, Glasgow.

H S. 2 dks; F: 15 ft (54 m); B: 164 ft (49.99 m); P: 38 ft (11.58 m).

1902 Dec: Completed for Greenshields, Cowie & Co, Liverpool.
1917 Acquired by China Mutual S.N.Co; as a war loss replacement.
1918 Feb 11: Missed by two torpedoes in the English Channel.
1923 June: Sold to Emmanuel A. Stavroudis and christened *Aspasia Stavroudi*. Registered at Chania.
1926 Became *Hoffplein* of N.V.S.M. 'Milligen', Rotterdam. Managed by G. A. Spliethoff.
1930 Jan 4: Wrecked on Skorpas Island en-route Narvik—Rotterdam with iron ore.

165 KNIGHT OF THE THISTLE

Sister to *Knight of the Garter* except:
B 1903. **T**: 6,675 g, 4,286 n.
D 455.8 ft (138.93 m).

1903 Built for Greenshields, Cowie & Co, Liverpool.
1917 Acquired with three other 'knights' by Ocean S.S.Co. as war loss replacements.
1917 Apr 26: Chased by a U-boat off south west Ireland.
1917 Dec 10: Foundered in the North Atlantic (42.19N, 56.50W) enroute New York—London.

166 KNIGHT TEMPLAR

B 1905 Chas. Connell & Co, Glasgow. **T**: 7,175 g, 4,602 n.
D 470 ft (143.26 m) × 58 ft (17.68 m) × 31.8 ft (9.69 m).
E Sgl scr, tpl exp, 3 cyls, 596 NHP, 11 kts. By D. Rowan, Glasgow.
H S. 2 dks; F: 51 ft (15.54 m); B: 169 ft (51.51 m); P: 38 ft (11.58 m).

1905 Built for Greenshields, Cowie & Co, Liverpool.
1917 Acquired by Ocean S.S.Co; same name.
1918 April 7: Torpedoed southwest of the Scilly Isles but reached Falmouth safely.
1925 Sold to Norway. Converted into a Whale oil carrier and floating refinery. Renamed *Orwell*. Owned by Tonsberg Hvalfangerei A/S, Tonsberg.
1954 Feb: Sold for scrapping at Hamburg.

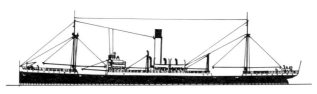

KNIGHT COMPANION

167 KNIGHT COMPANION

Sister to *Knight Templar* (166) except:
B 1913. **T**: 7,241 g, 4,625 n.
H F: 99 ft (30.17 m); B: 167 ft (50.9 m); P: 87 ft (26.52 m).
1913 Built for Greenshields, Cowie & Co, Liverpool.
1917 Acquired by Ocean S.S.Co; same name.
1917 June 11: Torpedoed in the Atlantic. Towed into Liverpool.
1933 Feb: Broken up in Italy.

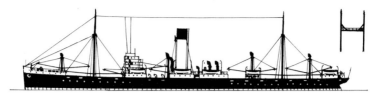

ACHILLES (III) and PHILOCTETES

168 ACHILLES (II)

B 1920 Scotts S.B.& E. Co, Greenock. **T:** 11,426 g, 7,199 n.
D 507.4 ft (154.65 m) × 63.2 ft (19.26 m) × 41.1 ft (12.53 m).
E Tw scr. 2 stm reduction geared turbines. 12 kts. By builder.
H S. 3 dks; F: 69 ft (21.03 m).
Cargo: 670,000 cu ft (18,972 cu m) bale plus 19,500 cu ft (5,380.2 cu m) refrigerated in 2 chambers.
P 4. Crew 70.

1920 Completed for Ocean S.S.Co. Cost £545,000.
Jan 8: Launched.
June 4: Placed on Far East–U.S.A. service.
1926 Dec: Taken over and used as transport for 1,000 horses and men during the China Affair'. *Achilles* steamed at full speed directly to Shanghai.
1940 Aug: Acquired by Admiralty. Converted into a destroyer depot ship. Because there was already the Battle of the River Plate *Achilles* the ship was renamed H.M.S. *Blenheim*. Armed with 4–4 in guns. Complement 674.
1948 Disposed of for breaking up at Barrow-in-Furness.

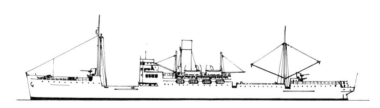

HMS PHILOCTETES

169 PHILOCTETES (I)

Sister to *Achilles* (168) except:
 T: 11,446 g, 7,187 n.
D 511.9 ft (156.03 m) × 63.2 ft (18.98 m) × 41.1 ft (12.53 m).
H F: 73 ft (22.2 m).

1922 May 25: Launched for the China Mutual S.N.Co.
Dec: Completed and placed with her sister on the Trans–Pacific service.
1940 Aug: Acquired by the Admiralty and converted into a destroyer depot ship. Became H.M.S. *Philoctetes*. Same armament and complement as *Blenheim*.
1948 Broken up at Newport, Monmouthshire.

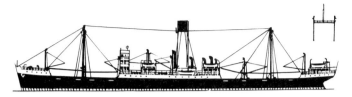

CALCHAS (II), DIOMED (IV), PERSEUS (II) and MENELAUS (III)

170 CALCHAS (II)

B 1921 Workman Clark & Co., Belfast. **T:** 10,304 g, 6,313 n.
D 490.8 ft (149.59 m) × 62.4 ft (19.02 m) × 39.6 ft (12.07 m).
E Tw. scr, 4 stm turbines dble reduction geared. Brown Curtis type. 6,500 SHP. 14 kts. By builder.
H S. 3 dks; F: 58 ft (17.68 m); B: 121 ft (36.88 m); P: 67 ft (20.42 m).
P 4 Crew: 70.

1921 Jan 11: Launched.
June 4: Completed for Ocean S.S.Co's Liverpool—Far East route. Cost £532,000.
1941 Apr 21: 10.40 am torpedoed by U-107 west south west of the Canary Islands. 31 dead. A first torpedo had killed 7 men in the engine room but *Calchas* remained afloat on an even keel but down by the stern, number 6 hold being flooded and taking in water. The crew and passengers were put into the lifeboats while a skeleton crew, under Captain Holden, remained aboard. The submarine surfaced beyond the lifeboats to prevent any attempt by *Calchas* to shell her. A second torpedo caused the ship to sink immediately and Captain Holden plus another 23 crew were lost.

171 DIOMED (IV)

Details as *Calchas* (170) except:
T: 10,453 g, 6,340 n.

1922 Built for China Mutual S.N.Co. Jan 14: Launched.
May 16: Completed and placed in the Liverpool—Far East service.
1952 Sept 2: Sold and dismantled at Dalmuir by W. H. Arnott Young.

172 PERSEUS (II)

Details as *Calchas* (170) except:
B 1923 Caledon S.B.&E Co, Dundee. **T:** 10,286 g, 6,336 n.
D 490.5 ft (149.5 m) × 62.3 ft (18.99 m).

1922 Built for China Mutual S.N.Co's Liverpool—Far East route. Aug 23: Launched.
1923 Feb: Completed.
1944 Jan 16: Torpedoed off Madras by the Japanese submarine I 165. Captain G. G. Rumble and all aboard were saved.

173 MENELAUS (III)

Details as *Calchas* (170) except:
B 1923 Caledon S.B.I E. Co, Dundee. **T:** 10,278 g, 6,334 n.
H F: 55 ft (16.76 m); B: 174 ft (53.03 m); P: 69 ft (21.03 m).

1923 May 1: Launched for Ocean S.S.Co.
Oct 11: Completed for the Liverpool—Far East Service.

1940 Collided with *City of London*, Ellerman Lines.

1942 May 1: On passage from Durban to Baltimore *Menelaus* was attacked at dawn by the German raider *Michel*, Captain Helmut von Ruckteschell. He used one of his motor torpedo-boats but to no avail and *Menelaus* ran out of range using smoke to hide her passage. When in captivity von Ruckteschell admitted that it was the only ship that had escaped him. *Menelaus* was fortunate because von Ruckteschell sank his victims without mercy leaving the survivors to fend for themselves. He was one of only two German Naval sea going officers to be tried for war crimes and died in prison while serving a ten year sentence.

1952 June 25: Arrived at Dalmuir for breaking up by W. H. Arnott Young & Co.

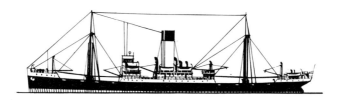

MACHAON (II) and DARDANUS (III)

174 **MACHAON** (II)

B 1920 Caledon S.B.& Co, Dundee. **T**: 7,806 g, 4,909 n.
D 459.2 ft (139.96 m) × 56.3 ft (17.16 m) × 32.5 ft (9.91 m).
E Sgl scr, tpl exp, 3 cyls, 571 NHP, 11 kts. By builder.
H S. 2 dks; F: 65 ft (18.81 m); B: 164 ft (49.99 m); P: 54 ft (16.46 m).

1920 Completed for Ocean S.S.Co. The first Holt vessel to have a soft nosed stem.
1935 Transferred to the Glen Line, renamed *Glenaffaric*.
1947 Sept: Returned to Holts. Reverted to *Machaon*.
1950 Jan: Back to Glen and renamed *Glenaffaric*.
1951 Jan 14: Arrived at Briton Ferry for breaking up by Thos. W. Ward. The price being £55,000. During demolition the vessel was damaged by fire.

175 **DARDANUS** (III)

Details as *Machaon* (174) except:
B 1923 Workman Clark & Co, Belfast. **T**: 7,823 g, 4,920 n.
D 459.5ft (140.06) × 58.4 ft (17.8 m) × 32.6 ft (9.94 m).
H F: 63 ft (19.2 m); P: 53 ft (16.15 m).

1923 Built for Ocean S.S.Co.
1935 Transferred to the Glen Line. Renamed *Flintshire*.
1939 Reverted to Holts, Ocean S.S.Co, and *Dardanus*.
1942 Apr 6: Sunk by a Japanese cruiser in the Indian Ocean off the coast of Golconda.

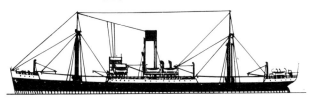

EUMAEUS (II), GLAUCUS (III), MERIONES, RHEXENOR (I), AUTOMEDON (I), AUTOLYCUS (II) and ADRASTUS (II)/EURYADES (II)

176 EUMAEUS (II)

B 1921 Caledon S.B. & E. Co, Dundee. **T:** 7,736 g, 4,849 n, 9,400 dwt.
D 459.2 ft (139.96 m) × 56.3 ft (17.16 m) × 32.5 ft (9.91 m).
E Sgl scr turb dbl reduction geared. 2 dbl ended boilers; 6,000 SHP. 14 kts. By Hawthorn Leslie & Co. Fuel 1,237 tons coal at 82 tons per day.
H S. 2 dks; 6 hatches; F: 65 ft (18.81 m); B: 164 ft (49.99 m); P: 54 ft (16.46 m).
P 12.
This class had the donkey boiler abaft the funnel.

1921 Built for the Ocean S.S.Co.
1941 Jan 14: *Eumaeus* left Liverpool on Dec. 29th 1940 for Cape Town. South west of Freetown the Italian submarine *Commandante Capellini* surfaced at 2,000 yards and opened fire while giving chase. The gunfire was aimed at the stern and bridge and four shells hit their targets but Captain J. E. Watson turned his stern to narrow the field of fire and put on top speed. Aboard *Eumaeus* for the voyage were 400 naval ratings in addition to the crew of 90, including the ship's army gunners. Despite machine gun fire from 700 yards *Eumaeus* kept on firing until every shell was used and one hit was observed on the enemy. *Eumaeus* was abandoned as the submarine closed in and torpedoed the ship, which was now well ablaze. 23 lives were lost.

177 GLAUCUS (III)

Details as *Eumaeus* (176) except:
B Hawthorn Leslie & Co, Newcastle. **T:** 7,644 g.
D 459.5 ft (140.06 m).
E By builder.

1920 Dec 9: Launched.
1921 Completed for Ocean S.S.Co.
1943 May 4: While in convoy hit Shell's *Macuba* in avoiding a collision with Ellerman's *City of Florence*. It was to be five years before Shell Oil were able to sue for the collision and they were awarded damages.
1955 July 26: Laid up at Bromborough Dock, Birkenhead pending a sale which failed to materialise.
Oct 29: Arrived at Milford Haven for breaking up by Thos. W. Ward.

178 MERIONES

Sister to *Eumaeus* (176) except:
B Hawthorn, Leslie & Co., Hebburn. **T:** 7,684 g, 4,810 n.
D 459.7 ft (140.12 m) × 58.4 ft (17.8 m) × 32.6 ft (9.94 m).
E By builder.

1922 Constructed for China Mutual S.N.Co.
1941 Jan 26: Sunk by German air attack off Cromer.

179 **RHEXENOR** (I)

Details as *Eumaeus* (176) except:
B 1922. Taikoo Dockyard & Engineering Co, Hong Kong. **T**: 7,957 g, 5,004 n.
D 459.6 ft (140.09 m) × 58.3 ft (17.77 m) × 32.6 ft (9.94 m).
E By builder.
H F: 32 ft (15.85 m); B: 162 ft (49.38 m); P: 53 ft (16.15 m).

1922 Built for Ocean S.S.Co.
1943 Feb 3: Torpedoed by U-217 south east of Bermuda.

180 **AUTOMEDON** (I)

Details as *Eumaeus* (176) except:
B 1922 Palmer's Co, Newcastle. **T**: 7,628 g, 4,724 n.
D 459.4 ft (139.9 m) × 58.4 ft (17.8 m) × 32.6 ft (9.94 m).
E By builder.
H F: 52 ft (15.85 m); B: 162 ft (49.38 m); P: 53 ft (9.94 m).

1922 Completed for Ocean S.S.Co.
1940 Nov 11: Sunk by the German raider *Atlantis* midway between the Nicobar Islands and Ceylon. Captain W. B. Ewan, 6 crew and 1 gunner were killed. (See the historical chronology for fuller details.)

181 **AUTOLYCUS** (II)

Details as *Eumaeus* (176) except:
T: 7,718 g, 4,859 n, 9,400 dwt. **B** Hawthorn Leslie & Co., Hebburn.
D 459.7 ft (140.11 m) × 58.3 ft (17.77 m).
H F: 57 ft (17.37 m); B: 162 ft (49.38 m); P: 57 ft (17.37 m).

1923 Built for China Mutual S.N.Co.
1942 Apr 6: Sunk by a Japanese cruiser east of Puri in the bay of Bengal. 18 killed.

182 **ADRASTUS** (I)/**EURYADES** (II)

Details as *Eumaeus* (176) except:
B 1923 Scott's S.B.& E. Co, Greenock. **T**: 7,905 g, 4,948 n, 9,900 dwt.
D 459.5 ft (139.9 m) × 58.1 ft (17.71 m) × 32.5 ft (9.91 m).
E By builder.
H F: 57 ft (17.37 m); B: 164 ft (49.99 m); P: 53 ft (16.15 m).

1923 Constructed for Ocean S.S.Co. At one phase in her career the boat deck lifeboats were paired one above the other. This was during her service as a Jeddah pilgrimage ship.
1927 June: Her captain hanged himself in his cabin as the ship approached Penang.
1951 July: Renamed *Euryades* in order to make the name available for *Adrastus* (II).
1954 Employed on the United States Pacific coast ports — Phillippines—East Indies route.
1954 Feb: Laid up in Holy Loch.
1954 Aug 10: Arrived at Faslane for scrapping by Metal Industries.

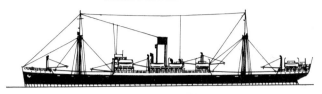

PHEMIUS (II)

183 PHEMIUS (II)

Sister to *Eumaeus* (176) except:
B 1921 Scotts S.B.& E. Co, Greenock. **T**: 7,669 g, 4,787 n. **D** 459.1 ft (139.93m) × 56.2 ft (17.13m) × 32.5 ft (9.91 m). **E** By builder. **H** F: 62 ft (18.89 m); B: 165 ft (50.29 m); P: 54 ft (16.46 m).

1921 Delivered to Ocean S.S.Co.

1932 May 14: Lost her funnel in a West Indies hurricane. Given a small temporary one and went to Hong Kong for repairs. Her tall funnel was reinstated.

1942 Operated Port Said-Malta under the command of Captain J. L. W. Johnstone.

1943 Dec 19: Torpedoed by U-515 south of Accra, West Africa. Five crew and 18 passengers killed.

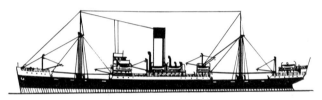

TROILUS (III)

184 TROILUS (III)

Sister of *Phemius* (183) except:
T: 7,648 g, 4,774 n.

1921 Built for China Mutual S.N.Co.

1942 June 5: A convoy of six ships, including *Troilus* left the Clyde to supply Malta. This was Operation Harpoon. In parallel Operation Vigorous would send 11 ships from Alexandria. Gibraltar was passed on the night of June 11–12. The escort, thereafter comprised one battleship, two aircraft carriers, two cruisers and eight destroyers plus a 'close in to Malta' escort of one more cruiser, nine destroyers and four fleet minesweepers together with six minesweeping motor-launches. The ships in the convoy were British: *Troilus, Burdwan* and *Orari*. Dutch: *Tanimbar*. American: *Chant* and *Kentucky*. In all 43,000 tons of cargo and oil. On June 14 *Tanimbar* was sunk; next day *Chant* went and after being hit, *Kentucky* was taken in tow. An air attack next disabled *Burdwan*. Rather than slow down both *Kentucky* and *Burdwan* had to be sunk. All that remained was *Orari*, which next struck a mine, and *Troilus*. *Orari* limped into port and *Troilus* arrived as the only unscathed ship. Operations Vigorous, from Alexandria had been reduced from eleven merchantmen down to six when Admiral Vian's group was recalled to base.

Troilus had borne a charmed life; she had seen Malta's Hurricane fighters shoot down 30 of her attackers and she had herself shot down four. Several high and low level air attacks had missed and a submarine which came in a periscope depth to the attack was sunk by one of the escorting destroyers.

1944 Aug 31: Torpedoed by U-859 east of Socotra Island, Indian Ocean en-route Colombo- –Aden–Liverpool. 24 lost.

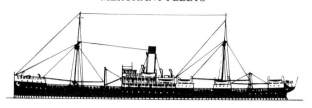

HECUBA (II)

185 HECUBA (II)

B 1901 Bremer Vulcan, Vegesack, Germany. **T:** 7,540 g, 4,811 n.
D 430 ft (131.06 m) × 54.3 ft (16.55 m) × 39.6 ft (12.07 m).
E Tw scr, Quad exp, 2 × 4 cyls; 496 NHP, 10 kts. By buider.
H S 3 dks and awning dk; **F:** 46 ft (14.02 m); **B:** 121 ft (36.88 m).
P None with Holts.

1901 Built for Norddeutscher Lloyd as *Brandenburg*.
1922 Acquired from the British Government, who had taken the ship over as a war loss reparation, and renamed *Hecuba*. The ship was not in a good state of repair and only completed 3 voyages for Blue Funnel.
1924 Aug: Sold to Italy for breaking up. Renamed *Ada* for the delivery voyage to the scrapyard.

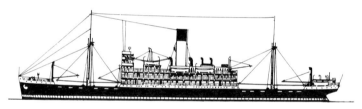

SARPEDON (IV), PATROCLUS (III), HECTOR (IV) and ANTENOR (III)

186 SARPEDON (IV)

B 1923 Cammell Laird & Co, Birkenhead. **T:** 11,321 g, 6,921 n, 11,400 dwt.
D 499 ft (152.09 m) × 62.3 ft (18.99 m) × 34.9 ft (10.64 m).
E Tw scr, 4 stm sgl reduction geared turbs. 15½ kts. By builder.
H S. 3 dks; **F:** 62 ft (18.90 m); **B:** 201 ft (61.26 m); **P:** 57 ft (10.64 m).
P 155 1st. Crew: 80.

1923 Built as the first of a class of 4 which were regarded by many as being among the best looking ships of their day.
1923 Feb 2: Launched. June 9: Maiden voyage Liverpool—Far East. On her trials *Sarpedon* took relief supplies to St. Kilda.
1927 During the 'China Affair' carried supplies and ammunition to Hong Kong.
1946 Jan 5: Took the first post war Australian sailing Liverpool—Brisbane. Pass 48.
1953 June 5: Arrived at Newport, Monmouthshire, for breaking up by John Cashmore & Co.

187 PATROCLUS (III)

Details as *Sarpedon* (136) except:
B Scotts S.B.&E. Co, Greenock. **T:** 11,314 g, 6,910 n.
D 498.8 ft (152.03 m).
H **F:** 60 ft (18.29 m); **B:** 195 ft (59.44 m); **P:** 57 ft (17.37 m).

1923 Mar 17: Delivered to the China Mutual S.N.Co. Yard No. 518. Liverpool—Far East.
1939 Became an Armed Merchant Cruiser.
1940 Nov 3: 22.55 hrs torpedoed by Otto Kretschmer in U-99 off the Bloody Foreland. Sank the next day. At the time *Patroclus* had stopped to pick up the survivors of the Armed Merchant Cruiser *Laurentic* (White Star). In all it took 7 torpedoes to dispatch the ship. There was later some controversy over the stopping of the ship alongside *Laurentic* when there was the distinct possibility of the submarine being in the area. 76 lost. *Laurentic* was herself going to the aid of Elder & Fyffes's *Casanare*. *U-99* sank all three.

188 HECTOR (IV)

Sister to *Sarpedon* (186) except:
B 1924 Scotts S.B.&.E. Co, Greenock. **T:** 11,198 g, 6,481 n.
D 498.8 ft (152.03 m). By builder.
H F: 60 ft (18.29 m); B: 195 ft (59.44 m).
Identification: No lifeboat on bridge deck derrick house. Three boats on boat deck.
1924 June 18: Launched. Sept 24: Maiden voyage Liverpool—Far East.
1940 Converted into an armed merchant cruiser.
1942 Apr 5: Sunk by Japanese air attack in Colombo Harbour.
1946 Refloated and beached. Condemned and sold for scrap. Broken up where she lay.

189 ANTENOR (III)

Sister to *Sarpedon* (186) except:
B 1925 Palmer's Co, Jarrow. **T:** 11,174 g, 6,809 n.
D 487.7 ft (151.70 m) × 62.2 ft (18.96 m) × 35 ft (10.67 m).
E By builder.
H P: 74 ft (22.55 m).
1924 Sept 30: Launched for China Mutual S.N.Co.
1925 Jan 15: Maiden voyage Liverpool—Far East. Three boats on bridge deck. No cowls to Bridge deck house derricks nor boat thereon.
1940 Troop ship.
1953 July 19: Sold to Hughes Bolckow and broken up at Blyth.

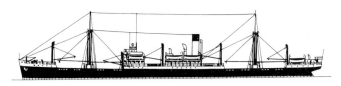

TANTALUS (II)

190 TANTALUS (II)

B 1923 Caledon S.B.& E. Co, Dundee. **T:** 7,777 g, 4,800 n, 9,500.
D 458.3 ft (139.61 m) × 58.2 ft (17.74 m) × 32.6 ft (9.94 m). Dft 28.3 ft (8.62 m).
E Sgl scr oil; 4 S.SA, 4,500 BHP: By Burmeister & Wain, Copenhagen.
H S. 2 dks; F: 64 ft (19.51 m); B: 159 ft (48.46 m); P: 52 ft (15.85 m).
Cargo 592,000 cu ft (16,763.6 cu m). Fuel: 1,110 tons oil.
1923 Built for Ocean S.S.Co.
1936 Transferred to Glen Line; renamed *Radnorshire*.
1939 Reverted to Ocean; became *Tantalus*.
1941 Dec 26: Sunk by air attack in Manila Bay.

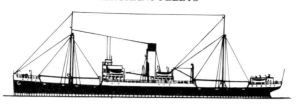

MEDON (I) and DOLIUS (I)

191 MEDON (I)

B 1923 Palmer's Co, Newcastle. **T**: 5,915 g, 3,268 n.
D 406.5 ft (123.90 m) × 52.2 ft (15.91 m) × 29.3 ft (8.93 m).
E Sgl scr, oil 4 S.SA; 652 NHP, 12 kts. By Burmeister & Wain, Copenhagen.
H S. 2 dks, 6 hatches. F: 45 ft (13.72 m); B: 130 ft (39.62 m); P: 38 ft (11.58 m).
1923 The company's first motorship. Owned by Ocean S.S.Co.
1942 Aug 10: Sunk north-east of Para by the Italian submarine *Reginaldo Giuliano*.
It was pitch black when *Medon* was abandoned and when daylight came the Italians surfaced and shelled the ship but failed to sink her. A torpedo was finally used. In the dark the lifeboats had separated; one was picked up after eight days but the other two were only rescued after five weeks adrift during which considerable hardship was endured; although all aboard them survived.

192 DOLIUS

Details as *Medon* (191) except:
B 1924 Scotts S.B. & E. Co, Greenock. **T**: 5,994 g, 3,645 n.
D Depth 28.4 ft (8.66 m).
E Sgl scr oil 2S.DA, 8 cyls plus 2 steam generators; 12 kts. By builder.

1924 Constructed for the Ocean S.S.Co. She was the first vessel to be fitted with part-steam and part-diesel engines. A larger set was later installed in *Eurybates* (205). The steam regenerators worked by having the exhaust gases from the main engines passed through 2 boilers, one at 180 lbs and one at 150 lbs. Oil burners fired the larger boiler when the main engine was not in use — as for example when manoeuvering. In service the engine showed over a 200,000 mile trial period, considerable fuel savings. *Dolius* averaged 11.53 kts on 8.67 tons oil per day.
1941 Apr 24: Straffed, bombed and damaged by German aircraft in the channel approaches to the Firth of Forth.
1943 Aug 5: Torpedoed by U-638 east of Belle Isle, Gulf of St. Lawrence. Escorts sank U-638

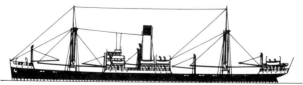

EURYMEDON (II), POLYDORUS (I) and MELAMPUS (I)

193 EURYMEDON (II)

B 1924 Caledon S.B.& E. Co, Dundee. **T**: 6,223 g, 3,858 n.
D 431.8 ft (131.61 m) × 54.7 ft (16.67 m) × 30.1 ft (9.17 m).
E Tw scr oil 4S.SA, 2 × 8 cyl. 951 NHP; 12 kts. By Buremister & Wain, Copenhagen.
H S. 2 dks; F: 45 ft (13.72 m); B: 122 ft (37.19 m); P: 40 ft (12.19 m).

1924 The first of a trio of similar appearance. Built for Ocean S.S.Co.
1940 Sept 25: Twice torpedoed by U-29 west of Ireland. The first torpedo hit the port side in the engine room. The second blew a hole in the corresponding position on the starboard side. This second one wrecked two lifeboats killing the passengers and crew in them. Next morning Captain J. F. Webster and crew members reboarded *Eurymedon*. The water in the engine room was at sea level and the ship was slowly settling on an even keel. A lifeboat from Donaldson's *Sularia* took them off and on the second day after being hit the ship sank. 28 lives were lost.

194 **POLYDORUS** (I)

Details as *Eurymedon* (193) except:
B 1924 Scotts S.B.& E. Co, Greenock. **T:** 6,256 g, 3,863 n.
D 429.9 ft (131.03 m) × 54.8 ft (16.7 m).
E Sgl scr, 2 double reduction geared turbs. Stm 220 lb 12 kts. By builder.
H B: 123 ft (37.49 m); P; 42 ft (12.80 m).

1924 Operated by N.S.M. 'Oceaan', Dutch flag.
1942 Nov 27: Torpedoed by U-176 off Freetown.

195 **MELAMPUS** (I)

Details as *Eurymedon* (193) except:
B 1924 Palmer's Co, Newcastle. **T:** 6,321 g, 3,904 n, 7,848 dwt.
D 449.5 ft (137 m) o.a. 428 ft (130.67 m) × 54.9 ft (16.73 m).
E As *Polydorus* (194). By builder.
H B: 127 ft (38.71 m); P: 43 ft (13.11 m).

1924 June: Operated under the Dutch flag by N.S.M. 'Oceaan'. Registered at Amsterdam.
1940 Registered at Willemstad under Allied control.
1950 Transferred to the British flag. Same name; Ocean S.S.Co.
1955 Laid up in Holy Loch.
1957 Oct 1: Arrived at Inverkeithing for breaking up by Thos. W. Ward.

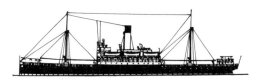

CENTAUR (II)

196 **CENTAUR** (II)

B 1924 Scott's S.B.& E. Co, Greenock. **T:** 3,066 g, 1,800 n.
D 315.7 ft (96.22 m) × 48.2 ft (14.69 m) × 21.5 ft (6.55 m).
E Sgl scr, oil, 4S.SA, 355 NHP, 6 cyl; 14 kts. By Burmeister & Wain, Copenhagen.
H S. 2 dks & shade dk.

1924 Built for Ocean S.S.Co's Singapore—Australia service.
1940 Converted into a hospital ship on loan to the Australian Government.
1943 May 14: Sunk at night by the Japanese I-174 off Brisbane, en-route Sydney—New Guinea. The ship was fully illuminated and painted in Red Cross colours. Only 64 out of 363 survived. Eighteen doctors and 12 nurses were drowned. *Centaur* sank in three minutes.

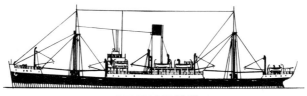

ASPHALION (I)

197 ASPHALION (I)

B 1924 Scott's S.B.& E. Co, Greenock. **T:** 6,274 g, 3,836 n.
D 431.7 ft (131.58 m) × 54.7 ft (16.67 m) × 30.1 ft (9.17 m).
E Sgl scr, 2 stm turbs, dbl reduction geared. 2 dbl ended boilers. Stm P: 220 lb, 12 kts. By builder.
H S, welded; 2 dks; F: 45 ft (13.72 m); B: 140 ft (42.67 m); P: 43 ft (13.11 m).
P 12.

1924 Completed for China Mutual S.N.Co.
1944 Feb 11: escaped Indian Ocean torpedo attack.
1959 June 27: Sold for scrap to Dah Cheong Hong Ltd, Hong Kong.

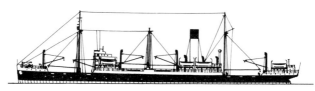

ALCINOUS (III)/PHEMIUS (III), STENTOR (III) and PHRONTIS (I)

198 ALCINOUS (II)/PHEMIUS (III)

B 1925 Scott's S.B.& E. Co, Greenock. **T:** 6,639 g, 4,131 n.
D 429.8 ft (131 m) × 54.8 ft (16.7 m) × 29 ft (8.84 m). Dft: 26.3 ft (8.02 m). 449 ft (136.85 m) o.a.
E Tw scr, oil 4S.SA 2 × 8 cyls; 1,200 NHP; 4,800 BHP; 14 kts. By Buremeister & Wain, Copenhagen. Fuel: 740 tons.
H S. 2 dks; C: 520,000 cu ft (147,248.4 cu m); F: 45 ft (13.72 m); B: 238 ft (75.54 m); P: 25 ft (7.62 m).
P 12.

1925 First of three sisters. Operated by N.S.M. 'Oceaan'. Registered at Amsterdam.
1950 Renamed *Phemius* when transferred to the British flag; now owned by Ocean S.S.Co.
1957 July 26: Arrived at Hong Kong for demolition.

199 STENTOR (III)

Details as *Alcinous* (198) except:
B 1926 Caledon S.B.& E. Co, Dundee. **T:** 6,634 g, 4,161 n, 7,700 dwt.
D 430.8 ft (131.31 m) × 55.8 ft (17.01 m).
E By North East Marine Eng. Co, Newcastle.
H F: 50 ft (15.24 m); B: 241 ft (73.46 m); P: 51 ft (15.54 m).

1926 Built for China Mutual S.N.Co.
1942 Oct 27: Torpedoed on her starboard side by *U-509* west of the Canary Isles enroute Freetown–U.K. *Stentor* was the lead ship (No 91 being the lead ship in the ninth column) in a convoy of 40 vessels. Captain Williams, 21 crew and 23 passengers died. Commodore Gastin, aboard *Stentor*, in charge of the convoy, also died when the ship sank in eight minutes. The survivors were picked up by H.M.S. *Woodruff*.

200 **PHRONTIS** (I)

Details as *Alcinous* (198) except.
B 1925 Caledon S.B.& E. Co, Dundee. **T**: 6,635 g, 4,136 n.
D 429.5 ft (130.91 m).

1926 Operated by N.S.M. 'Oceaan'. Amsterdam.
1958 Sold to M. Bakhashab, Saudi Arabia. Renamed *Ryad*.
1958 Aug 25: Arrived Hong Kong for scrapping.

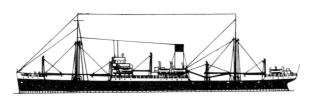

PEISANDER (I) and PROMETHEUS (III)

201 **PEISANDER** (I)

B 1925 Caledon S.B.& E. Co, Dundee. **T**: 6,225 g, 3,884 n.
D 431.8 ft (131.61 m) × 54.7 ft (16.67 m) × 30.1 ft (9.17 m).
E Tw scr, oil 4S.SA 2 × 8 cyl; 12 kts; by Burmeister & Wain, Copenhagen.
H S 2 dks; F: 45 ft (13.72 m); B: 122 ft (37.19 m); P: 40 ft (12.19 m).

1925 Delivered to Ocean S.S.Co.
1942 May 17: Torpedoed by U-653 off Nantucket.

202 **PROMETHEUS** (III)

Sister of *Peisander* (201) except:
B 1925 Scott's S.B.& E. Co, Greenock. **T**: 6,256 g, 3,872 n.
D 431.2 ft (131.43 m).
1925 Built for Ocean S.S.Co.
1942/43 Took part in the North Africa Sicily and Salerno landings.
1957 Sold for £100,000 to Panama. Renamed *Janus*, delivered to Hamburg. Owned: Janus Compagnia de Nav S.A.
1959 Jan: Sold to Italian breakers after fire damage.

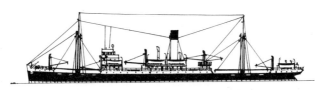

ORESTES (IV) and IDOMENEUS (II)

203 **ORESTES** (IV)

B 1926 Workman Clark & Co, Belfast. **T**: 7,845 g, 4,809 n, 9,070 dwt.
D 477.5 ft (145.54 m) o.a., 459.6 ft (140.09 m) bp × 58.4 ft (17.80 m) × 32.6 ft (9.94 m). Dft 28.3 ft (8.63 m).
E Tw scr, oil, 4S.SA 2 × 4 cyl; supercharged. 6,000 BHP;. 14½ kts. By Burmeister & Wain, Copenhagen.
H S. 2 dks; F: 62 ft (18.90 m); B; 168 ft (51.21 m); P: 50 ft (15.42 m).
P 12 plus 800 unberthed pilgrims.

1926 Completed for Ocean S.S.Co.

1942 May: Attacked by a Japanese seaplane off Madras. Four bombs missed the zig-zagging ship and her accurate anti-aircraft fire drove off the enemy.

June: Attacked by 3 Japanese submarines 90 miles south of Sydney. The ship was hit by two shells. Depth charges were dropped over the stern, damaging one of the submarines and the chase was broken off.

1946 Reconditioned at Rotterdam at the end of her war service.

1954 Mar: Her cargo of sisal caught fire at Walsh Bay, Sidney. It was exitinguished at the end of two days.

1963 Aug 11: Arrived at Mihara, Japan, to be broken up.

204 **IDOMENEUS** (II)

Sister to *Orestes* (203) except:

T: 7,857 g, 4,813 n.

H F: 63 ft (19.2 m); B: 162 ft (49.38 m).

1926 Built for the China Mutual S.N.Co.

1962 Apr 6: Arrived at Genoa for scrapping.

XANTHUS

205 **XANTHUS**

B 1927 Cammell Laird & Co, Birkenhead. **T:** 213 g, 91 n.

D 102.8 ft (31.33 m) × 22.7 ft (6.92 m) × 10.1 ft (3.08 m). 108 ft (32.92 m) o.a.

E Sgl scr, 2 cyl comp; Stm P 130 lb, 8 kts. By A. G. Mumford, Colchester.

H S. 1 dk.

1927 June: Built for Alfred Holt & Co. but transferred during the year to Ocean S.S.Co. Used as an oil separation barge in the River Mersey.

1959 Sold to T. Routledge, Seaforth. Renamed *Crosby Dale*. Tank barge.

1968 June: Towed to Dalmuir by Alexandra's tug *Egerton* for breaking up by W. H. Arnott Young & Co.

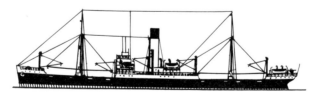

EURYBATES (II)

206 **EURYBATES** (II)

B 1928 Scott's S.B.& E. Co, Greenock. **T:** 6,436 g, 3,988 n.

D 431.9 ft (131.64 m) × 54.8 ft (16.70 m) × 29.1 ft (8.87 m).

E Tw scr oil and steam. Oil: 2S.SA 2 × 5 cyl; steam: 4 cyl quad exp with 1 regenerator; 2,500 BHP. 13½ kts at 105 rpm. Scott-Still type by builder. Constructed with high tensile steel.

1928 Built for the Ocean S.S.Co. The novel part steam part diesel engines created much

interest but were found to require too much maintenance. *Eurybates'* engines had twice the power of those installed in *Dolius* (192).

1948 Re-engined by Harland & Wolff using her original oil engines only.
1958 July 15: Arrived at Ghent for breaking up by Van Heyghen Freres.
1964 March: Sold for breaking up.

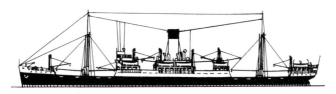

AGAMEMNON (III), MENESTHEUS (II), DEUCALION (III),
MEMNON (III) and AJAX (III)/SARPEDON (V)

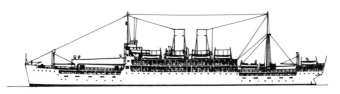

AGAMEMNON (III) and MENESTHEUS (II)

207 **AGAMEMNON** (III)

B 1929 Workman Clark (1928) Ltd, Belfast. **T:** 7,593 g, 4,806 n.
D 478.3 ft (145.79 m) o.a. 459.8 ft (140.15 m) bp × 59.4 ft (18.10 m) × 29.3 ft (8.93 m). Depth 35.3 ft (10.76 m). Dft 28.4 ft (8.66 m).
E Tw scr oil 2 × 8 cyl 4S.SA by Burmeister & Wain, Copenhagen. 1,295 NHP. 14 kts.
H S. special steel; F: 60 ft (18.29 m); B: 180 ft (54.86 m); P: 44ft (13.41 m).

1929 Built for Ocean S.S.Co, for Liverpool—Far east service with continental ports visited on the inbound leg. Also round-the-world service.
1940 Became a naval mine layer.
1943 Converted at Vancouver into a Pacific fleet recreation ship. Sailors took their local leave aboard her. *Agamemnon* had a cinema-theatre, brewery and swimming amenities..
1947 March: Reverted to commercial service.
1963 March 26: Broken up at Hong Kong.

208 **MENESTHEUS** (I)

Sister to *Agamemnon* (207) except:
B 1929 Caledon S.B.& E. Co, Dundee. **T:** 7,715 g, 4,796 n.
D 460 ft (140.21 m). Dft 28.6 ft (8.72 m).
H F: 57 ft (17.37 m); B: 181 ft (55.17 m); P: 63 ft (19.2 m).

1929 Built for Ocean S.S.Co.
1940 Became a naval minesweeper.
1943 Converted into a naval recreation ship. Similar to her sister.
1946 July: Left Yokohama for U.K. and de-commissioning.
1948 Returned to her owners for commercial service.
1953 April 16: Abandoned on fire after an engine room explosion, off the coast of California.
May 5: Arrived in tow at Long Beach, California.
June 10: Condemned for breaking up.

209 DEUCALION (III)

Sister of *Agamemnon* (207) except:
B 1930 Hawthorn Leslie & Co, Newcastle. **T:** 7,740 g, 4799 n.
D 460 ft (140.21 m).
H F: 51 ft (15.54 m); B: 177 ft (53.95 m).

1930 Built for Ocean S.S.Co.
1940 Dec 21/22: Damaged by air attack at Gladstone Dock, Liverpool.
1941 July: Achieved a round convoy voyage between Gibraltar and Malta. When leaving Malta the ship was inexplicably shelled by shore batteries without damage however minutes later a mine was set off by the port side paravane which sprung some of *Deucalion's* plates. Later that day the ship was attacked by Italian Marchetti bombers; both of whose torpedoes missed, one by a mere three feet and the other scraped the ship's side. One of the Italians was shot down. The periscope of a submarine was then spotted by the arrival of an escorting destroyer and a circling Sunderland enabled *Deucalion* to escape.
1942 Aug 12: Sunk by air attack while in convoy for Malta. Sank 5 miles west of Cani Rocks, Gallita Island. Commanded by Capt. Ramsey Brown, D.S.C.
Deucalion was high level bombed by 5 Heinkel aircraft seven miles north of the island. One was shot down. The first direct hit went through number 5 hold and out of the side of the ship into the sea where it exploded lifting *Deucalion* almost out of the water and deluging the ship. No. 1 hold filled with water and No. 5 hold had 9 ft in it. Captain Brown kept the ship steaming towards Malta. Enemy reconaissance planes found her once more and three aircraft made a low level attack. Three near misses shook the ship. The second aircraft sent an aerial torpedo into No. 6 hold snapping the propeller shaft and igniting the high octane fuel destined for Malta. Within moments the stern was a blazing inferno and all aboard abandoned ship; rafts being launched for the poop crew who were trapped. H.M.S. *Bramhan* picked up the survivors.

210 MEMNON (IV)

Sister of *Agamemnon* (207) except:
B 1931 Caledon S.B.& E. Co, Dundee. **T:** 7,731 g, 4,765 n.
D 460 ft (140.21 m).
H F: 56 ft (17.07 m); B: 179 ft (54.56 m); P: 46 ft (14.02 m).

1931 Delivered to the China Mutual S.N.Co.
1941 Mar 11: Torpedoed by U-106 north east of Cape Blanco, Cape Verpe Islands. Five killed. *Memnon* sank in 15 minutes.

211 AJAX (III)/SARPEDON (V)

Sister of *Agamemnon* (207) except:
B 1931 Scott's S.B.& E. Co, Greenock. **T:** 7,797 g, 4,803 n.
D 459.6 ft (140.09 m) × 59.3 ft (18.07 m) × 29.2 ft (8.9 m). 478.3 ft (145.78 m) o.a.
H F: 51 ft (15.54 m); B: 178 ft (54.25 m); P: 46 ft (14.02 m).

1931 Built for Ocean S.S.Co.
1957 Transferred to the Glen Line. Renamed *Glenlochy*.
1958 Reverted to Ocean S.S.Co, became *Sarpedon*.
1962 Aug: Arrived Hong Kong to await scrapping (often 18 months).

BLUE FUNNEL LINE

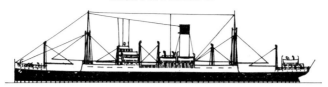

MARON (I), CLYTONEUS (I), MYRMIDON (III) and POLYPHEMUS (III)

212 MARON (I)

B 1930 Caledon S.B.& E. Co, Dundee. **T:** 6,701 g, 4,114 n.
D 433 ft (131.98 m) × 56.3 ft (17.16 m) × 26.3 ft (8.02 m).
E Tw scr oil; 4 S.SA 2 × 6 Cyl 637 NHP; 13½ kts. By North East Marine Eng. Co.
H S 2 dks; F: 47 ft (14.32 m); B: 256 ft (78,03 m); P: 44 ft (13.41 m); C: 530,000 cu ft (49,237 cu m) G.

1930 First of a class of four. Built for China Mutual S.N.Co.
1942 Nov 13: Torpedoed by U-81 off Oran.

213 CLYTONEUS (I)

Sister to *Maron* (212) except:
B Scotts S.B. & E. Co, Greenock. **T:** 6,663 g, 4,110 n.
D 432.5 ft (131.83 m).
H F: 50 ft (15.24 m); B: 260 ft (79.25 m); P: 43 ft (13.11 m).

1930 Delivered to Ocean S.S.Co.
1941 Jan 8: On passage from the Dutch East Indies for Liverpool *Clytoneus* was south of Rockall when an air attack began. Two near misses stopped the main engines. The next attack, from only 250 ft set the sugar in No. 2 hold furiously ablaze. More near misses opened up her seams and the Blue Funneller commenced to settle by the stern. The whole attack lasted only eight minutes.

214 MYRMIDON (III)

Sister of *Maron* (212) except:
B 1930 Scott's S.B.& E. Co, Greenock. **T:** 6,663 g, 4,110 n.
D 432.5 ft (131.83 m).
E By builder.
H F: 50 ft (15.24 m); B: 260 ft (79.25 m); P: 43 ft (13.11 m).

1930 Completed for Ocean S.S.Co.
1941 Mar 13: Damaged by a mine at Liverpool.
1942 Sept 5: Torpedoed by U-506 off Cape Palmas, Liberia.

215 POLYPHEMUS (III)

Sister of *Maron* (212) except:
B 1930 Scott's S.B.& E. Co, Greenock. **T:** 6,671 g, 4,117 n.
D 430.5 ft (131.22 m).
H F: 45 ft (13.72 m); B: 252 ft (76.81 m); P: 42 ft (12.80 m).

1930 Operated by N.S.M. 'Oceaan'.
1941 See *Automedon* (180) and 1940 Nov 11 Chronology entry.
1942 May 26: Torpedoed twice in five seconds by U-135 north of Bermuda en-route Sydney, Australia, via Halifax for Liverpool. *Polyphemus*, Captain Koningstein, had aboard 14 survivors from the Norwegian *Norland*, 8,134 g. Of a total of 75 only 30 were saved.

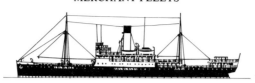

GORGON (II) and CHARON (II)

216 GORGON (II)

B 1933 Caledon S.B.& E. Co, Dundee. **T**: 3,533 g, 2,120 n.
D 336 ft (102.41 m) o.a., 320.3 ft (97.63 m) bp × 51.2 ft (15.61 m) × 21.6 ft (6.58 m). Dft: 20.7 ft (6.31 m).
E Sgl scr oil 2S.DA 6 cyl. 12 kts. By Burmeister & Wain, Copenhagen. 580 NHP.
H S 2 dks and shelter dk; B: 88 ft (26.82 m).

1933 Built for Ocean S.S.Co's and West Australian S.N.Co. (Bethell, Gwynn & Co) joint Singapore-West Australian ports service.
1936 Wholly owned by Ocean.
1942 Feb 3: Sailed with 300 passengers from Singapore three days prior to the surrender to Japanese forces. Attacked by high level bombers on six occasions. Two direct hits set *Gorgon* on fire one blaze being adjacent to the ammunition store. Chief Officer J. Bruce discovered a third bomb in the hold embedded in bags of flour. With the aid of two army men the bomb was dumped over the side.
1942 Apr 14: Damaged by Japanese bombers during the American landings at Milne Bay, New Guinea.
1964 July 21: Last sailing from Fremantle.
1964 Aug: Sold for breaking up at Hong Kong.

217 CHARON (II)

Sister of *Gorgon* (216) except:
B 1936. **T**: 3,703 g, 2,217 n. **H** B: 95 ft (28.96 m).

1936 Built for Ocean S.S.Co. Same service as her sister.
1964 March: Sold for breaking up at Singapore. Re-sold to become *Seng Kong No. 1* owned Chan Kai Kit, Panama.
1965 Aug: Broken up.

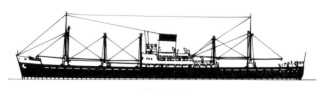

JASON (II)

218 JASON (III)

B 1940 Cantieri Riuniti dell Adriatico, Monfalcone. **T**: 6,310 g.
D 449.5 ft (137 m) × 60.9 ft (18.5 m) × 25.9 ft (7.89 m).
E Sgl scr, oil.
H S, 2 dks; F: 121.4 ft (37).

1939 Ordered by N.S.M. 'Oceaan'.
1940 May 9: Trials were carried out under the Dutch flag.
May 10: Taken over by the Italian Government. Renamed *Sebastiano Veniero*.
June 10: Italy entered the war.
1941 Together with all captured and sequestrated ships the *Sebastiano Veniero* was operated by the German Mittelmeer Reederei G.m.B.H. (Mediterranean SS Co.) Same name. Black hull light grey uppers.
1941 Dec 9: Torpedoed south of Navarino by H.M.S. *Torbay* and H.M.S. *Porpoise*. The ship was beached but became a total loss. The ship had the distinction of serving with Blue Funnel for one day only. She was in fact never officially handed over.

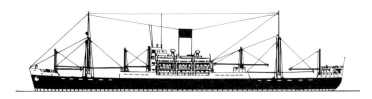

PRIAM (IV)/PHEMIUS (IV) and TELEMACHUS (III)

219 **PRIAM** (IV)/**PHEMIUS** (IV)

B 1941 Caledon S.B. & E. Co, Dundee. **T**: 9,975 g, 5,944 n.
D 512.8 ft (156.3 m) o.a., 486.1 ft (148.16 m) × 66.4 ft (20.24 m) × 32.3 ft (9.84 m).
E Tw scr, oil, 2S.DA 2 × 6 cyl. By John G. Kincaide & Co, Greenock.
H S 2 dks, 3rd dk forward; F: 55 ft (16.76 m); B: 212 ft (64.62 m); P: 43 ft (13.11 m).

1939 Keel laid. While still under hull construction the vessel was requisitioned by the Admiralty. Work on her stopped.
1941 The Admiralty decided to complete the ship to her original specifications because the cost of conversion into the intended escort carrier was too great. Ocean S.S.Co. took her into service under her intended name.
1948 Transferred to the Glen Line; renamed *Glenorchy*.
1970 Reverted to Blue Funnel; renamed *Phemius*.
1971 May: Broken up at Kaohsiung, Taiwan.

220 **TELEMACHUS** (III)

Sister to *Priam* (219) except:
T: 9,061 g, 5,314 n.
H F: 52 ft (15.85 m); B: 214 ft (65.23 m); P: 45 ft (13.72 m).

1940 Feb 1: The keel was laid as *Telemachus* for the Ocean S.S.Co. Due to the war work on her was slow. She was requisitioned and, while still on the stocks, renamed *Empire Acitvity*. Because of the low level on hull work it was found to be economically feasible to complete her as an escort carrier. She therefore emerged as H.M.S.*Activity* with 15 aircraft and 2 × 4 in guns. Complement 700. Speed 18 kts. She was used initially as a deck landing training ship and then on the Atlantic and Arctic convoys.
1944 Apr: In the Arctic her aircraft, operating with those of H.M.S. *Avenger* and H.M.S. *Tracker*, sank three U-boats. The convoy reached Russia without loss.
1945 Employed as a Far East aircraft ferry. Took aircraft out of the British Pacific fleets and flew them off for delivery upon arrival. Later *Activity* ran a shuttle service from Ceylon

with aircraft spares and supplies.

1946 Purchased 'as lies' by the Glen Line. Converted back to virtually her original design by Palmers Hebburn Co. Ltd.

1947 Sept 11: Proceeded on her commercial trials.

Sept 12: Handed over as *Breconshire.*

1967 Broken up at Kobe, Japan.

Telemachus did not, therefore, actually serve under the Blue Funnel.

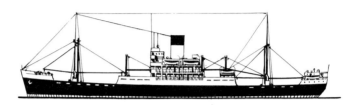

TELEMACHUS (IV)/GLAUCUS (IV)

221 TELEMACHUS (IV)/GLAUCUS (IV)

B 1943 Caledon S.B.& E. Co, Dundee. **T:** 8,265 g, 4,817 n.

D 489 ft (149.05 m) o.a., 462.2 ft (140.88 m) bp × 61.4 ft (18.71 m) × 31.9 ft (9.72 m).

E Sgl scr oil, 2S.DA 8 cyl. By J. G. Kincaid & Co, Greenock.

H S 2 dks + 3rd forward; F: 44 ft (13.41 m); B: 190 ft (57.91 m); P: 38 ft (11.58 m).

1943 Built as a direct replacement if slightly smaller version, of *Telemachus* (220). Completed for Ocean S.S.Co.

1957 Transferred to Glen Line. Renamed *Monmouthshire.*

1963 Renamed *Glaucus,* Ocean S.S.Co.

1964 Chartered to China Navigation Co; renamed *Nanchang.*

1968 Broken up at Hong Kong.

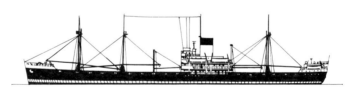

RHEXENOR (II) and STENTOR (IV)

222 RHEXENOR (II)

B 1945 Caledon S.B.& E. Co, Dundee. **T:** 10,199 g, 6,022 n, 10,800 dwt.

D 496 ft (151.17 m) o.a., 475.8 ft (145.02 m) × 64.4 ft (19.63 m) × 40 ft (12.19 m). Dft: 29.9 ft (9.11 m).

E Sgl scr, oil 2S.DA 8 cyl 1,320 NHP. 15 kts. By John G. Kincaid & Co, Greenock.

H S 2 dks + 3rd forward; F: 38 ft (11.58 m); P: 42 ft (12.8 m).

P 12

1945 Completed for China Mutual S.N.Co. The vessel was laid down as one of the fast Empire class. Purchased on the stocks and completed to Holt requirements.

Rhexenor was used on the Australian run with her extensive refrigerated capacity.

1975 Sold for breaking up. For the delivery voyage she was called *Hexeno* by the removal of the first and last letters.

223 **STENTOR** (IV)

Details as *Rhexenor* (222) except:
B 1946. **T**: 10,203 g, 6,053 n.
H F: 36 ft (10.97 m); P: 38 ft (11.58 m).

1946 Similarly acquired and completed for Ocean S.S.Co.
1958 Transferred to the Glen Line. Renamed *Glenshiel.*
1963 Reverted to *Stentor* but owned by China Mutual S.N.Co.
1975 Apr 1: Sold at Singapore for breaking up at Taiwan. Renamed *Tento* for the delivery voyage. Oddly she appears in Lloyds Register under this name which she held for one week. Apr 6: Arrived Taiwan for scrap.
Note: To replace *Stentor* (IV) on the Australian berth *Memnon* (288) was renamed *Stentor.*

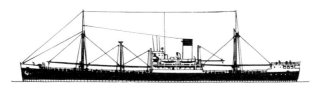

MEDON (II)

224 **MEDON** (II)

B 1942 Harland & Wolff, Belfast. **T**: 7,376 g, 4,408 n.
D 448.2 ft (135.91 m) o.a., 431.4 ft (131.49 m) bp × 57.3 ft (17.46 m) × 33.6 ft (10.24 m).
E Sgl scr oil; 4S.SA 6 cyl. 12 kts. By builder.
H S 2 dks + 3rd forward.

1942 Built as *Empire Splendour*, Ministry of War Transport. G. Heyn & Sons as managers.
1946 Acquired by Blue Funnel. Renamed *Medon*. Assigned to Ocean S.S.Co.
1962 Nov 23: Laid up in the River Fal.
1963 Sold to Liberian buyers. Renamed *Tina*, Olistim Nav Cia, Monrovia.
1968 Sold to Sanspyridon Shipping Co, Cyprus. (Olistim as managers).
1970 Broken up.

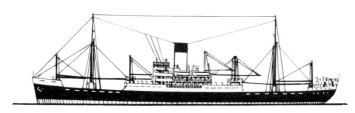

CALCHAS (III), ANCHISES (III)/ALCINOUS (IV), AENEAS (II), AGAPENOR (II), ACHILLES (IV)/ASPHALION (II)/POLYPHEMUS (V)/ ASPHALION, ASTYANAX (II), CLYTONEUS (II), CYCLOPS (III)/AUTOMEDON (III), AUTOLYCUS (III), ANTILOCHUS (II), AUTOMEDON (II), LAERTES (IV)/IDOMENEUS (III), BELLEROPHON (III), ASCANIUS (III), ATREUS (II), ALCINOUS (III)/POLYDORUS (III), LAOMEDON (II), EUMAEUS (IV), ADRASTUS (II), ELPENOR (II) and LYCAON (II)/GLAUCUS (V)

225 CALCHAS (III)

B 1947 Harland & Wolf, Belfast. **T**: 7,639 g, 4,526 n, 9,300 dwt.
D 487 ft (148.44 m) o.a., 462.9 ft (141.09 m) bp × 62.3 ft (18.98 m) × 31.7 ft (9.66 m). Dft: 28.4 ft (8.65 m).
E Sgl scr, oil 2S.DA, 8 cyl. 6,800 BHP, 15½ kts. Harland & Wolff-Burmeister & Wain type. By builder.
H S, 2 dks; F: 44 ft (13.41 m); B: 190 ft (57.91 m); P: 41ft (12.5 m).
P 12−18.

1946 Aug 27: Launched by Mrs Lawrence D. Holt. Known as the *Anchises* class Mark A1, she was the first of a class of 21 vessels spread over seven years and which constituted Holt's post war re-building programme.
1947 Jan: Delivered ahead of *Anchises* to become the leader into service. Owned by China Mutual S.N.Co.
1957 Renamed *Glenfinlas*, Glen Line.
1962 Nov: Reverted tó *Calchas*.
1971/2 Operated by Elder Dempster Lines.
1973 July: Damaged by a five day fire at Port Kelang, Malaysia. Found to be beyond economic repair.
Oct 23: Arrived in tow at Kaohsiung to be broken up.

226 ANCHISES (III)/ALCINOUS

Details as *Calchas* (225) except:
B 1947 Caledon S.B.& E. Co, Dundee. **T**: 7,642 g, 4,474 n.
E By John G. Kincaid, Greenock.

1946 Sept: Launched.
1947 Apr: Completed for Ocean S.S.Co. Her delivery was behind schedule.
May: Maiden voyage from Birkenhead to the Far East three months later than *Calchas.*
1949 June: Bombed in the Whangpo River by Chinese Nationalist fighter bombers. The engine room was flooded and the ship settled by the stern in shallow water. Refloated and towed up river to discharge. Attacked again, this time unsuccessfully. Towed to Kobe, Japan, for repairs.
1973 Jan: Renamed *Alcinous*. This can lead to confusion with *Alcinous* (240). The name *Anchises* was thereby released for allocation to *Anchises* (308).
1974 Aug: Transferred to the Glen Line without change of name.
Nov: Reverted to Blue Funnel's China Mutual S.N.Co.
1975 Sept 5: Arrived Kaohsiung for breaking up.

227 AENEAS (II)

Details as *Calchas* (225) except:
B 1947 Caledon S.B. & E. Co, Dundee. **T**: 7,641 g, 4,473 n.
E By John G. Kincaid & Co, Greenock.

1947 Sept: Completed for China Mutual S.N.Co.
1972 July: Broken up at Taiwan.

228 AGAPENOR (II)

Details as *Calchas* (225) except:
B 1947 Scott's S.B. & E. Co, Greenock. **T**: 7,664 g, 4,460 n.
D 463 ft (141.12 m).
E By Harland & Wolff, Belfast.

1947 June: Completed for China Mutual S.N.Co.

1967 June: Trapped by the Israeli—Egyptian Six-Days War in the Suez Canal. See *Melampus* (289) for fuller details. After being abandoned to the insurance underwriters the ship became the property of Agapenor War Risks Ltd.

1975 May 20: Towed to Port Said thence to Dhekelia to unload ammunition then to Trieste to discharge the balance of her cargo, having been sold to the Greek Grecomar Shipping Agency Ltd. Renamed *Nikos* she was operated by Faynav Shipping Co, Panama.

July 27: Arrived at Piraeus for overhaul.

1981 Sold for demolition.

229 ACHILLES (IV)/ASPHALION (II)/POLYPHEMUS (V)/ASPHALION

Details as *Calchas* (225) except:
B 1948 Caledon S.B.& E. Co, Dundee. **T:** 7,632 g, 4,449 n.
E By John G. Kincaid & Co, Greenock.

1947 Dec: Delivered.

1948 Jan: M/v for Ocean S.S.Co. The 28th ship to be constructed for them by Caledon.

1949 Apr: Transferred to the Glen Line. Renamed *Radnorshire*.

1962 Dec: Returned to Blue Funnel. Became *Asphalion* because the name had been bestowed upon *Achilles* (283).

1966 Jan: Transferred to N.S.M. 'Oceaan'; renamed *Polyphemus*.

1972 Nov: Reverted to Ocean S.S.Co as *Asphalion*.

1975 Oct: Sold to Gulf (Shipowners) Ltd, London. Renamed *Gulf Anchor*.

1979 Broken up at Kaohsiung, Taiwan.

230 ASTYANAX (II)

Details as *Calchas* (225) except:
B 1948 Scott's S.B.& E. Co, Greenock. **T:** 7,654 g, 4,481 n.
D 463 ft (141.12 m).
E By John G. Kincaid, Greenock.
H F: 50 ft (15.24 m); B: 195 ft (59.43 m); P: 64 ft (19.51 m).

1948 Apr: Delivered to China Mutual S.N.Co.

1957 Nov: Transferred to Glen Line; renamed *Glenfruin*.

1962 Sept: Returned to Blue Funnel as *Astyanax*.

1972 Dec: Arrived at Kaohsiung for breaking up.

231 CLYTONEUS (II)

Sister to *Calchas* (225) except:
B Caledon S.B.& E. Co, Dundee. **T:** 7,620 g, 4,434 n.
E By John G. Kincaid & Co, Greenock.

1948 Aug: The first vessel of the Mark A2 class of six ships which were built with 'tween deck accommodation for Far East pilgrims to Jeddah. They had a wood clad main deck, port holes and extra ventilators in addition to sanitary and kitchen areas. The lifeboats of this class were all doubled one atop the other. When *Gunung Djati* (291) entered service the pilgrim capacity of the Mark A2 class was removed and the additional lifeboats were taken out. *Clytoneus* was owned by Ocean S.S.Co.

1971 Dec: Operated by Elder Dempster Lines, same name.

1972 June: Arrived Kaohsiung for scrapping.

232 CYCLOPS (III)/AUTOMEDON (III)

Sister to *Calchas* (225) except:
B 1948 Scott's S.B. & E. Co, Greenock. **T**: 7,632 g, 4,476 n.
D 463 ft (141.12 m).
E By builder.

1948 Dec: Delivered to Ocean S.S.Co.
1955 Sept: Outward bound for Kobe out of Liverpool came in collision with Henderson's *Prome* south-west of Holyhead. Put back into the Mersey for repairs and resailed ten days later.
1975 Modified radar fitted to the funnel top. Several ships with bridge top radar suffered from a wide area of blindness aft of the funnel. The first step was to equip new ships with a tall radar mast forward of the funnel. This was costly and so the older ships had it afixed to the funnel foretop.
1975 July: Renamed *Automedon* to release the name for the new vessel that had just been launched as *Cyclops* (313).
1975 Dec: Transferred to Elder Dempster Lines, same name but in their colours.
1977 Jan-Mar: Chartered to the Nigerian National Line.
1977 Aug: Broken up at Dalmuir by W. H. Arnott Young & Co.

233 AUTOLYCUS (III)

Details as *Calchas* (225) except:
B 1949 Vickers Armstrong Ltd, Newcastle. **T**: 7,635 g, 4,438 n.
E By Harland & Wolff, Glasgow.

1949 May: Delivered to China Mutual S.N.Co.
1974 Nov: Transferred to Elder Dempster Lines, same name.
1975 June: Laid up at Bromborough Dock, Birkenhead.
1975 Oct: Chartered to the Nigerian National Line.
1976 Sold to Gulf (Shipowners) Ltd, London; renamed *Gulf Trader*. Later registered as being owned by Gulf Shipping Lines, Liverpool. Chartered again to the Nigerian National Shipping Line whose funnel colours she bore.
1978 June: Arrived at Taiwan for breaking up.

234 ANTILOCHUS (II)

Sister of *Calchas* (225) except:
T: 7,635 g, 4,479 m.

1949 May: Built for Ocean S.S.Co.
1975 Transferred to Elder Dempster Lines; same name.
1977 Sold to Gulf (Shipowners) Ltd, London; renamed *Gulf Orient*.
1978 Sold for breaking up by Al Noor Steel Ltd.
May 9: Arrived at Gadani Beach.

235 AUTOMEDON (II)

Details as *Calchas* (225) except:
B Vickers Armstrong Ltd, Newcastle. **T**: 7,636 g, 4,439 n.
E By John G. Kincaid, Greenock.

1949 Aug: Delivered to Ocean S.S.Co.
1971 Dec: Collided in fog with the Greek *San George* in the River Scheldt. After a survey it was decided to dispose of her for scrap. Repaired on the Tyne to a state of sea-worthiness for her voyage to Taiwan.
1972 Mar: Broken up at Kaohsiung.

236 LAERTES (IV)/IDOMENEUS (III)

Details as *Calchas* (225) except:
B Vickers Armstrong Ltd, Newcastle. **T:** 7,664 g, 4,533 n.
D 487.3 ft (148.53 m).
E By John G. Kincaid & Co, Greenock.

1950 Oct: Completed as the final vessel of the Mark A2 type. Operated by N.S.M. 'Oceaan', Amsterdam.
1972 Aug: Transferred to Blue Funnel; renamed *Idomeneus.*
1975 Operated by Elder Dempster Lines; same name.
1976 June: Sold to Gulf Shipping Lines; renamed *Gulf Voyager.*
1978 May 8: Arrived Gadani Beach, Karachi, for breaking up by Al Noor Steel Ltd.

237 BELLEROPHON (III)

Sister of *Calchas* (225) except:
B 1950 Caledon S.B.& E. Co, Dundee. **T:** 7,707 g, 4,485 n.
E 7 cyl 2S.SA. By John G. Kincaid, Greenock.
H F: 47 ft (14.32 m); B: 186 ft (56.69 m); P: 40 ft (12.19 m).

1950 Oct: Delivered to Ocean S.S.Co. Designated Mark A3.
1957 Transferred to the Glen Line; renamed *Cardiganshire.*
1957 Reverted to Blue Funnel and *Bellerophon*, China Mutual S.N.Co.
1975 Transferred to Elder Dempster Lines; same name.
1976 Sold to Saudi-Europe Line Ltd. Became *Obhor.*
1978 Chartered for the making of a film. Temporarily called *Bell* for the period.
1978 Sept 23: Arrived at Gadani Beach, Karachi, for breaking up.

238 ASCANIUS (II)

Sister of *Calchas* (225) except:
B 1950. **T:** 7,692 g, 4,545 n.
E 7 cyl; 2S.SA.
H F: 48 ft (14.63 m); B: 187 ft (57 m); P: 40 ft (12.19 m).

1950 Nov: Built for Ocean S.S.Co.
1972 Transferred to Elder Dempster Lines: renamed *Akosombo.*
1973 Reverted to Blue Funnel and *Ascanius* but ownership changed to China Mutual S.N.Co.
1976 Sold to Saudi-Europe Line Ltd; renamed *Mastura.*
1978 Apr 4: Arrived at Blyth for demolition by Hughes Bolckow Ltd.

239 ATREUS (II)

Details as *Calchas* (225) except:
B 1951 Vickers Armstrong Ltd, Newcastle. **T:** 7,800 g, 4,545 n.
D 487.2 ft (148.5 m).
E 7 cyl, 2S.SA; by John G. Kincaid & Co, Greenock.
H F: 48 ft (14.63 ft).

1951 Nov: Delivered to China Mutual S.N.Co.
1977 Oct: Sold to Sherwood Shipping Co, Singapore. Renamed *United Valiant.* The same group purchased *Glaucus* (245).
1979 Feb 23: Broken up at Kaohsiung, Taiwan.

240 ALCINOUS (III)/POLYDORUS (III)

Sister to *Calchas* (225) except:
B 1952 Vickers Armstrong Ltd, Newcastle. **T:** 7,799 g, 4.538 n.
D 487.2 ft (148.5 m).
E 7 cyl 2S.SA. By John G. Kincaid & Co, Greenock.
H F: 48 ft (14.63 m); B: 190 ft (57.91 m); P: 41 ft (12.5 m).

1952 Apr: Completed for Ocean S.S.Co. It was originally intended to call this ship *Cadmus*.
1960 Aug: Transferred to N.S.M. 'Oceaan' as *Polydorus*.
1973 Nov: Reverted to Blue Funnel. Her radar was fitted to a mast during May. This lifted the vision clear of the funnel.
1976 Apr: Sold to S. H. Alatas & Co.; renamed *Johara*. Alatas & Co. were agents at Jeddah and the tactic was to avoid port delays at that port and to use the priority granted to domiciled ownership.
Nov: Reverted to her original status and name.
1977 Nov: Sold to Hesperus Navigation Corp, Monrovia; renamed *Matina*. Panamanian flag.
1978 Apr 23: Arrived Gadani Beach for scrapping.

241 LAOMEDON (II)

Details as *Calchas* (225) except:
B 1953 Vickers Armstrong Ltd, Newcastle. **T:** 7,684 g, 4,580 n.
D 487.2 ft (148.5 m).
E By Harland & Wolff, Belfast 7 cyl 2S.SA.
H F: 48 ft (14.6 m).

1953 Built for China Mutual S.N.Co.
1977 March: Sold to Regent Navigation Corp, Panama. Maldives Shipping as managers. Renamed *Aspasia*.
1978 Apr 20: Left Kuwait for Pakistan for demolition.
Nov: Broken up at Gadani Beach, Karachi.

242 EUMAEUS (IV)

Sister to *Calchas* (225) except:
B 1953 Caledon S.B. & E. Co, Dundee. **T:** 7,681 g, 4,566 n.
D 487.2 ft (148.5 m).
E 7 cyl 2S.SA. By Harland & Wolff, Belfast.
H F: 46 ft (14.6 m).

1953 Dec: Delivered to Ocean S.S.Co. The first ship of a class of four Mark A4. This class had a poop hatch in place of the poop locker. To accommodate the hatch the derrick posts were located further forward.
1962 Transferred to N.S.M. 'Oceaan', Amsterdam.
1978 Jan 31: Arrived at Kaohsiung for breaking up by Hai Kwang.

243 ADRASTUS (II)

Details as *Calchas* (225) except:
B 1953 Vickers Armstrong Ltd, Newcastle. **T:** 7,859 g, 4,573 n.
D 487.2 ft (148.5 m).
E 7 cyl 2S.SA. By Harland & Wolff, Belfast.
H F: 48 ft (14.63 m).

1953 Dec: Completed for Ocean S.S.Co. The lead ship of the four class Mark A4.

1961 Jan: Transferred to N.S.M. 'Oceaan'; same name.

1975 Nov: Reverted to Blue Funnel.

1978 Feb: Acquired by Rhodeswell Shipping Co. S.A., Limassol, Cyprus. Renamed *Anassa.*

1981 Sept: Sold for breaking up at Gadani Beach, Karachi. She was the last survivor of the 21 *Anchises* class.

244 **ELPENOR** (II)

Sister to *Calchas* (225) except:
B 1954. **T:** 7,757 g, 4,509 n.
E 7 cyl, 2S.SA.
H F: 48 ft (14.6 m).

1954 Delivered to China Mutual S.N.Co.

1978 June: Sold to Cremorne Bay Shipping Co, Liberia. Renamed *United Concord.* Delivered to Flushing. Panama flag.

1979 Broken up at Taiwan.

245 **LYCAON** (II)/**GLAUCUS** (VI)

Sister to *Calchas* (225) except:
B 1954 Vickers Armstrong Ltd, Newcastle. **T:** 7,859 g, 4,567 n.
E 7 cyl 2S.SA. By John G. Kincaid, Greenock.
H F: 48 ft (14.63 m).

1954 June: Completed for the China Mutual S.N.Co.

1960 Transferred to N.S.M. 'Oceaan'; same name.

1975 Jan: Reverted to the British flag but under Elder Dempster Line's ownership.

1977 Dec: Renamed *Glaucus* in order to release the name *Lycaon* for re-use. See *Lycaon* (317).

1977 Mar: Sold to Marlborough Maritime Inc, Monrovia (Gulf Group) but flew the Singapore flag. Renamed *United Vanguard.*

1979 May 12: En-route Sharjah—Bassein suffered engine failure and a ruptured sea water cooling pipe. The vessel was abandoned. 31 crew were saved but one was lost.

May 14: *United Vanguard* sank.

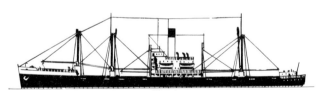

POLYDORUS (II)/TALTHYBIUS (III), POLYPHEMUS (IV)/TANTALUS (IV), MARON (II)/RHESUS (II), MENTOR (II), MEMNON (V)/GLAUCUS (IV) and MYRMIDON (IV)

246 **POLYDORUS** (II)/**TALTHYBIUS** (III)

B 1945 Permanente Metals Corp. (Shipyard No. 1) Richmond, California.
T: 7,671 g, 4,567 n, 10,750 dwt.
D 455.2 ft (138.74 m) o.a., 439.1 ft (133.83 m) bp, × 62.1 ft (18.92 m) × 34.5 ft (10.51 m). Dft: 28.6 ft (8.72 m).
E Sgl scr 2 dbl reduction geared turbines by Westinghouse Elect. & Manuf., Pittsburgh. 15 kts.

H S 2 dks; F: 87 ft (26.51 m). 7 watertight bulkheads, 5 holds. 6 deep tanks were fitted abaft the shaft tunnel for extra fuel oil or water ballast.

P As designed these vessels had accommodation for 28 anti-aircraft gunners. Crew: 62.

1944 Dec: Completed as *Salina Victory,* United States Maritime Commission. Type VC2-S-AP2 type.

1946 Purchased by Blue Funnel. Operated by N.S.M. 'Oceaan'. Renamed *Polydorus.*

1960 Transferred to Ocean S.S.Co. Renamed *Talthybius.*

1971 In Elder Dempster colours on the West African service; then laid up at Bromborough Dock, Birkenhead.

1971 Dec: Scrapped by Nan Feng Co, Taipei, Taiwan.

247 **POLYPHEMUS** (IV)/**TANTALUS** (IV)

Details as *Polydorus* (246) except:
T: 7,674 g, 4,562 n.

1945 June: Built as *MacMurray Victory* for U.S.M.C.

1946 Acquired by Alfred Holt & Co. Operated by N.S.M. 'Oceaan' as *Polyphemus.*

1960 Transferred to Ocean S.S.Co. Renamed *Tantalus.*

1969 Mar: Laid up in the River Fal. Sold Greek for scrap. Named *Pelops* for the delivery voyage with cargo to Taiwan. Broken up at Kaohsiung.

248 **MARON** (II)/**RHESUS** (II)

Details as *Polydorus* (246) except:
B Shipyard No. 2. **T**: 7,713 g, 4,546 n.
D 441.3 ft (134.51 m).

1945 Aug: Built as *Berywn Victory.* For U.S.M.C.

1947 Acquired by China Mutual S.N.Co. Renamed *Maron.*

1957 Renamed *Rhesus.* Same owners.

1960 Nov: Laid up.

1962 Sold and renamed *Pacific Telstar,* Overseas Maritime Company Inc. Monrovia.

1974 Feb 1: Arrived Kaohsiung for breaking up by China Steel Corp.

249 **MENTOR** (II)

Sister of *Polydorus* (246) except:
T: 7,642 g, 4,547 n.
D 441.5 ft (134.56 m).

1945 Aug: Constructed as *Carthage Victory* for U.S.M.C.

1947 Renamed *Mentor* when acquired by Ocean S.S.Co.

1967 Sept 20: Sold for £80,000 to Seawave Nav. Corp., Greece. Renamed *Vita,* Cullum Cia. Nav. S.A. Panama.

1969 Became *Viva,* same owners.

1971 Renamed *Syra,* same owners.

1971 Sept: Broken up at Split.

250 **MEMNON** (V)/**GLAUCUS** (V)

Sister of *Polydorus* (246) except:
T: 7,711 g, 4,567 n.
D 441.3 ft (134.51 m).

1945 June: Delivered as *Phillips Victory* for U.S.M.C.

1946 Acquired by Ocean S.S.Co. Renamed *Memnon*.
1957 Became *Glaucus*.
1962 Sold and renamed *Persian Ferdowsi*. Owned by Iranian Lloyd Co. Ltd, Khorramsshar.
1965 Became *Kashan*. Same owner but now shown as owned by Iranian Shipping Lines.
1966 Sold to become *Eleni K*. Paul J. Frangoulis & A & I Cliafas, Piraeus.
Oct: Arrested by the Iranian authorities for alleged debts when still *Kashan*. Detained at Bandar Shapur for 38 days and then released as being clear of debt. Out at sea the ship stopped for boiler repairs only to be re-arrested because, it was said, that her Greek crew had slipped cables and sailed without permission in the night. The arresting party of the Iran navy consisted of a destroyer, 5 frigates, 3 launches and a helicopter. *Eleni K*, although stationary, was fired upon.
1968 Sold. Renamed *Pirouzi,* still under Iranian colours. Did not sail.
1969 May: Left for breaking up at Hong Kong, as a wreck damaged vessel, in tow of the Japanese tug *Amaryllis*.
June: Arrived Hong Kong.

251 MYRMIDON (IV)

Details as *Polydorus* (246) except:
T: 7,715 g, 4,569 n.
H F: 89 ft (27.12 m).

1945 Aug: Delivered as *Ripon Victory* to U.S.M.C.
1947 Acquired by China Mutual S.N.Co. Renamed *Myrmidon*. It had originally been intended that Ocean S.S.Co, would be the owners.
1971 Sept: Broken up at Kaohsiung, Taiwan, by Tien Cheng Steel Manufacturing Co, Taipei.

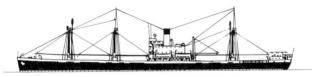

EUMAEUS (III)/EURYADES (III), EURYMEDON (III), EURYPLUS (II), TROILUS (IV), TYDEUS (II), TALTHYBIUS (II), TANTALUS (III) and TITAN (III)

252 EUMAEUS (III)/EURYADES (III)
B 1943 Bethlehem Fairfield Shipyard, Baltimore, Maryland. **T**: 7,308 g, 4,379 n.
D 441.6 ft (134.6 m) o.a., 423.5 ft (129.08 m) × 57 ft (17.37 m) × 34.8 ft (10.61 m).
E Sgl scr tpl exp, 3 cyl, 2,500 IHP, 11 kts. By General Mach'y Corp. Hamilton, Ontario.
H S 2 dks; C: 562,608 cu ft (171,482.9 cu m) grain. 499,573 cu ft (152,269.8 cu m) bale. F: 1,819 tons oil at 30 tons per day.
P 45 as designed but accommodation later increased by 36 anti-aircraft gunners. Total 81.

1943 Launched as *Simon B. Elliott* for U.S.M.C. Completed as *Samnesse*, Ministry of War Transport. Managed by Alfred Holt.
1947 Acquired by Holts. Renamed *Eumaeus*. Owned by China Mutual S.N.Co.
1952 Mar: Transferred to Glen Line, initially as *Eumaeus* then renamed *Glenshiel*.
1957 Reverted to Blue Funnel. Became *Euryades*; China Mutual S.N.Co.
1961 Sold. Renamed *Marine Bounty* owned by Bounty Shipping Co, Hong Kong.
1966 Feb 25: Went aground at Hasieshan, China. Refloated but driven ashore again. Abandoned and then broke in two. The ship was carrying a cargo of coal from Chingwantao to Singapore.

253 **EURYMEDON** (III)

Details as *Eumaeus* (252) except:
T: 7,314 g, 4,405 n.
E By Worthington Pump & Machinery Co, Harrison, New Jersey.

1943 Launched as *Matthew Brush* for U.S.M.C. Completed as *Samoa*, Ministry of War Transport, bare boat charter. Managed by Alfred Holt & Co.
1947 Acquired, renamed *Eurymedon* for China Mutual S.N.Co.
1952 Apr: Transferred to Glen Line. Became *Glenlogan*.
1957 Reverted to Blue Funnel and *Eurymedon*.
1958 Sold to Etolika Cia. Nav. S.A., Piraeus. Renamed *Angelos*. Flew the Costa Rican flag.
1964 Became *Mimosa*, Michael A. Araktingi, Lebanon.
1966 Sold and renamed *Alplata*, Alplata Shipping Corp, Monrovia.
1967 Changed hands again to become *Anka,* Maria de Lourdes Shipping Co, Cyprus.
1972 Broken up.

254 **EURYPYLUS** (II)

Details as *Eumaeus* (252) except:

T: 7,292 g, 4,380 n.
1943 Launched as *Augustine Herman* for War Shipping Administration branch of the U.S.M.C. Renamed *Samsette* upon transfer to British ownership, bare boat charter. Managed by Alfred Holt for Ministry of War Transport.
1947 Purchased by Holts. Renamed *Eurypylus*; China Mutual S.N.Co.
1950 Transferred to Glen Line; renamed *Pembrokeshire*.
1957 Reverted to Blue Funnel and *Eurypylus*.
1960 Because *Kota Bahru*, Federal Shipping Company, Hong Kong.
1966 Renamed *Cresta*, Cresta Shipping Co, Inc. Panama.
1968 Feb: Broken up at Kaohsiung, Taiwan.

255 **TROILUS** (IV)

Details as *Eumaeus* (252) except:
T: 7,287 g, 4,375 n.
D 441.7 ft (134.3 m) o.a., 423.9 ft (129.2 m).

1943 Launched as *Martha C. Thomas*, War Shipping Administration. Transferred to British bare boat management under 'Lend Lease' and renamed *Samharle*, Ministry of War Transport. Alfred Holt & Co. as managers.
1947 Acquired for Ocean S.S.Co, renamed *Troilus*.
1958 Sold to Panama. Became *Green River*, Cia. de Nav. San Agustin S.A. but registered in Liberia for crewing purposes.
1963 Broken up at Osaka.

256 **TYDEUS** (II)

Details as *Eumaeus* (252) except:
B 1944. T: 7,234 g, 4,345 n.
D as *Troilus*.

1944 Completed as *Samjack*, M.O.W.T. Alfred Holt as managers.
1947 Acquired by Blue Funnel. Renamed *Tydeus*.
1950 Transferred to Glen Line; became *Glenbeg*.
1958 Sold to Panama. Became *Roan*, Forman Shipping & Trading Inc.
1960 Renamed *Jucar*, West African Carriers Corp., Monrovia.
1967 Sept: Broken up at Mihara, Japan.

257 **TALTHYBIUS** (II)

Details as *Eumaeus* (252) except:
B 1943. **T:** 7,291 g, 4,380 n.
D As *Troilus.*
E By Elliott Machy. Corp, Baltimore, Maryland.

1943 Launched as *Peter Cooper,* W.S.A. Transferred to Great Britain. Renamed *Samarkand.* Alfred Holt as managers.
1947 Acquired and renamed *Talthybius,* owned by Ocean S.S.Co.
1954 Transferred to Glen Line. Became *Gleniffer.*
1958 Sold to Liberian owners. Named *Dove,* Colombine Shipping Co.
1965 Dec: Became *Patraic Sky,* Patriarch Steamship Co, Monrovia.
1971 Broken up at Split, Yugoslavia.

258 **TANTALUS** (III)

Details as *Eumaeus* (252) except:
T: 7,297 g, 4,385 n.
D As *Troilus.*

1943 Launched as *John T. Clark,* W.S.A. To Britain. Renamed *Samcleve* before completion. Assigned to Alfred Holt & Co. as managers.
1947 Became *Tantalus,* owned by Ocean S.S.Co.
1958 Renamed *Urbania,* Ditta Luigi Pittaluga Vapori, Genoa.
1965 Sold to Henry Coe and Clerici S.P.A. Genoa. Renamed *Cocler.*
1975 Jan: Sold to Italsider S.p.A.; allocated to Vado Scali e Bacini, Vado, for demolition.

259 **TITAN** (III)

Details as *Eumaeus* (252) except:
T: 7,297 g, 4,385 n.
D As *Troilus.*

1943 Launched as *James Carroll,* W.S.A. Completed as *Samgara* for M.O.W.T. Managed by Alfred Holt & Co.
1947 Purchased and renamed *Titan,* Ocean S.S.Co.
1950 Transferred to Glen Line. Became *Flintshire.*
1958 Reverted to *Titan,* Ocean S.S.Co.
1962 Sold to Tidewater Commercial Co. Inc, Monrovia. Renamed *Titanus.*
1969 Dec: Broken up at Mihara, Japan.

DANAE

260 **DANAE**

B 1945 W. Pickersgill & Son Ltd, Sunderland. **T:** 54 g.
D 71 ft (21.64 m) o.a., 65 ft (19.81 m) bp × 17 ft (5.18 m) × 7.4 ft (2.25 m). Dft: 8 ft (2.44 m).
E Sgl scr 2 cyl comp. Stm P: 140 lb. 9 kts. By J. Dickinson & Sons, Sunderland.
H S 1 dk.

1945 Built as harbour tug *TID 155.*
1947 Acquired by Holts for harbour duties at Hong Kong. Renamed *Danae.*
1961 Sold to Sarawak Co. (1959) Ltd, Kuching; renamed *Hailey.* Based at Sibu.
1985 Deleted.

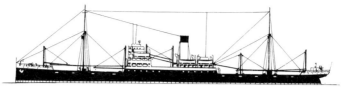

DARDANUS (IV), DEUCALION (IV), DOLIUS (II) and DYMAS (I)

261 DARDANUS (IV)

B 1920 Harland & Wolff, Glasgow. **T:** 9,503 g, 5,802 n, 14,000 dwt.
D 485.6 ft (148.01 m) × 62.3 ft (18.99 m) × 35.8 ft (10.91 m). Dft 29.8 ft (9.08 m) 502 ft (153 m) o.a.
E Tw scr oil, 4S.SA 2 × 8 cyl, 5,250 BHP; 12½ kts at 115 rpm. Burmeister & Wain Type by builder.
H S 2 dks and awning dk; F: 58 ft (17.98 m); B: 153 ft (46.63 m); P: 40 ft (12.19 m). C: 511,000 cu ft (14,470 cu m) bulk; Fuel: 1,300 tons oil on 19½ per day.
P 12 Crew: 75.

1920 Built as *Glenapp*, Glen Line for their Far East service which terminated at Vladivostok. When built she was the largest motorship in the world and with her nine sisters was also the most important group of oil engined ships yet built. The crew accommodation was of a very high standard. One draw back to these pioneers was the comparatively slow service speed of the day. At the time of their introduction to service Glen was part of the Royal Mail S. P. conglomerate. Thus three sisters went to Royal Mail and two to Holland American Line as a part of the North Pacific joint service.
1929 Superchargers were fitted to all four.
1949 Feb: Transferred to Ocean S.S.Co; renamed *Dardanus*. Employed on Far East to Australia service. Prior to this her post war route had been U.K.—North Pacific west coast ports.
1956 Laid up at Holy Loch, Scotland.
1957 July 19: Arrived at Inverkeithing for breaking up by Thos. W. Ward.

262 DEUCALION (IV)

Details as *Dardanus* (261) except:
T: 9,513 g, 5,859 n.

1920 Completed for the Glen Line as *Glenogle*.
1949 Feb: Transferred to Ocean S.S.Co; renamed *Deucalion*.
1956 Jan: Arrived Briton Ferry for demolition.

263 DOLIUS (II)

Details as *Dardanus* (261) except:
T: 9,802 g, 5,938 n.

1920 Sept: Launched.
1922 Completed as *Glengarry* for the Glen Line.
1922 Nov: Grounded in the Whangpo River; refloated after the discharge of her cargo into lighters.
1925 Collided at Leith with the tug *Heathercock*.
1939 March: Renamed *Glenstrae* in order to make the name available for a new *Glengarry*.
1940 Sept: Damaged by air attack in the Royal Docks, London.
1949 Feb: Transferred to the Ocean S.S.Co; renamed *Dolius*.
1952 July: While leaving Gladstone Dock, Liverpool, for Glasgow where the balance of the inbound cargo was to be discharged *Dolius* hit the dock wall and sustained hull plate damage. Further examination revealed that the starboard thrust block casing was cracked. The ship, because of her age was sold for demolition.
1952 Aug 20: Arrived at Briton Ferry for demolition by Thos. W. Ward.

264 DYMAS (I)

Details as *Dardanus* (261) except:
B 1922. **T**: 9,461 g, 5,789 n.

1922 Apr: Built as *Glenbeg* for the Glen Line.
1949 Transferred to Ocean S.S.Co, became *Dymas*.
1954 Apr 8: Arrived at Dalmuir for breaking up by W. H. Arnott Young & Co.

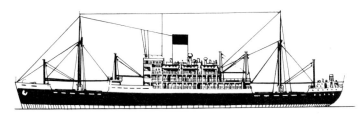

PELEUS (II), PYRRHUS (III), PATROCLUS (IV)/PHILOCTETES (II)
and PERSEUS (III)

265 PELEUS (II)

B 1949 Cammell Laird & Co, Birkenhead. **T**: 10,093 g, 5,888 n, 11,000 dwt.
D 515.5 ft (157.12 m) o.a., 489.4 ft (149.17 m) bp × 68.3 ft (20.82 m) × 35.2 ft (10.73 m).
E Sgl scr, 3 steam Parsons turbines, dbl reduction geared. 14,000 NHP 15,000 SHP, 18½
kts. Stm P: 570 lb at 850°F. 2 Foster-Wheeler water tube boilers. By builder.
H S 2 dks; F: 59 ft (17.98 m); B: 235 ft (71.63 m); P: 55 ft (16.76 m); 6 holds 26 derricks.
P 35.

1948 Sept 3: Launched.
1949 Delivered to Ocean S.S.Co.
1972 Feb 18: Arrived Taiwan for demolition.

266 PYRRHUS (III)

Details as *Peleus* (265) except:
T: 5,898 n.
H F: 53 ft (16.15 m); B: 219 ft (66.75 m); P: 24 ft (7.31 m).

1949 July: Delivered to Ocean S.S.Co.
1964 Nov 12: Afire at Huskisson Dock, Liverpool. Several hours to extinguish.
1972 Sept 19: Arrived Taiwan for scrapping.

267 PATROCLUS (IV)/PHILOCTETES (II)

Details as *Peleus* (265) except:
B 1950 Vickers Armstrong & Co, Newcastle. **T**: 10,109 g, 5,923 n.
E By Vickers Armstrong, Barrow. Stm P: 540 lb.

1950 Jan 22: Completed for the China Mutual S.N.Co.
Feb 11: Maiden voyage.
1962 Nov 28: Went aground Tokyo Bay
1967 Feb: Caught fire at Glasgow; safely extinguished.
1973 Transferred to Glen Line; renamed *Glenalmond*.
1973 Reverted to China Mutual S.N.Co. Renamed *Philoctetes*.
1973 Feb 13: Arrived Taiwan for breaking up by Chai Tai Steel Enterprises.

268 PERSEUS (III)

Details as *Peleus* (265) except:
B 1950 Vickers Armstrong & Co, Newcastle. **T:** 10,109 g, 5,923 n.
E By Vickers Armstrong, Barrow.
H F: 54 ft (16.4 m); B: 221 ft (67.36 m); P: 27 ft (8.23 m).

1949 Oct 22: Launched.
1950 Apr 4: Delivered to China Mutual S.N.Co.
Apr 21: Maiden voyage.
1973 Jan 5: Arrived Kaohsiung for demolition.

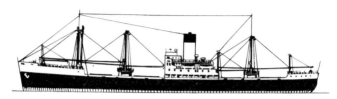

*ULYSSES (V), TEIRESIAS (II)/TELEMACHUS (V) and
TEUCER (IV)/TELAMON (III)*

269 ULYSSES (V)

B 1949 Joseph L. Thompson & Sons, Sunderland. **T:** 8,976 g, 5,303 n.
D 473.8 ft (144.41 m) o.a., 453 ft (138.02 m) bp × 61.6 ft (18.77 m) × 38 ft (11.58 m).
E Sgl scr 3 stm turbs dbl reduction geared. Stm P: 490 lb.
H S 2 dks + 3rd forward; F: 102 ft (31.1 m); P: 40 ft (12.19 m).

1949 Jan: Launched as *Silverholly*, S. & J. Thompson's Silver Line.
July: Completed as *Ulysses*, China Mutual S.N.Co.
Aug: Maiden voyage Birkenhead—Far East. At the end of the trip further alterations were made.
1971 Sold to N. D. Papalios, Aegis Group; renamed *Aegis Saga*. Cypriot flag. Apsyrtos Shipping Co. as owners.
1974 Feb 18: Left Singapore for scrapping in China.

270 TEIRESIAS (II)/TELEMACHUS (V)

Details as *Ulysses* (269) except:
B 1950. **T:** 8,924 g, 5,272 n.
H P: 48 ft (14.63 m).

1950 Launched as *Silverelm*, S. & J. Thompson's Silver Line. Completed as *Teiresias* for N.S.M. 'Oceaan', Amsterdam.
1960 Transferred to British flag; renamed *Telemachus*. Owned by Ocean S.S.Co.
1971 Sold to the Aegis Group, N. D. Papalios; became *Aegis Courage*. Cypriot flag. Anax Shipping Co. as owners.
1973 Jan 25: Sailed from Yawata, Kyushu Japan, for breaking up in China.

271 TEUCER (IV)/TELAMON (III)

Details as *Ulysses* (269) except:
B 1950. **T:** 8,922 g, 5,273 n.
H P: 48 ft (14.63 m).

1950 Launched as *Silverlaurel* for S. & J. Thompson's Silver Line. Completed as *Teucer* for N.S.M. 'Oceaan'.
1960 Transferred to the British flag; renamed *Telamon*. Owned by the China Mutual S.N.Co.
1971 Sold to the Aegis Group, N. D. Papalios; became *Aegis Epic*. Cypriot flag. Owned by the Apsyrtos Shipping Co.
1973 Dec: Broken up.

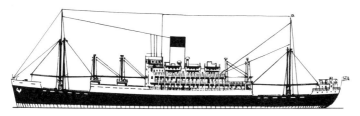

HELENUS (II), JASON (IV), HECTOR (V), IXION (III)

272 HELENUS (II)

B 1949 Harland & Wolff, Belfast. **T:** 10,125 g, 5,922 n.
D 522.6 ft (159.29 m) o.a., 496.3 ft (151.27 m) bp × 69.3 ft (21.12 m) × 34.7 ft (10.58 m). Dft 30.11 ft (9.18 m).
E Sgl scr, 3 dbl reduct. geared turbs. 14,000 SHP 106 rpm. 18½ kts. 2 oil fired Foster-Wheeler blrs. Stm P: 525 lb, 850°F.
H S 2 dks; F: 51 ft (15.54 m); B: 265 ft (80.77 m); P: 26 ft (7.92 m) 7 holds 25 derricks.
P 29/31.

1949 Oct: Delivered to the Ocean S.S.Co. This class had the then greatest shaft horse power of any sgl scr vessel. Australian service.
Nov 9: During loading for her maiden voyage at Gladstone Dock, Liverpool, a fire broke out ashore. *Helenus* and *Dardanus* (261) were loading at No. 2 branch while *Pyrrhus* (266) and *Calchas* (225) were discharging in No. 1 Branch. The last two ships were towed to safer berths. *Helenus* (and *Dardanus*) had to sail partly loaded. She left on Nov 12.
1978 July 11: Arrived Kaohsiung for breaking up.

273 JASON (IV)

Details as *Helenus* (272) except:
B 1950 Swan, Hunter & Wigham Richardson Ltd, Wallsend. **T:** 10,160 g, 5,936 n.
E Wallsend Slipway, Wallsend.
H F: 47 ft (14.32 m).

1950 Feb 19: Maiden voyage for the Australian service of China Mutual S.N.Co.
1972 May 23: Broken up at Kaohsiung.

274 HECTOR (V)

Details as *Helenus* (272) except:
B 1950. **T:** 10,125 g, 5,992 n.
H F: 51 ft (15.54 m).

1949 July: Launched by Mr. Clement Atlee.
1950 Mar: Completed for the Australian service of the Ocean S.S.Co.
Apr 25: Maiden voyage.
1972 July 5: Arrived Kaohsiung for demolition.

275 **IXION** (III)

Details as *Helenus* (272) except:
B 1951. **T**: 5,919 n.

1951 Jan: Completed for Ocean S.S.Co. Australian service.
1972 March: Sold to Salvamiento y Demolici S.A. at Villaneuva y Geltru, Spain for breaking up.

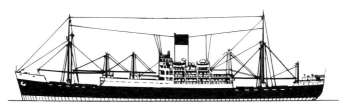

NESTOR (IV)/ORESTES (V), NELEUS (II) and THESEUS (II)

276 **NESTOR** (IV)/**ORESTES** (V)

B 1952 Caledon S.B. & E. Co, Dundee. **T**: 7,802 g, 4,368 n, 9,500 dwt.
D 489.9ft (149.32 m) o.a., 464.9 ft (141.7 m) bp, × 64.3 ft (19.6 m) × 31.1 ft (9.48 m) Dft: 28.6 ft (8.71 m).
E Sgl scr, 3 dbl reduct geared turbs by Metropolitan Vickers, Manchester. Stm P: 680 lb. 2 Foster-Wheeler blrs 600 lb 950°F.
H S 2 dks + 3rd forward; F: 48 ft (14.6 m); B: 202 ft (61.57 m); P: 38 ft (11.58 m).

1952 Oct: Delivered to Ocean S.S.Co. for Australian service.
1968 Transferred to the Glen Line; renamed *Glenaffric.*
1970 Reverted to Blue Funnel; became *Orestes.*
1971 Sold to the Aegis Group, N. D. Papalios. Renamed *Aegis Dignity.* Owned by Adelais Maritime Co, Cyprus. Later Kimon Cia Nav S.A. Piraeus.
1973 Nov 21: Sold to Chinese shipbreakers; left Singapore for Whampoa.

277 **NELEUS** (II)

Details as *Nestor* (275) except:
B 1953.

1953 Feb: Completed for China Mutual S.N.Co.
Mar 21: Maiden voyage.
1971 Sept 14: Sold to Akamas Shipping Co, Cyprus. Renamed *Aegis Fable.*
1972 Became *Aegis Trust,* Alicarnassos Shipping Co, Cyprus.
1974 Mar 17: Left Niigata, Japan for demolition at Shanghai.

278 **THESEUS** (II)

Details as *Nestor* (275) except:
B 1955. **T**: 7,804 g, 4,242 n.
D 490 ft (149.35 m) o.a.

1955 Built for Ocean S.S.Co.
1971 June 21: Sold to the Aegis Group, N. D. Papalios; renamed *Aegis Myth.* Owned by the Alkividis Shipping S.A., Panama. Registered at Famagusta, Cypriot flag.
1972 Renamed *Aegis Care*, owned by Syracusae Maritime Co; same group.
1973 Nov 4: Left Singapore for Shanghai to be broken up.

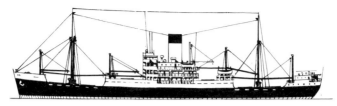

DEMODOCUS (II), DIOMED (V), DOLIUS (III), ANTENOR (IV)/DYMAS (II), ACHILLES (V)/DARDANUS (V) and AJAX (IV)/DEUCALION (V)

279 **DEMODOCUS** (II)

B 1955 Vickers Armstrong, Walker Naval Yard, Newcastle. **T:** 7,968 g, 4,558 n.
D 491.5 ft (149.81 m) o.a., 452.9 ft (138.04 m) bp × 62.4 ft (19.02 m) × 35.3 ft (10.76 m).
Dft: 28.5 ft (8.69 m).
E Sgl scr, oil 2S.SA 6 cyl 8,000 BHP; 15 kts. By Harland & Wolff, Belfast.
H S 2 dks; F: 49 ft (14.93 m); B: 192 ft (58.52 m); P: 40 ft (12.19 m).
P 12.

1955 Aug: Built for the Ocean S.S.Co. The first of a class of three ships designated Mark A5.
1970 June: Transferred to the Glen Line; renamed *Glenroy.*
1972 Apr: Reverted to Blue Funnel as *Demodocus.*
1973 Apr: Sold to Nan Yang Shipping Co, Macao; renamed *Hungsia.* Operated by Dawn Maritime Corp, Panama. This was, in effect, Chinese controlled.
1979 Became *Hong Qi 137,* Bureau of Maritime Transport Administration, China, Canton.
1985 Still in Lloyds Register.

280 **DIOMED** (V)

Details as *Demodocus* (279) except:
B 1956 Caledon S.B. & E. Co, Dundee. **T:** 7,980 g, 4,267 n.
E By J. G. Kincaid & Co, Greenock.
H B: 193 ft (58.83 m); P: 41 ft (12.5 m).

1956 Sept: Delivered to the China Mutual S.N.Co. the 34th ship by Caledon for Alfred Holts. Equipped as a cadet training ship.
1970 June: Transferred to the Glen Line; renamed *Glenbeg.*
Oct: Caught fire; extinguished in five hours.
1972 May: Reverted to China Mutual S.N.Co. and *Diomed.*
1973 Feb: sold to Nan Yang Shipping Co, Macao; became *Kaising.* Registered at Mogadishu, Somali flag. Operated by Golden City Maritime Corp. S.A. a member of the Ocean Tramping Co. of Panama.
1983 Broken up at Kaohsiung, Taiwan.

281 **DOLIUS** (III)

Details as *Demodocus* (279) except:
B 1956 Harland & Wolff, Belfast. **T:** 7,960 g, 4,262 n.

1956 Jan: Built for Ocean S.S.Co.
1970 Nov: Transferred to Glen Line. Renamed *Glenfruin.*
1972 Apr: Reverted to Holts and *Dolius,* Ocean S.S.Co.
1972 Nov: Sold to Nan Yang Shipping Co, Macao; renamed *Hungmien.* Somali flag as was *Diomed* (280).
1977 Sold to the Bureau of Maritime Transportation, China; renamed *Hong Qi 119.*
1985 Renamed *Zhan Dou 51*; same owners. Based Guanzhou. Still in service.

282 ANTENOR (IV)/DYMAS (II)

Details as *Demodocus* (279) except:
B 1957. **T**: 7,965 g, 4,276 n. **E** By J. G. Kincaid, Greenock. **H** F: 47 ft (14.33 m); B: 201 ft (61.26 m); P: 40 ft (12.19 m).
1956 Oct 4: Launched.
1957 July: Completed for the Ocean S.S.Co. The first of a class of three ships designated Mark A6.
1970 Nov: Transferred to the Glen Line; renamed *Glenlochy.*
1972 June: Reverted to Blue Funnel; became *Dymas.*
1973 Apr: Sold to Nan Yang Shipping Co, Macao; renamed *Kaiyun.*
1976 Sold to Highseas Nav. Corp. S.A., Panama. Same name.
1982 Broken up.

283 ACHILLES (V)/DARDANUS (V)

Sister to *Demodocus* (279) except:
B 1957. **T**: 7,969 g, 4,287 n.
E By J. G. Kincaid, Greenock.
H As *Antenor.*

1957 Oct: Delivered to Ocean S.S.Co.
1972 May: Renamed *Dardanus.*
1973 Apr: Became *Kiago*, Nan Yang Shipping Co, Macao, Somali flag.
1977 Operated by the Highseas Navigation Corp. S.A. Panama.
1982 June 5: Arrived at Calcutta for demolition.

284 AJAX (IV)/DEUCALION (V)

Details as *Demodocus* (279) except:
B 1958. **T**: 7,969 g, 4,268 n.
E By J. G. Kincaid, Greenock.
H As *Antenor.*

1958 Completed for China Mutual S.N.Co.
1972 May: Renamed *Deucalion.*
1973 Feb: Sold to Brilliance S.S.Co, became *Kailock.* Owned by Nan Yang Shipping Co, Macao.
1982 Aug: Arrived at Taiwan for scrapping.

MENELAUS (IV), MENESTHEUS (II), MACHAON (III), MEMNON (VI)/STENTOR (V), MELAMPUS (II) and MARON (III)/RHEXENOR (III)

285 MENELAUS (IV)

B 1957 Caledon S.B. & E. Co, Dundee. **T**: 8,538 g, 4,698 n.
D 494.8 ft (150.81 m) o.a., 455.4 ft (138.81 m) bp × 65.4 ft (19.93 m) × 36.1 ft (11 m). Dft 28.10 ft (8.81 m).
E Sgl scr, oil 2S.SA; 6 cyl, 8,500 BHP; 16½ kts. By Harland & Wolff, Belfast.

H S 2 dks; F: 48 ft (14.63 m); B: 184 ft (56.08 m); P: 34 ft (10.36 m). C: 566,083 cu ft (16,029.8 cu m).

1957 Sept: Built for Ocean S.S.Co. Sept 29: trials.
1972 Tranferred to Elder Dempster. Renamed *Mano,* operated by the British & Burmese S.N.Co.
1977 Switched to Elder Dempster Lines; renamed *Oti* to match in with others of the 'O' class. Elder Dempster now operated all of the Blue Funnel 'M' class, with the exception of *Melampus* (289), with names commencing with the letter 'O'.
1978 Sold to Thenamaris Maritime Inc, Pireaus. Operated as *Elstar* by Leon Rivera Lines, Cyprus.
1979 Feb 27: Arrived in South Korea for scrapping.

286 **MENESTHEUS** (II)

Sister to *Menelaus* (285) except:
B 1958. **T**: 8,510 g, 4,873 n.

1958 Feb: Completed for Ocean S.S.Co.
1977 Transferred to Elder Dempster. Became *Onitsha.*
1978 Sold to Thenamaris Maritime Inc, Piraeus. Renamed *Elisland*; operated by Palermo Shipping Co, Cyprus.
1979 Mar 19: Arrived at Kaohsiung for breaking up by Lung Fa Steel & Iron Co.
Apr 12: Demolition commenced.

287 **MACHAON** (III)

Sister of *Menelaus* (285) except:
B 1959. **T**: 8,529 g, 4,650 n.
E By J. G. Kincaid, Greenock.

1959 Apr: Completed for Ocean S.S.Co.
1975 Transferred to N.S.M. 'Oceaan'. Same name
1977 Transferred to Elder Dempster. Renamed *Obuasi.*
1978 Sold to Thenamaris Maritime Inc, Piraeus; renamed *Elsea.* Passed virtually immediately to Tartan Shipping Ltd, Monrovia, to become *Med Endeavour.*
1979 Broken up at Kaohsiung.

288 **MEMNON** (VI)/**STENTOR** (V)

Sister of *Menelaus* (285) except:
B 1959 Vickers Armstrong, Newcastle. **T**: 8,504 g, 4,873 n.
D 494.5 ft (150.72 m).
E By Harland & Wolff, Belfast.

1959 Completed for China Mutual S.N.Co.
1975 Renamed *Stentor.* See *Stentor* (223). Employed, therefore, on the South East Asia—Australia services.
1977 Transferred to Elder Dempster Lines; became *Owerri.*
1978 Sold to Thenamaris Maritime Inc, Piraeus. Operated by Henlow Shipping Corp. as *Europe.* Cost £172,000.
1982 July 3: Laid up at Stylis.
1987 Renamed *Primus* for last voyage.
1988 Feb 5: Arrived Alang, India, and scrapped.

289 **MELAMPUS** (II)

Sister to *Menelaus* (285) except:
B 1960 Vickers Armstrong, Newcastle. **T:** 8,509 g, 4,668 n.
D As *Memnon* (288). **E** By J. G. Kincaid & Co, Greenock.

1959 Dec 15: Launched.
1960 June: Completed for Ocean S.S.Co.
1967 June: Trapped in the Great Bitter Lake, Suez Canal when the Canal was blocked during the Suez crisis caused by the 'Six Days War' between Israel and her Arab neighbours. Fifteen vessels were trapped in the Bitter Lakes and one, *Observer*, (Marine Carriers Corp.) in Lake Timseh. The ships involved were:

Agapenor (Blue Funnel) *Munsterland* (Hamburg Amerika Line)
Melampus (Blue Funnel) *Nippon* (Svenska Ostasiatiska)
Nasr (United Arab Maritime) *Nordwind* (C. Macksprang)
African Glen (Farrell Lines) *Port Invercargill* (Port Line)
Boleslaw Bieurut (Polish Ocean) *Scottish Star* (Blue Star Line)
Djakarta (Polish Ocean) *Sindh* (Messageries Maritimes)
Killara (Transatlantic Red. A/B) *Vassil Levsky* (Nav Maritime Bulgare)
Lednice (Czechoslovak Danube Line)

1971 Jan: The trapped ships were abandoned to the underwriters who then sold them to the Grecomar Shipping Agency Ltd. although Farrell Line's vessel was later sunk by gunfire.
1975 May 20: After the clearing of the Canal *Melampus* left in tow for Trieste. After overhaul she passed to the Korissianev Shipping Co. S.A. and became *Annoula II*, D. N. Leventakis as Agent.
1982 Nov: Arrived and anchored at Gadani Beach, Karachi.
1983 Broken up.

290 **MARON** (III)/**RHEXENOR** (III)

Details as *Menelaus* (285) except:
B 1960. **T:** 8,529 g, 4,649 n. **E** By J. G. Kincaid & Co, Greenock.

1960 Feb 26: Launched. April: Delivered to Ocean S.S.Co.
1975 Became *Rhexenor* on the South East Asia-Australia service. ✗ FREEMANTLE / SINGAPOR PENANG / MALACCA / FREM
1977 Transferred to Elder Dempster Lines. Renamed *Opobo*.
1978 Sold to Thenamaris Marine Inc, Piraeus. Renamed *Elfortune*. Operated by Belton Shipping Corp, Monrovia; because *Europe II*.
1984 Sold to Trade Shipping Ltd, Malta. Same name. Laid up at Piraeus.
1987 Apr: At Aliaga for breaking up.

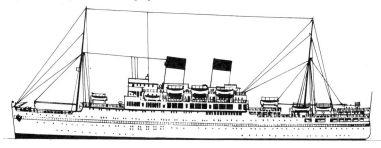

GUNUNG DJATI

291 **GUNUNG DJATI**

B 1936 Blohm & Voss, Hamburg. **T:** 16,662 g, 9,981 n.
D 578 ft (176.17 m) o.a., 550 ft (167.64 m) bp × 72 ft (21.95 m).

E Tw scr, 8 sgl reduct stm turbs; 14,200 SHP; 2 Benson blrs. Stm P: × 25.1 ft (5.14 m) 1,150 lb at 900°C. 18 kts. **H** S 3 dks. **P** 150 1st. 250 Tst. Crew: 250.

1936 July 16: Launched as *Pretoria* for the Deutsche Ost-Afrika Linie. Dec 19: Maiden voyage Hamburg—Southampton—South Africa.
1939 Accommodation ship for the German Navy at Hamburg.
1945 Taken over by the British for trooping. Renamed *Empire Doon*. Managed by Orient Line for Ministry of War Transport. Laid up due to boiler defects.
1949 Reboilered with Foster Wheeler water-tube equipment. All the auxilliary machinery was renewed by John I. Thornycroft at Southampton. Having been brought up to troopship standards she was renamed *Empire Orwell* in recognition of Orient Line management. She, thus, maintained the M.O.W.T's 'Empire', the Troopship's 'River' and Orient's 'O' nomenclature.
1958 Chartered to Pan—Islamic S.S.Co, Karachi, for pilgrimage work. At the end of the season laid up in the Kyles of Bute.
Nov: Sold to Alfred Holt & Co for the same service. It was intended to call the ship *Dardanus* but she entered service as *Gunung Djati*, being the name of the leading Javanese Haji and an Islamic missionary. Owned Ocean S.S.Co. Refitted for Holt's by Barclay Curle, Glasgow. Troop accomodation being replaced by Indonesian pilgrim type beds. Pass: 106 1st. 2,000 pilgrims.
1959 March 7: Left Liverpool for Djarkarta to join *Tyndareus* in the service.
1962 At the termination of three seasons the vessel was sold to the Government of Indonesia for the same service.
1965 Sold to P. T. Maskapai Pelajaran 'Sang Saka', Djakarta. Same name.
1968 Transferred to Pan-Islamic S.S.Co, Karachi, same name. Continued on the Mecca Pilgrimage service.
1973 Converted to diesel at Hong Kong.
1975 Refitted at Hong Kong.
1980 Returned to the Indonesian flag. Because a naval accommodation ship. Renamed *Kri Tanjung Pandan*, Pendant 971.
1984 Still in service but no longer seagoing.

CENTAUR (III)

292 **CENTAUR** (III)

B 1964 John Brown & Co. (Clydebank) Ltd. **T:** 8,262 g, 4,409 n.
D 480.9 ft (146.58 m) o.a. × 66.3 ft (20.2 m) × 38.9 ft (11.85 m) Dft 26.4 ft (8.04 m).
E Tw scr, oil 2 × 11 cyl 2S.SA turbocharged with poppet valves. 9,250 BHP each at 180 rpm. By Burmeister & Wain, Copenhagen.
H S 1 dk and shelter dk; F: 43 ft (13.11 m); P: 250 ft (76.2 m). Stabilisers. C: 4,500 sheep, 700 cattle. 47,130 cu ft (1,334.58 cu m) insulated. 10 derricks and 3 deck cranes (the company's first). Swimming pool lido. **P** 190 1st. Crew 98.

1963 June 20: Launched by Mrs D. Brand, wife of the Prime Minister of Western Australia.
1964 Completed at a cost of £2.5 million for Ocean S.S.Co.
Jan 20: Maiden voyage Liverpool—Sydney. Placed on the three-weekly service Fremantle—Western Australia ports—Singapore. Her first Australian sailing was, however, on charter to an Australian Chambers of Trade mission.

1967 Transferred to China Mutual S.N.Co. Ltd ownership.

1973 Nov: Transferred to the ownership of the Eastern Fleets Ltd section of the group, managed by the Straits S.S.Co. but in Blue Funnel colours.

1978 Owned by Blue Funnel (S.E.A) Pte Ltd, Singapore.

1981 Sept 15: Final departure out of Fremantle. The ship had been losing money for some time and her passengers had taken to the air while the specialised livestock carriers had taken away her cargo capabilities. Singapore interport cruises became her inadequate mainstay.

1982 Chartered to St. Helena Shipping Co, to replace their *St Helena* (ex *Northland Prince*) which had been requisitioned for Falkland Islands service during the war with the Argentine.

1983 Oct: The option to purchase *Centaur* was not exercised due to the need for a more modern ship. Their own *St Helena* returned from her Falklands service during the month.

1985 Sold to Shanghai Hai Xing Shipping Co., China. Renamed *Hai Long*.

1986 Transferred to Hai Xing Shipping Co., (Cosco) Shanghai. Renamed *Hai Da*. Still in service.

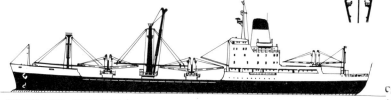

BECAME CHINA NA

PRIAM (V), *PEISANDER (II)*, *PROTESILAUS (II)*, *PROMETHEUS (IV)*, 'KWANGHO *PHRONTIS (II)*, *PATROCLUS (V)*, *PERSEUS (IV)* and *PHEMIUS (V)*

293 PRIAM (V)   BECAME CHINA NAV'S 'KWANGSI' UNTIL 1981

B 1966 Vickers Armstrong, Newcastle. (Walker-on-Tyne). **T:** 12,094 g, 6,471 n.
D 563.8 ft (171.85 m) o.a., 521 ft (158.8 m) bp × 77.9 ft (23.74 m) × 44 ft (13.41 m). Dft 30·ft (9.14 m).
E Sgl scr oil 2S.SA 9 cyl; 22,500 BHP; 21 kts. By Burmeister & Wain, Copenhagen.
H S 2 dks; F: 94 ft (28.65 m); P: 197 ft (60.04 m). C: 768,000 cu ft (2174.74 cu m) g. 20,165 cu ft (571 cu m) insulated. 150 containers.

1966 Completed for the Ocean S.S.C. The lead ship in a class of eight of which 4 were initially placed in Glen Line colours.

1978 After only 12 years these ships were outmoded by the rise in container ships and four were sold enblock to C. Y. Tung. They were *Priam, Peisander, Prometheus* and *Protesilaus*. Renamed *Oriental Champion*, Panocean Shipping, Liberia.

1980 Transferred to Carterfold Shipping Co; same name. C. Y. Tung.

1982 Sold to Vanderhoff Shipping Co, Panama; same name.

1984 To Island Investment & Agency Corp. Ltd. and Wattling Nav. Inc., Panama. Same name.

1985 Dec 11: Left Bahrain in tow for scrapping at Kaohsiung.

294 PEISANDER (II)

Sister to *Priam* (293) except:
B 1967. **D** 563.11 ft (171.64 m) o.a. **H** P: 197 ft (60.04 m).

1967 Mar: Delivered to Ocean S.S.Co.

1972 Transferred to China Mutual S.N.Co Ltd.

1978 Became *Oriental Exporter,* Panocean Shipping Co, Liberia.

1981 Transferred to Carland Shipping Ltd, Hong Kong; Renamed *Main Express.* Panama.

1981 Sold to Foreland Shipping Ltd, Monrovia. Panamanian flag.

1984 Sold to Island Investment & Agency Corp. & Wattling Nav. Inc., Liberia. Renamed *Oriental Exporter.*

1986 Sept 10: Arrived Kaohsiung for scrap.

295 PROTESILAUS (II)

Sister to *Priam* (293) except: **B** 1967. **D** 563.11 ft (171.64 m).

1967 July: Built for China Mutual S.N.Co.
1978 Because *Oriental Importer,* Balcombe Co, Ltd, Hong Kong. The Panocean Shg Co., both C. Y. Tung group.
1979 To Carbrook Shg Ltd. C. Y. Tung.
1982 Transferred to Flint Shipping Ltd, Panama. Same name.
1984 To same owners as 293. C. Y. Tung group.
1985 June 1: Struck by two Iran/Iraq rockets en-route Damman-Kuwait. July 25; Left for Kaohsiung and broken up.

296 PROMETHEUS (IV)

Sister to *Priam* (293) except: **B** 1967. **D** 563.11 ft (171.63 m).

1967 June: Completed for Ocean S.S.Co.
1972 To China Mutual S.N.Co. Ltd.
1979 Sold to C. Y. Tung. Renamed *Oriental Merchant,* Blound Co. Ltd. Hong Kong.
1980 Sold to Panocean Shipping Co. Inc, Liberia. Became *Oriental Merchant No. 1.* Transferred to Calm Isle Shipping Ltd, Hong Kong. Reverted to *Oriental Merchant.*
1984 To same owners as 293.
1986 March 21: Arrived Kaohsiung for scrapping.

297 PHRONTIS (II)

Sister to *Priam* (293) except:
B 1967 Mitsubishi Heavy Industries, Nagasaki. **T**: 12,299 g, 6,573 n.
E By builder. 9 cyl 18,900 BHP.

1967 Built as *Pembrokeshire* for the Glen Line.
1972 To Ocean S.S.Co. Renamed *Phrontis.*
1972 Transferred to China Mutual S.N.Co.
1978 Chartered to Wilhelm Wilhelmsen.
1982 Sold by China Mutual to Gulf Shipping Lines, London, renamed *Gulf Osprey.*
1983 Sold to Islamic Republic of Iran Shg Lines. Renamed *Iran Ejtehad.* Still in service.

298 PATROCLUS (V)

Sister to *Priam* (293) except:
B As *Phrontis* (297).

1967 Completed for the Glen Line as *Glenalmond.*
1973 Transferred to China Mutual S.N.Co. Renamed *Patroclus.* Operated a joint service with the Swedish East Asia Co. and wore their funnel colours.
1974 Transferred to N.S.M. 'Oceaan'.
1978 Came back to a British registry. Laid up at Liverpool and then placed on the Ben-Ocean Joint Service.
1982 Feb: Sold to Rajab & Co, Jeddah, Saudi Arabia. Renamed *Rajab 1.*
1984 July 18: Arrived Port Rashid on fire. Sold locally. Renamed *Sahar,* Molasses Trading & Export Co. Nov 26: Broken up at Gadani Beach.

299 PERSEUS (IV)

Sister to *Priam* (292).

1967 Completed for the Glen Line as *Radnorshire.*
1973 Transferred to China Mutual S.N.Co. and renamed *Perseus.*
1978 Sold to John Swire's China Navigation Co, in whom Holts had a substantial interest. Renamed *Kwangsi.*
1981 Became *Asia Dragon.* Owners not specified.
1982 Sold to the Saudi Venture Corporation, Jeddah. Became *Saudi ZamZam.* Owners changed to Saudi Falcon Nav. Co. Still in service.

300 PHEMIUS (V)

Sister to *Priam* (292) except:

1967 Jan: Built for Glen Line as *Glenfinlas*.
1972 Transferred to Blue Funnel. Renamed *Phemius*.
1978 Sold to China Navigation Co. Became *Kweichow*. AUST/NZ PORTS MANILA HONG KONG
1983 Sold to Saudi Venture Corp. Renamed *Saudi Kawther*. Still in service. AND BACK TO AUST/NZ

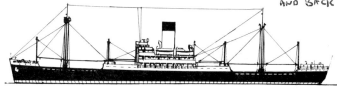

SARPEDON (VI) and DARDANUS (VI)

301 SARPEDON (VI)

B 1939 Nederlandsche Scheepvaarts Maats, Amsterdam. **T**: 7,151 g, 3,455 n.
D 507 ft (154.53 m) oa 476.3 ft (145.18 m) bp × 66 ft (20.12 m) × 38 ft (11.58 m).
E Tw scr, oil 2S.SA 2 × 6 cyls, 12,000 BHP. 17 kts. By Burmeister and Wain, Copenhagen.
H S. 2 dks, 3rd clear of machinery; F: 47 ft (14.32 m); B: 208 ft (63.40 m); P: 45 ft (13.72 m);
6 holds; 8 bulkheads. **C**: 652,147 cu ft (18,467 cu m) g; 28,227 cu ft (799.3 m) ins; 24 derricks.

1939 Built for the Glen Line as *Denbighshire*.
1942 Took part in the Malta Convoys and was damaged and set on fire at Valletta.
1945 Served in the Pacific fleet train.
1967 Transferred to the China Mutual S.N.Co; renamed *Sarpedon*.
1969 Aug 11: Arrived Kaohsiung. Sold for £49 per light ton and broken up.

302 DARDANUS (VI)

Sister to *Sarpedon* (301) except:
B 1940 Burmeister & Wain, Copenhagen. **T**: 9,311 g, 4,811 n.
H 3 dks; F: 53 ft (16.15 m); B: 215 ft (65.53 m); P: 70 ft (21.33 m).
C 637,587 cu ft (18,054.5 cu m) g, 69,387 cu ft (1,964.8 cu m) ins. Fuel 1,608 tons.

1940 May: When completing as *Glengarry* for the Glen Line the vessel was seized when the Germans overran Denmark.
Nov 5: Renamed *Meersburg*; operated by Hamburg American Line. Depot ship to U-boat flotillas 25 & 27.

HANSA (SCHIFF 5)

1942 Converted into an Armed Merchant Cruiser by Wilton-Fijnoord, Rotterdam.
1945 Renamed *Hansa* (Schiff 5) when commissioned by the German Navy. Never operational.
May 4: Recovered by the British at Kiel. Renamed *Empire Humber*.
1946 Delivered to the Glen Line and reverted to *Glengarry*.
1970 Transferred to Blue Funnel and renamed *Dardanus*.
1971 Once again became *Glengarry* but only in order to be sold for breaking up in Japan at Sakaide.

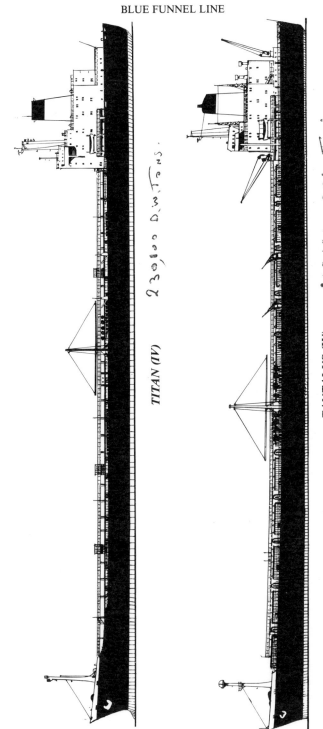

TITAN (IV)   230,000 D.W. Tons.

TANTALUS (IV)   215,680 D.W. Tons.

O.B.O. CARRIER.

303 **TITAN** (IV)

B 1972 A/B Gotaverken, Gothenburg. **T**: 113,551 g, 90,609 n, 230,099 dwt.
D 1,090.3 ft (332.32 m) obb, 1,050 ft (320.05 m) bp × 149.9 ft (45.70 m) × 67.9 ft (20.69 m).
E Sgl scr, 2 Stal-Laval Stm Turbs dbl reduct. geared. 32,450 SHP, 15½ kts.
H S 1 dk. Raised fore deck 66.27 ft (20.2 m). 8 compartments.

1972 Oil Tanker. Built for Ocean Titan Ltd.
1973 Shown as being owned by Elder Dempster Lines, Liverpool.
1975 Sold to Mobil Shipping and Transportation Co, Monrovia; renamed *Mobil Condor*.
1982 June 8: Sold to Nissho Iwai Corp. for breaking up by Dongkuk Steel Mill, Pusan, Korea.
Titan's sister ships were *Thorshavet*, Thor Dahl; *Veni*, Smedvigs; *Birta Onstad*, Onstad and *World Princess*, World Tankers.

304 **TANTALUS** (V)

B 1972 Nippon Kokan, Tsu. **T**: 120,787 g, 98,631 n, 215,680 dwt.
D 1,074.7 ft (327.57 m) obb, 1,017.13 ft (310.02 m) bp × 164.2 ft (50.05 m) × 62.9 ft (19.17 m).
E Sgl scr 2 stm turbs dbl reduct. geared; 30,000 SHP, 15½ kts. By Mitsubishi Heavy Industries Ltd, Nagasaki.
H S 1 dk. Raised fore deck 167.3 ft (51 m); 1 hatch on; 5 holds; 11 hatches; C: 258,930 cu m liquid; 119,350 cu m grain.

1972 Built for China Mutual S.N.Co. Oil/Ore carrier.
1978 July: Laid up.
Nov: Brought back into service.
1982 April 23: Laid up at Ocean Dock, Southampton.
1984 June: Sold for £4.7 million to Bulk Shipping, Norway. Renamed *Tantra*. Owned by Orca Shipping Co., Cyprus.
1987 Sold to Yellow Diamond Co., Cyprus. Renamed *Antarctica*.

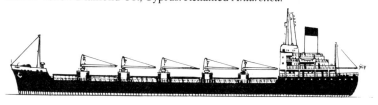

ACHILLES (VI), AGAMEMNON (IV), ANTENOR (V), ANCHISES (V) and AJAX (V)

305 **ACHILLES** (VI)

B 1972 Mitsui S.B. & E. Co, Fujingata, Japan. **T**: 16,406 g, 10,420 n, 26,725 dwt.
D 551.3 ft (168.04 m) o.a. × 75 ft (22.86 m) × 46 ft (14.02 m).
E Sgl scr oil, 6 cyl 2S.SA, 11,600 BHP, 15½ kts. By Mitsui-Zosan.
H S 1 dk; F: 52 ft (15.8 m); P: 123 ft (37.49 m); 6 holds and top side tanks. C: 1,279,243 cu ft (36,224.3 cu m) g. Hatches have MacGregor steel covers. 5 8-ton cranes.

1972 Completed for Blue Funnel Line Ltd. Ocean S.S.Co. as managers.
1974 Recorded as being owned by Elder Dempster Lines Ltd.
1977 Transferred to Blue Funnel Bulkships Ltd.
1978 June: To Silverdale Shipping Co, Bermuda.
1983 Operated by Flores Maritime Pte, Singapore. Same name.
1988 Still in service. Same name.

306 **AGAMEMNON** (IV)

Sister to *Achilles* (305) except:
T: 16,402 g.

1972 Delivered. Owned by Ocean Fleets Ltd. Managed by Elder Dempster Lines.
1974 Shown as owned by Elder Dempster Lines but retained the Blue Funnel colours.
1977 Transferred to Blue Funnel Bulkships Ltd.
1978 Became *Protoporos*, Protoporos Maritime Corp, Greece.
1984 May: Renamed, *Alicia,* Placido Shipping Corp., Greece.
1985 Became *Annaba,* U.S.S.R.-Black Sea Shipping Co., Odessa.
1988 Still in service.

307 **ANTENOR** (V)

Sister to *Achilles* (306) except:
T: 16,406 g.

1973 Delivered. Owned by Ocean Fleets Ltd.
1974 Owned by Elder Dempster Lines.
1977 Transferred to Blue Funnel Bulkships Ltd. thence to Elder Dempster Lines.
1978 Sold to Mermaid Sea Carriers Corp, Liberia; renamed *Sideris.*
1988 Still in service.

308 **ANCHISES** (V)

Sister to *Achilles* (306) except:
B 1973.

1973 Completed for Ocean Fleets Ltd.
1977 Transferred to Blue Funnel Bulkships Ltd.
1984 Jan: Sold to the U.S.S.R. with delivery at Lisbon. Renamed *Aytodar,*
U.S.S.R.-Black Sea Shipping Co. Still in service.

309 **AJAX** (V)

Sister to *Achilles* (306) except:
B 1973.
1973 Built for Ocean Titan Ltd. Blue Funnel colours.
1977 Transferred to Blue Funnel Bulkships Ltd.
1984 March: Sold to U.S.S.R. with delivery at the end of present commitments.
Renamed *Adler.* U.S.S.R. – Black Sea Shipping Co. Still in service.

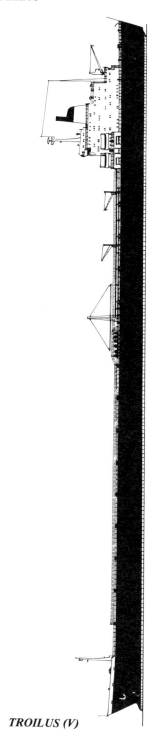

310 **TROILUS** (V)

B 1974 Mitsui S.B. & E. Co, Chiba. **T:** 141,288 g, 107,013 n, 273,516 dwt. **D** 1,087.7 ft (331.5 m) × 183.9 ft (56.06 m) × 86.6 ft (26.4 m). Dft 66.4 ft (20.24 m). **E** Sgl scr 1 dbl reduct. geared stm turb, 36,000 SHP, 15½ kts; By Kawasaki, Kobe. **H** S 1dk. **C:** 328,000 cu m.

1974 Completed for Ocean Troilus Ltd.
1975 Sold for $43,750,000. Renamed *Al-Dhrafrah*, owned by Al-Dhrafrah Tanker Co, Monrovia.
1985 Sold to Smith Tak International Ocean Towage & Salvage Co. Renamed *Alda*. Nov 9: Arrived Kaohsiung for breaking up.

TROILUS (V)

134

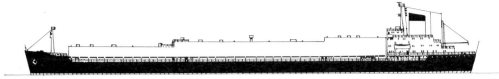

HELENUS (III)

311 **HELENUS** (III)

B 1973 Burmeister & Wain, Cophenagen. **T:** 30,078 g, 22,422 n, 51,072 dwt.
D 718 ft (218.85 m) o.a. × 100.2 ft (30.54 m) × 55.77 ft (17 m) Dft 39.6 ft (12.07 m).
E Sgl scr oil, 7 cyl 2S.SA 31,100 SHP, 15 kts. By builder.
H S 1 dk; F: 66.7 ft (20.2 m); P: 144 ft (43.9 m).

1973 Built as a bulk carrier for Rea Ltd (as in 312) and managed by Ocean Titan Ltd.
1977 Owned by Ocean Helenus Ltd.
1978 Converted into an automobile transporter (as above) to fulfill a two year contract with Japan.
1983 Sold, still as a car carrier, to Eurocolor Shipping Ltd, Cyprus. Renamed *Seafarer*.
1988 Still in service.

HECTOR (VI)

312 **HECTOR** (VI)

Sister to *Helenus* (311) except:

1973 Built for Cory Maritime Services; operated as a Blue Funnel ship.
1979 Sold to Cast Motorvessels Ltd, renamed *Cast Orca*.
1982 Became *Tramco Asia*, Ocean Tramping Co, Hong Kong.
1983 Sold to Armadora Maribella S.A., Greece; renamed *Marijeannie*.
1988 Still in service.

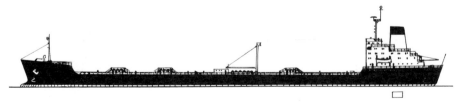

CYCLOPS (IV) and CLYTONEUS (III)

313 **CYCLOPS** (IV)

B 1975 Van der Geissen-de Noord B.V, Krimpen, Netherlands. **T:** 32,576 g, 22,605 n. 56,050 dwt.
D 689.1 ft (210.3 m) obb × 106 ft (32.31 m) × 53.3 ft (16.26 m). Dft 40.7 ft (12.41 m).
E Sgl scr, oil, 2S.SA, 7 cyl, 18,500 SHP, 16¾ kts. By Burmeister & Wain, Copenhagen.
H S 1 dk; F: 77.1 ft (23.5 m); B: 132.2 ft (40.3 m). C: 73,717 cu m liquid.

1975 Nov: Built for Ocean Titan Ltd. Product carrier.
1977 Transferred to Blue Funnel Bulkships Ltd.
1982 Dec 18: Laid up in the River Fal. The largest vessel yet to be laid up there.
1983 May 26: Arrived at Falmouth for handing over to Pequat Shipping Corporation, Greece. Renamed *Procyon.*
1988 Still in service.

314 **CLYTONEUS** (III)

Sister to *Cyclops* (313) except:
B 1976

1975 June 14: Launched for Ocean S.S.Co. Product carrier.
1976 Aug 6: Delivered to Ocean Titan Ltd.
1977 Transferred to Blue Funnel Bulkships Ltd.
1985 Dec: Sold to Transpetrol Nav. Pte Ltd., Singapore. Renamed *Affinity.*
1987 Sold to Transporti Internazionali Petroliferi S.p.A., Italy. Renamed Cervino. Still in service.

CHARON (III)

315 **CHARON** (III)

B 1975 Sasebo Heavy Industries, Sasebo. **T:** 24,512 g, 14,865 n, 41,855 dwt.
D 636.8 ft (194.11 m) o.a. × 99.9 ft (30.46 m) × 49.5 ft (15.09 m). Dft 37.8 ft (11.52 m).
E Sgl scr, Sulzer oil 2S.SA, 7 cyl, 14,000 BHP, 14¾ kts.
H S 1 dk.

1976 Jan: Operated by Koninklijke N.S.M. 'Oceaan'; note addition of the 'Royal' prefix to the name.
1985 Renamed *Finesse L,* Ceres Hellenic Shipping Enterprises, Greece.
1985 Renamed *Finesse,* Inter Mexico Brokers Inc. In service.

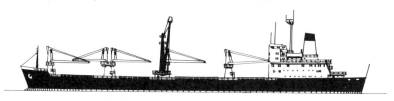

LAERTES (VI) and LYCAON (III)

316 **LAERTES** (V)

B 1976 Kherson Shipyard, Kherson, U.S.S.R. **T:** 11,804 g, 6,285 n.
D 533.2 ft (162.5 m) obb × 74.2 ft (22.6 m) × 43.9 ft (13.39 m). Dft 30.2 ft (9.19 m).
E Sgl scr 2S.SA 6 cyl, B & W 10,600 BHP, 18.3 kts. By Bryansk Engine Works. The engine room is unmanned and is controlled from the bridge.
H S. 2 dks; F: 42 ft (12.8 m); C: 21,340 cu m g; 5 hatches, 1 63-tonne heavy lift derrick, 7 12-tonne cranes, 6 of which operate in tandem. 404 containers. Funnel rectangular.

1976 Constructed for China Mutual S.N.Co, a vessel of the *Dnepr* class. Purchased to meet

the need for a sharp growth in container capacity. Originally intended for service with N.S.M. 'Oceaan'. The name 'Amsterdam' was still displayed as the port of registry when the ship arrived in the River Mersey.

1977 Jan 6: Delivered to Birkenhead. Placed on the Japan—Persian Gulf route.
1982 Transferred to Elder Dempster Lines and placed on the West African berth.
May: Requisitioned for service during the Falklands War.
1983 Sold to the Dimskal Shipping Co, Panama; renamed *Evia Luck*.
1987 Became *Vigor*, Sponge Maritime Co, Cyprus.

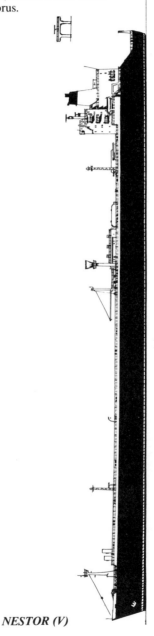

317 **LYCAON** (III)

Sister to *Laertes* (316).

1976 Dec. 22: Handed over to the China Mutual S.N.Co.
1977 Jan 6: Arrived at Birkenhead twenty minutes later than *Laertes*.
1979 Chartered for work in the Caribbean and South American trading.
1983 Laid up at Falmouth. Elder Dempster colours.
Apr: Chartered by the Ministry of Defence for the Falklands War. A helicopter pad has been installed.
1985 Transferred to Blue Funnel Bulkships Ltd.
1985 Renamed *Chrysovalandon Faith*, Mersey Transport Inc., Panama.
1985 Became *Eleftheria K*, Estuary Shipping, Panama.

NESTOR (V)

318 NESTOR (V)

B 1977 Chantiers de L'Atlantique, St-Nazaire. **T:** 78,951 g, 51,244 n, 78,641 dwt.
D 902.2 ft (275.01 m) oa × 138.02 ft (42.07 m) × 89.93 ft (27.41 m) Dft 40.3 ft (12.30 m).
E Sgl scr, 2 Stal-Laval geared turbines; 34,000 SHP, 19¾ kts at 109 rpm. 2 Foster-Wheeler Verolome blrs. By Chantiers & Ateliers de St-Nazaire, Penhoet.
H S. 1 dk; C: 122,255 cu m liquid.

1977 A liquid gas carrier. Oct 4: Handed over to Odyssey Trading Co, a subsidiary of Ocean Trading Fleets Ltd. Cost £62.4 million.
Dec 9: On completion went into immediate lay up at Loch Striven, Scotland. The ship was delivered in Blue Funnel colours but was chartered for 20 years by Pacific Indonesia LNG Co. for a service between Indonesis and California. The U.S. Dept of Energy had approved the plan in Dec. 1977. The payment formula dealing with base price and subsequent escalations was concluded in Sept 1978. However the receiving terminal is delayed in completion. Has only been back to builders for modifications.
1988 Still laid up together with *Gastor*, the sister ship owned by the Nedlloyd group. Shell have an option to purchase her.

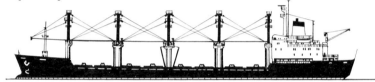

MENELAUS (V)/BARBER MENELAUS, MEMNON (VII)/BARBER MEMNON,
MELAMPUS (III) and MENESTHEUS (III)/BARBER MENESTHEUS

319 MENELAUS (V)/BARBER MENELAUS/MENELAUS

B 1977 Mitsubishi Heavy Industries, Nagasaki. **T:** 16,031 g, 8,666 n, 21,242 dwt.
D 540 ft (164.6 m) obb × 85.3 ft (26 m) × 46.6 ft (14.2 m). Dft 34.8 ft (10.62 m).
E Sgl scr, 2S.SA, 7 cyl Mitsubishi-Sulzer type RND76M. 14,300 BHP at 116, rpm. By builder's Kobe works.
H S. 1 dk, 7 bulkheads, 5 holds, 9 twin hatches; F: 84 ft (25.6 m); P: 112 ft (34.2 m); C: 30,335 cu m g; Cont: 773 × 20 ft (6.1 m); 9 Velle type derricks, 1 × 10 tonnes, 5 × 22 tonnes and 3 × 35 tonnes. Bow thrust propeller fitted. Crew: 39.

1977 Apr 16: Launched. July: Delivered on charter to Liner Holdings. Owned by Airlease International Nominees (Moorgate) Ltd, a British Petroleum subsidiary. BP substituted these four 'M' class merchantmen for the cancellation of two super tankers and Ocean took them over on virtually a lifetime lease. Constructed as multi-purpose ships.
1980 Dec 14: Renamed *Barber Menelaus.* Operated by Barber Blue Sea and managed by Ocean Fleets. Barber funnel colours.
1882 Sold to Barber Menelaus Shipping Corp, Liberia; same name.Ocean Fleets managers.
1984 Reverted to *Menelaus* when she returned to European waters. Owned by Airlease International Nominees (Moorgate) Ltd.
1985 Feb 8: Transferred to Elder Dempster Lines Ltd. Present fleet.

320 MEMNON (VII)/BARBER MEMNON/MEMNON

Sister to *Menelaus* (319).
1977 Aug: Delivered to Liner Holdings. Owned by Airlease International Nominees (Moorgate) Ltd.
1980 Renamed *Barber Memnon*, operated by Barber Blue Sea. Managed by Elder Dempster Lines. Panamanian flag.
1982 Owned by Barber Menelaus Shipping Corp, Liberia; same name.
1984 Still in service now as *Memnon*. Same owners as 319. For charter to Lloyd Brasiliero was temporarily renamed *Lloyd San Francisco.*
1985 Reverted to *Memnom*, owned by Airlease International Nominees (Moorgate) Ltd. Ocean Fleets managers. Present fleet.

321 **MELAMPUS** (III)

Sister to *Menelaus* (319).

1977 Nov: Delivered to Ocean Fleets Ltd. Owned by Airlease International Nominees (Moorgate) Ltd.

1980 Operated by Barber Blue Sea, Elder Dempster Lines as managers.

1983 Sold to Menelaus Shipping Corp, Liberia; same name.

1985 Transferred to Elder Dempster Lines Ltd. Present fleet.

322 **MENESTHEUS** (III)/**BARBER MENESTHEUS/MENESTHEUS**

Sister to *Menelaus* (319).

1977 Dec: Delivered to Ocean Fleets Ltd. Owned by Airlease International Nominees (Moorgate) Ltd.

1980 Nov 4: Renamed *Barber Menestheus*. Operated by Barber Blue Sea. Managed by Elder Dempster Lines.

1983 Sold to Barber Menestheus Shipping Corp, Panama; same name. Dec: Renamed *Menestheus*.

1984 Apr 18: Chartered to Woermann Line for West Africa sevice. Same owners as 319. Chartered to Lloyd Brasiliero. Renamed *Lloyd Parana*.

1985 Jan 29: Reverted to *Menestheus*. Elder Dempster services.

1986 Feb: Renamed *Apapa Palm*. Same owners. Present fleet.

PLUMLEAF

323 **PLUMLEAF**

B 1960 Blyth DD & SB Co, Blyth. **T:** 12,549 g, 7,418 n.

D 560 ft (170.69 m) oa, 534 ft (162.76 m) bp × 72.1 ft (21.98 m) × 39.1 ft (11.91 m).

E Sgl scr, oil, 2S.SA 6 cyl, 9,500 BHP, Doxford. By N. E. Marine Eng Co, West Hartlepool.

H S. 1 dk; F: 69 ft (21.03 m); B: 36 ft (10.97 m); P: 118 ft (35.96 m).

1968 Aug: Oil tanker. Laid down as *Corheath* for William Cory & Son. Chartered while on the stocks by the Admiralty for use as a Fleet replenishment oiler. Renamed *Plumleaf* to conform with their 'Leaf' nomenclature.

1977 With the winding up of Cory Maritime *Plumleaf* passed into the ownership of Blue Funnel Bulkships.

1984 On Admiralty charter.

1986 Replaced by *Oakleaf*. Dec 17: Arrived at Kaohsiung. Scrapped by Cheng Yung Enterprises.

AENEAS (III)

324 **AENEAS** (III)

B 1972 Astilleros Espanoles S.A, Seville. **T:** 15,498 g, 11,227 n.

D 598.8 ft (182.6 m) oa, 563.9 ft (171.68 m) bp × 73.5 ft (22.4 m) × 46.5 ft (14.2 m).

E Sgl scr, Sulzer diesel type RND 68, 6 cyls; 9,900 BHP; 15½ kts. By builder.

H S. 1 dk; 4 × 15 ton Hagglund electro-hydraulic deck cranes; F: 52 ft (15.9 m); P: 100 ft (30.5 cm); C: 1,270,551 cu ft (35,978 cu m) bulk.

1972 Built as *Cunard Carrier*, Eskalduna Type 27, for Cunard—Brocklebank Bulk Carriers.

1978 Aquired by Silverdale Co. Ltd, Ocean Fleets as managers; Renamed *Aeneas*.

1984 To Caroline Maritime Pte Ltd, Singapore; same name. Later to Transocean Maritime Agencies, Singapore.

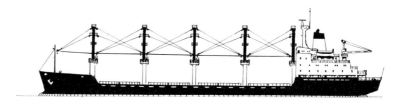

MARON (IV), MENTOR (III) and MYRMIDON (V)

325 **MARON** (IV)

B 1980 Scotts S.B. & E. Co, Greenock. **T**: 16,482 g, 8,872 n, 21,300 dwt.

D 539.9 ft (164.57 m) obb × 85.3 ft (26 m) × 49.6 ft (14.2 m). Dft 35 ft (10.67 m).

E Sgl scr, oil, 7 cyl Scotts-Sulzer type RND 76M, 16,800 BHP at 122 rpm. 18 kts. By builder.

H S 2 dks; C: 1,021,734 cu ft (28,932 cu m) b. Cont: 795 which includes 76 refrigerated by plug in sockets; F: 1,687 tonnes. Crew 36. A bow thrust propeller is fitted. 5 holds.

1980 May 9: Delivered. During the ship's trials she suffered from excessive vibration aft. This was cured by the addition of 3 flow improvement fins at the stern.

Maiden voyage: Middlesborough—West Africa. Although having a traditional Blue Funnel name *Maron* is owned by Elder Dempster Lines and bears their funnel colours although the water line is in the familiar flesh-red of Alfred Holt ships. The cost of the three ships was £36 million.

1981 Nov 22: Renamed *Studland Bay* during a charter period.

1982 Reverted to *Maron*.

1987 Sold to Al-Mubarak (Shg & Trading Co) then to Omega Ltd, both Bermuda. Renamed *Baltic Adventurer*

326 **MENTOR** (III)

Sister to *Maron* (375).

1979 Aug 8: Launched.

1980 July: Delivered to Elder Dempster Lines. West African service.

1981 Dec 5: Chartered to Overseas Containers and renamed *City of London* for the COBRA service.

1982 Dec 20: Laid up in the River Fal as *Mentor.*

1984 March: Present fleet; due to return to COBRA service.

1985 April: To Hake Shipping Co. Ltd, Cyprus; renamed *Normannia.*

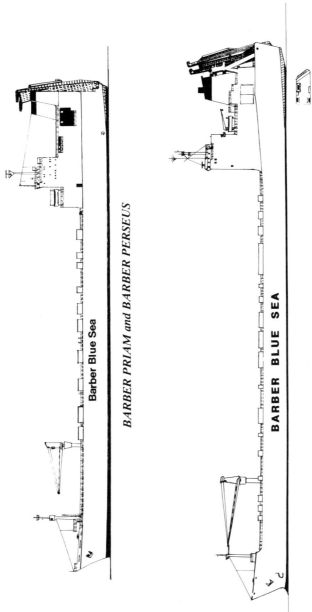

Barber Blue Sea

BARBER PRIAM and BARBER PERSEUS

BARBER BLUE SEA

BARBER HECTOR

327 **MYRMIDON** (V)

Sister to Maron (325).

1980 Feb 19: Launched. Nov 4: Delivered to Elder Dempster Line.
1981 Chartered to Compagnie General Maritime for Caribbean round voyage.
1982 June 22-Oct 28: Falkland Islands charter to Ministry of Defence.
1984 Nov: Renamed *Cape Town Carrier* during charter, to Maritime Associated Carriers.
1985 Feb 7: Reverted to *Myrmidon,* Ocean Transport & Trading PLC.
These three ships have not seen service in the Blue Funnel livery and are included because of their Ocean Fleet ownership and the fact that they bear Alfred Holts names. With the seemingly constant switching of ships on a company basis, such as is practised today, the ancestory is better defined by name rather than registered owner.
1986 Feb: Sold to Nigerian Green Lines Ltd, Lagos. Renamed *Bello Folawiyo.*

328 **BARBER PRIAM**

B 1979 Mitsubishi Heavy Industries, Nagasaki. **T**: 21,747 g, 11,999 n, 32,037 dwt.
D 749.67 ft (228.5 m) oa, 693.9 ft (211.5 m) bp × 105.83 ft (32.26 m) × 66.3 ft (20.2 m).
E Sgl scr, oil, 9 cyl. 30,150 BHP at 122 rpm, 20.5 kts. Sulzer type by builder at Kobe.
H S. 3 dks part 4th is moveable 'tween dks. 2 thwart ship propeller one fore the other aft.
Crew: 43.

1978 Nov 17: Launched for Ocean Transport & Trading Co. Ro-Ro type with stern ramp. Fitted to carry a wide range of cargoes but without refrigerated space.
1984 Owned Odysseus Shipping. International Corp, Panama.
1986 Owned by Ocean Transport & Trading PLC; Sold to the United States Military Sea Lift Command for $25 million. One 13 RoRo's bought. May 20: At Hampton Roads for handing over. Renamed *Cape Henry.*

329 **BARBER PERSEUS**

Details as *Barber Priam* (328) except:
32,435 dwt.

1979 Feb 7: Launched. June delivered. Owned by Speakshaw Ltd. with Ocean Fleets as managers. Later owned by Barber Menelaus Shipping Corp, Panama.
1985 Owned by Perseus Shipping Ltd, Panama.
1988 Present fleet.

330 **BARBER HECTOR**

B 1984 Hyundai Heavy Industries, South Korea. **T**: 30,400 dwt.
D 859.6 ft (262 m) obb × 105.84 ft (32.26 m) × 68.9 ft (21 m). Dft: 38.4 ft (11.7 m).
E Sgl scr, oil, 8 cyl MAN-B&W type 8L90GB. 20.5 kts at 94 rpm on 105 tonnes fuel per day. By HEMCO (Hyundai Eng. and Mchy. Co.).
H S. 4 dks + 2 hoistable. Fuel: 8,000 cu m. Crew 31. Bow and stern thrust propellers to reduce dependancy on tugs.
1983 Nov 16: Launched.
1984 Apr: Delivered for North America—Far East—Persian Gulf 90 day round the world service. The world's largest Roll on-Roll off ferry. Carries heavy lorry loads of up to 420 tons axle weight. Capacity for 630 cars. Containers: 2,464 TEU of which only 200 are to plug-in refrigeration equipment. Bale cargo capacity is 72,000 cu m.
The two sister ships *Barber Tampa* and Barber *Texas* are owned by the Wilhelmsen and Swedish East Asiatic partners.
1988 Present fleet. These two *Barber* ships alone carry a blue funnel in service.

Special Charters

These two ships were given Holt names with the prefix R.S meaning Roll on and Store. Containers being lifted from their parking lot by special fork lift tractors and stowed aboard ship on deck fitted guide lines. They are included solely because of the Holt names which they then bore.

R.S. IXION and R.S. JASON

331 **R.S IXION**

B 1977 Kurushima Dock Co, Imbari. **T:** 4,627 g, 2,859 n, 7,218 dwt.
D 372.34 ft (113.49 m) oa, 355 ft (108.21) bp × 57.77 ft (17.61 m) × 29.59 ft (9.0 m).
E Sgl scr, oil 2S.SA 6 cyl, 4,500 BHP; 17 kts. By Kobe Hatsudoki K.K.
H S 1 dk; F: 49.21 ft (15 m); P: 51.18 ft (15.6 m); 333 × 20 ft (6.1 m) containers. 2 holds.

1977 Launched as *R.S One*, owned by Class Container Lines, Liberia. Chartered prior to completion by Blue Funnel for a Roll-on, Roll-off service between Ellesmere Port and Jeddah. Painted in Holt colours and renamed *R.S Ixion*.
1979 Feb: Improvements at the port of Jeddah enabled the container traffic to be transferred to Overseas Container Line, 34.1% Ocean owned. The chartered ships were thereby released. Sold to Prescott Investors Inc. Passed to the U.S.S.R-Latvian Shipping Co; renamed *Kapitan Tomson*.
1984 Still in service.

332 **R.S JASON**

Sister to *R.S. Ixion* (329) except:
T: 4,633 g, 2,859 n, 7,424 dwt.

1977 Completed for the World Patent Corp. as *R.S Jason*. Chartered to Ocean Fleets.
1979 Sold to Prescott Investors Inc. Passed to U.S.S.R-Latvian Shipping Co, Riga. Renamed *Kapitan Yakovlev*.
1984 Present fleet.

Miscellaneous vessels

333 ARGO

B 1875 Scott & Co, Greenock. **T**: 580 g.
D 208 ft (63.4 m) × 26.3 ft (7.99 m) × 16 ft (4.88 m).
E Sgl scr, comp, 600 IHP, 11 kts. By builder.
H Iron, 1 dk; F: 14 ft (4.27 m).

1875 Built and used as Alfred Holt's private yacht. Also used as a cadet training ship with tutoring facilities.

1881 Sold to French owners for non commercial use.

Other East India Ocean S.S. Company ships.

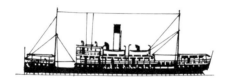

334 RANEE

B 1881 Ramage & Ferguson, Leith. **T**: 617 g, 378 n.
D 185 ft (25.9 m) × 27.1 ft (8.26 m) × 13.6 ft (4.14 m).
E Sgl scr, comp, 2 cyl, 99 RHP, 9 kts. By T. Richardson & Sons, Hartlepool.
H Iron, 1 and shelter dk; F: 31 ft (9.45 m); P: 41 ft (12.5 m).

1881 Built for Sarawak & Singapore Steamship Co.
1892 Acquired by the East India Ocean S.S.Co., having run on charter to Alfred Holt since 1888.
1899 Transferred to Norddeutscher Lloyd with the remainder of the E.I.O. ships. Initially renamed *Labuan* but reverted to *Ranee*.
1900 To Siam as *Bin Seng* then resold to Mrs Quah Seh Quan as *Pin Seng*.
1907 Transferred to Eastern Shipping Co, Penang on its formation.
1921 Sold to un-named Chinese buyers; same name.
1923 Broken up.

335 KONGSEE

B 1878 C. Mitchell & Co, Newcastle **T**: 1,072 g, 696 n.
D 248 ft (75.59 m) × 31.2 ft (9.51 m) × 17.9 ft (5.45 m).

E Sgl scr, comp inv, 2 cyl, 200 HP; Stm P: 75 lb, 10 kts. By R & W Hawthorne, Newcastle.
H Iron. 2 dks; F: 30 ft (9.14 m); B: 61 ft (18.59 m); P: 30 ft (9.14 m).

1878 Oct: Built for Netherlands Indies Steam Navigation Co, Batavia.
1890 Acquired by T. C. Bogaardt, Singapore and operated by him within the Blue Funnel network.
1893 Operated by N.S.M. 'Oceaan' in order to trade to the Dutch East Indies out of Singapore.
1898 Sold by Bogaardt to Tan Kim Tinn, same name.
1899 Sold to Philippine owners at Manila; U.S. flag.
1901 Renamed the U.S. Army's *Liscum*.
1922 Renamed *Nuestra Senora de Alba*, Tuason & Sampedro, Manila.
1934 Sold to Yung Shun S.S.Co, Newchwang, China; renamed *Yung Shun*.
193? Broken up at Shanghai.
Note: Straits S.S.Co. records show this ship as Holt owned beween 1891—1895.

336 BANJERMASSIN

B 1886 Wigham Richardson & Co, Newcastle. **T:** 428 g, 261 n.
D 174 ft (53.03 m) × 23.7 ft (7.22 m) × 12.2 ft (3.71 m).
E Sgl scr, tpl exp, 80 HP, 9 kts. By builder.
H Iron. 1 dk and shelter dk; F: 35 ft (10.36 m); P: 60 ft (18.29 m).

1886 June: Completed for Kho Soen Tjio Ang Eng, Banjermassin. Employed by T. C. Bogaardt between that port and Singapore for Holt's account.
1889 Holts took title to the ship.
1892 Transferred to N.S.M. 'Oceaan'.
1896 Transferred to East India Ocean S.S.Co.
1899 Acquired, with the remainder of the fleet, by Norddeutscher Lloyd; renamed *Sulu*.
1900 Sold to Philippine owners; renamed *Tan Auco*.
1901 Mar 3: Lost on Patras Sandbank, Philippines.

337 DEVONHURST

B 1874 C. Mitchell & Co, Newcastle. **T:** 1,559 g, 1,235 n.
D 280 ft (85.34 m) × 33.3 ft (10.15 m) × 24.6 ft (7.5 m).
E Sgl scr, comp, 2 cyl; 200 HP, Stm P: 80 lb. 10 kts. By N.E. Marine, Sunderland.
H Iron 2 dks; F: 41 ft (12.5 m); P: 56 ft (17.07 m).

1874 Built for H. Katz, Singapore, for Singapore—Calcutta—Nizagapatnam service.
1878 Sold to Netherlands India Steam Navigation Co, same name.
1882 Owned by Atjeh S.S.Co, London; Singapore based.
1888 Acquired by T. C. Bogaardt and operated for Blue Funnel.
1891 Mar 8: Collided with and sank Burrell & Son's *Strathendrick* (1).
1892 Holts took title to the ship in readiness to transfer it to East India Ocean S.S.Co.
1893 To E.I.O SS Co.
1896 Sold to Japan; became *Kubo Maru*.
1897 Wrecked on Kyushu.

NORMANBY

338 NORMANBY

B 1874 Henderson Coulborn, Renfrew. **T:** 976 g, 664 n.
D 220.4 ft (67.18 m) × 27.8 ft (8.47 m) × 14.9 ft (4.54 m).
E Sgl scr, comp inv, 2 cyl, 160 HP; Stm P: 65 lb. 10 kts. By builder.
H Iron. 2 dks.

1874 July: Completed for Eastern & Australian S.S.Co.
1880 Sold to J. S. Neave, Singapore.
1884 Acquired by Ong Kew Ho, Singapore.
1891 Became part of T. C. Bogaardt's fleet and operated by him for Alfred Holt who then took title to the ship in order to transfer it to the Dutch trade.
1892 Operated by N.S.M. 'Oceaan'.
1893 Dec 5: Wrecked en-route Manila—Singapore near Pulu Bintang.

339 MAHA VAJIRUNIS

B 1881 C. Mitchell & Co, Newcastle. **T:** 1,176 g, 704 n.
D 253 ft (77.1 m) × 32.2 ft (9.81 m) × 17.5 ft (5.33 m).
E Sgl scr comp inv, 2 cyl; 230 HP, 10 kts. By Wallsend Slipway, Newcastle.
H Steel. 2 dks; F: 47 ft (14.3 m); B: 61 ft (18.59 m); P: 44 ft (13.41 m).

1881 Built for Atjeh S.S.Co, London. Based Singapore and chartered to T. C. Bogaardt.
1891 The shares in the ship were held by Holts but the vessel was operated by Haacke & Co between Padang (Sumatra)—Penang (Malay States)—Singapore.
1893 Operated by N.S.M. 'Oceaan', same route. The freight rates were too fiercely competitive, being undercut by the Dutch K.P.M. ships until rice was being carried at 5 cts per kilo.
1894 Koninklijke Paketvaart Maats took over the ship.
1907 Out of register.

340 CHARON

B 1896 Workman Clark & Co, Belfast. **T:** 1,920 g, 1,237 n.
D 278 ft (84.73 m) × 41.1 ft (12.53 m) × 20.8 ft (6.34 m).
E Sgl scr, tpl exp, 149 NHP, 9½ kts. By builder.
H Steel. 2 dks. F: 26 ft (7.92 m); B: 74 ft (22.5 m).

1896 Built for the East Ocean S.S.Co.
1899 Transferred with the remainder of the fleet to Norddeutscher Lloyd; renamed *Bangkok*.
1911 Became *Kiodo Maru No 13*, Awakoku Kiodo K.K, Tokushma, Japan.
1918 Recorded as owned by Uchida Kisen K.K.
1922 Renamed *Kyodo Maru No 13*, owned by Ogina Kaisyo K.K, Takoaka.
1933 Owned by Oginuno Kaisho K.K, Fushiki. Same name.
1945 War loss in home waters; probably by torpedo attack.

China Mutual Ships Owned Prior to Holt Take Over

CM1 **OOPACK** (I)

B 1883 D & W Henderson & Co, Glasgow. **T**: 2,708 g, 1,735 n.
D 350 ft (106.68 m) × 41.8 ft (12.74 m) × 23.5 ft (7.16 m).
E Sgl scr, 2 cyl comp; 319 NHP, 2 dbl ended blrs, 80 lb. By builder.
H I. 2 dks; F: 42 ft (12.8 m); B: 64 ft (19.51 m); P: 12 ft (3.66 m).

1883 Built for China Mutual S.N.Co. Cost £59,000. Glasgow—London—Hong Kong service. Voyage 41 days.
1983 Sold to Nippon Yusen K.K., renamed *Nagoya Maru*.
1928 June 25: Wrecked south of Hakodate, Japan.

CM2 **NINGCHOW** (I)

Details as *Oopack* (CM1) except:
B 1884.

1884 Built for China Mutual S.N.Co. Cost £59.000.
1899 Sold to the Bombay & Persia S.N.Co, Bombay. Renamed *Monsoori*.
1909 June: Broken up at Genoa by L. Pittaluga S.A.

CM3 **CHING WO** (I)

B 1885 R. Dixon & Co, Middlesborough. **T**: 2,526 g, 1,566 n.
D 320 ft (97.54 m) × 38 ft (11.58 m) × 25.7 ft (7.83 m).
E Sgl scr, tpl exp, 3 cyl, 282 NHP, 2 dbl ended blrs, 142 lb. 10 kts. By T. Richardson & Sons, West Hartlepool.
H I. 2dks; F: 41 ft (12.5 m); B: 60 ft (18.29 m); P: 24 ft (7.31 m).

1885 Built for China Mutual S.N.Co.
1893 Sold to Nippon Yusen K.K. Renamed *Wakanoura Maru*.
1943 Aug 10: Torpedoed by U.S. submarine east of Sakhalin Island.

CM4 **KAISOW**

B 1885 J. L. Thompson & Sons, Sunderland. **T**: 3,099 g, 1,921 n.
D 350 ft (106.68 m) × 40.9 ft (12.47 m) × 25.8 ft (7.86 m).
E Sgl scr, tpl exp, 3 cyl, 433 NHP, 2 dbl ended blrs, 160 lb. 10 kts. By T. Richardson, Hartlepool.
H S. 2 dks; F: 42 ft (12.8 m); B: 68 ft (20.73 m).

1885 Built for the China Mutual S.N.Co.
1894 Sold to Japan. Renamed *Matsuyama Maru*, Nippon Yusen K.K.
1924 July 11: Sank west of Goto Islands enroute Keelung—Yokohama.

CM5 **MOYUNE**

Details as *Kaisow* (CM4) except:
B 1886. **T**: 2,784 g, 1,726 n.
D 346.9 ft (105.73 m) × 41.2 ft (12.56 m) × 25.5 ft (7.77 m).
H F: 47 ft (14.32 m); B: 78 ft (23.77 m); P: 53 ft (16.15 m).

1866 Dec: Delivered to China Mutual S.N.Co.
1894 Became *Shibata Maru*, Nippon Yusen K.K.
1896 Sold to the Japanese Government, Lighthouse Department. Same name.
1908 Sold to Hong Kong owners; same name.
1910 Sold to Turkey. Renamed *Mahmoud Chefket Pasha*.
1915 Sunk by war action.
1921 Salved. Became *Ararat*.
1923 Renamed *Mahmut Sevket Pasha*, a modernised spelling of her 1910 name.
1935 Broken up.

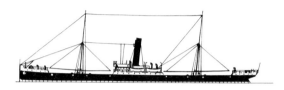

KEEMUN and PAK LING

CM6 **KEEMUN**

B 1890 J. L. Thompson & Sons, Sunderland. **T**: 3,162 g, 1,997 n.
D 361.6 ft (110.22 m) × 41.7 ft (12.71 m) × 24.5 ft (7.47 m).
E Sgl scr, tpl exp, 3 cyl, 442 NHP, 2 dbl ended blrs, 160 lb. 10 kts. By J. Dickinson, Sunderland.
H S. 2 dks; F: 48 ft (14.63 m); B: 100 ft (30.48 m); P: 24 ft (7.31 m).

1890 Nov: Delivered to China Mutual S.N.Co.
1897 Sold to the Donaldson Line, same name. Price £26,000.
1900 Sold to Belgium. Renamed *Patrie*. F. Schepens & G. Tonnelier, Antwerp.
1901 Became *Patria*, J. H. Andressen Successores, Oporto.
1905 Sold to Greece. Became *Patricia*. G. S. Patrikios, Argostoli.
1907 Jan 18: Sunk in collision off the Haisborough Lightship.

CM7 **PAK LING**

Details as *Keemun* (CM6) except:
T: 3,321 g, 2,059 n.
D 362 ft (110.34 m).

1890 Completed for China Mutual S.N.Co.
1894 Sold to Nippon Yusen K.K. Renamed *Yamaguchi Maru*.
1916 May 15: Wrecked on the Japanese coast.

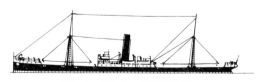

PING SUEY and KINTUCK

CM8 **PING SUEY**

B 1890 Barclay Curle & Co, Glasgow. **T:** 3,079 g, 1,982 n.
D 365 ft (111.25 m) × 41.5 ft (12.74 m) × 26 ft (7.92 m).
E Sgl scr, tpl exp, 3 cyl, 750 NHP 180 lb. 10 kts. By builder.
H S. 2 dks; F: 48 ft (14.63 m); B: 92 ft (28.04 m); P: 21 ft (6.4 m).

1890 May: Delivered to China Mutual S.N.Co.
1898 Sold to the Argentine Government; renamed *Guardia Nacional.* Used as a barracks ship at Buenos Aires.
1941 Became *Ombu,* same owner. (Lloyds recorded the ship as dismantled in 1933).
1945 Sold to Linea Argentina-Sud Africa S.A, Eugen Eugenides manager. Renamed *Ciudad del Cabo* (i.e. Cape Town).
1950 Broken up at Buenos Aires.

CM9 **KINTUCK**

B 1891 R. Dixon & Co, Middlesborough. **T:** 3,854 g, 2,389 n.
D 360 ft (109.72 m) × 45.2 ft (13.78 m) × 27.4 ft (8.38 m).
E Sgl scr, tpl exp, 3 cyl, 483 NHP. 2 dbl ended blrs, 160 lb. 10 kts. By T. Richardson & Sons, Hartlepool.
H S. 2 dks; F: 49 ft (14.93 m); B: 96 ft (29.26 m); P: 21 ft (6.40 m).

1891 May: Completed for China Mutual S.N.Co.
1892 Sold to Nippon Yusen K.K. Renamed *Kinshu Maru.* (The name was originally recorded as *Kinshiu Maru.*)
1904 April 25: Sunk north of Gensan by Russian warships.

CM10 **OOLONG**

B 1893 London & Glasgow Co, Glasgow. **T:** 3,593 g, 2,283 n.
D 360 ft (109.72 m) × 44.2 ft (13.47 m) × 26.9 ft (8.2 m).
E Sgl scr, tpl exp, 3 cyl, 297 NHP. 2 sgl ended blrs, 160 lb. 10 kts. By builder.
H S. 2 dks; F: 44 ft (13.41 m); B: 72 ft (21.95 m); P: 17 ft (5.18 m).

1893 Aug: Completed for China Mutual S.N.Co.
1898 Sold to Bucknall Bros; renamed *Bucentaur*
1911 Became the Japanese *Saikai Maru,* Katsuda Kisen K.K, Kobe.
1930 Renamed *Shoehi Maru,* Nippon Kosen K.K, Kobe..
1934 Broken up.

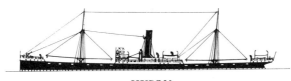

HYSON

CM11 **HYSON**

B 1896 Workman Clark & Co, Belfast. **T:** 4,510 g, 2,931 n.
D 410 ft (124.97 m) × 48.1 ft (14.66 m) × 27.4 ft (8.35 m).
E Sgl scr, tpl exp, 3 cyl, 600 NHP, 2 dbl ended blrs, 180 lb. 11 kts. By builder.
H S. 2 dks; F: 47 ft (14.32 m); B: 108 ft (32.92 m); P: 45 ft (13.72 m).

1896 Delivered to China Mutual S.N.Co.
1903 Sold to Apcar & Co, Calcutta. Renamed *Aratoon Apcar.*
1912 Sold with the Apcar fleet to British India S.N.Co, same name.
1932 Broken up in China.

NOTES

NOTES

NOTES